3ds max® Lighting

Nicholas Boughen

Wordware Publishing, Inc.

Library of Congress Cataloging-in-Publication Data

Boughen, Nicholas.
   3ds max lighting / by Nicholas Boughen.
     p. cm.
   Includes index.
   ISBN 1-55622-401-X (pbk., companion CD-ROM)
   1. Computer animation.   2. 3ds max (Computer file).   3. Computer graphics.   I. Title.
   TR897.7.B665 2004
   006.6'96—dc22   2004018413
                                      CIP

ISBN 1-55622-401-X

10 9 8 7 6 5 4 3 2 1
0409

All inquiries for volume purchases of this book should be addressed to Wordware Publishing, Inc., at the above address. Telephone inquiries may be made by calling:

(972) 423-0090

Being a man with a family who sees too little of him,
I must dedicate this book, of course,
To my wife, Victoria,
And to my children, Michael and Katherine,
Who have asked for attention so many times
While I sat,
Zombie-like,
Glued to my evening's work.

Contents

Contents

Part III
Creating Lighting

Contents

Acknowledgments

First and foremost, I wish to thank my publisher, Wes Beckwith, for his endless encouragement, support, and enthusiasm. I am grateful for the confidence he placed in me to complete this project to a high standard and on schedule. Thanks to all the other Wordware folks for their contributions and efforts on this book, especially Beth Kohler, who trains her eagle eye on the text, eschewing obfuscation at every turn.

Secondly, I'd like to thank Marnie Marshall, lighting artist and MAX lighting expert at Electronic Arts in Vancouver, British Columbia, who read over the manuscript, checking for technical errors and lack of clarity.

I'd like to acknowledge the contributions of Jessica Chambers, technical director at the Shadbolt Centre for the Arts in Burnaby, British Columbia, Canada. Thanks to Jessica for the use of her head in Chapter 1 and the use of her theater facilities to photograph some of the lighting concepts I attempt to describe herein.

Thanks to Rainmaker's Brian Moylan, director of digital imaging, for endless support and enthusiasm for the job, for keeping it real, and for encouraging personal projects such as this, which sometimes take time and focus away from the pressure-cooker of daily production work.

Numerous others have contributed in some part to this book. From hyper-talented lighting designers and college professors back in the mists of time to the 3D artists of the world. Some of these people I work with every day and others I know only by reputation, but from all I constantly learn new tricks and techniques. Every step down the path has led to this book, and so here it is. I hope you enjoy it. I hope, especially though, that this book brings you some new skill or understanding and helps improve your lighting in some small way.

Introduction

This book is separated into three main parts: Part I, "Lighting Theory," Part II, "3ds max Lighting Tools," and Part III, "Creating Lighting." Part I covers the fundamentals of what light is, how it acts and reacts in our world, and what those reactions look like. Part II covers the virtual lighting equipment available to achieve your 3ds max lighting goals. Part III deals with how to use those tools to create the lighting we desire. Theory is first in this book because it is fundamental to using the tools. In fact, any artist using any toolkit can make good use of the theoretical section of this book. The qualities of light do not change, regardless of what software you are using.

While reading this book, you will find areas where repetition occurs. Lighting a scene involves the application of numerous tools, methods, and properties that are all interlinked. Although I have endeavored to separate each element into chapters for easy comprehension, they nonetheless overlap here and there. I found that a small measure of repetition is preferable to constantly referring the reader to other chapters.

Why Write This Book?

I have had the privilege of working with some incredibly talented artists, yet some of them have not grasped the simplest lighting principles. The final scene is beautiful to be sure, but many artists run into two main problems lighting those scenes. One is that while the lighting is perfect and beautiful, it may have taken hours to accomplish through a system of trial and error. The other problem is that the lighting is imperfect, perhaps disobeying the laws of physics. It just looks wrong. The artist or viewer may not be able to put their finger exactly on the problem, but even an untrained eye has spent a lifetime experiencing the properties and qualities of light. You can't fool the audience. Understanding a few principles can solve this problem for the artist.

I have a 20-year background in practical lighting for stage and video. My studies derive from those of artists throughout history who have labored to understand the properties and qualities of light so they might incorporate those qualities into their own works. It seems natural that 3D artists should begin from the same point as painters, sculptors, and photographers, especially since 3D art embodies all three of these disciplines.

Good lighting can make the difference between a good shot and a great one. I would like to see more artists equipped with a strong enough understanding of lighting to make them masters of their art. To that end, I wish to share the tidbits of knowledge and experience I have acquired over the years through my own studies.

Why Read This Book?

If you have ever looked at a photograph and been unable to decipher the light sources, direction, and color, or if you have been unable to replicate this lighting within MAX, this book will help you. If you have ever thought your lighting looked flat, boring, meaningless, inane, incomprehensible, stale, clichéd (stop me any time), overused, cheesy, CG, fake, or derivative, reading this book might be a good move. If you have ever wondered how to make objects stand out from the background, how to demonstrate all the minute detail you have spent weeks modeling, or how to make a shot feel sad, angry, or joyous, you might take some time to look through these pages. If you have seen the work of some great 3D artists and marveled at how photo-real everything looks and wished you could add that sense of realism to your work, read on.

Good lighting is crucial to the final look of your shot. Even a poorly designed, marginally textured object can still look like it really exists if the lighting is good. On the other hand, a beautifully designed, painstakingly modeled and textured object, if lit poorly, will be easily identified as computer generated.

Screw Physics!

Physics nitpickers, beware. This section may offend some readers.

Lighting can be a very contentious issue. That is not to say that it is very complex or difficult to learn. It is not. But it can be difficult to talk about. This is mainly because there is a certain breed of people who just can't let reality go. I teach that a shadow may have a certain color based on a number of different environmental factors. Someone nit-picks that shadows don't actually have any color, being, themselves, the simple absence of light. (This is technically true, but quite unimportant to CG lighting.) I teach that certain light types behave a particular way. Some physics snob claims it's all wrong and lectures me about angstroms, electromagnetic wavelengths, photons, and wave theory.

It comes down to a few simple arguments. First, computer-generated imagery is fake. It is therefore not real and subsequently is not obliged to live by real laws of physics. Second, it is unimportant what hacks and tricks you had to pull and what physics you had to ignore as long as things turned out the way you intended and the final render looks great. Third, did you really purchase this book for a lecture on angstroms, electromagnetism, and the behavior of up quarks and down quarks? Or is it the art of computer-generated lighting we're talking about?

Hopefully by the time you have reached this paragraph, you have either tossed this book in the bin because you are a nit-picking physics snob and I have deeply offended your sense of reality (yay!), or you have come to the conclusion that there will be some "bending" of the laws of physics here. As a matter of fact, I plan to outright break, smash, and stomp some physics simply to amuse myself. Does it matter so long as the final render looks photo-real? Well, does it?

Physics is important to lighting for a number of reasons, not least of which is that it explains why light and shadow behave the way they do, but it is not there to fetter our artistic endeavors, our tastes, or even our baser need to get a render done quickly. Let's face it: If we were constrained to using lighting tools that only obeyed the laws of physics, frames would take days, weeks, or months to render instead of minutes.

Physics helps us understand how real things work so that we know how to build tools and techniques that approximate those realities. Of course the goal is to approximate them so well that they look completely photo-real. This approximation is likely to be a big compromise that is made up of completely impossible tools and techniques, cheats, fakes, hidden truths, and some seriously great compositing work post-render consisting of motion blur, film grain, smoke, dust, nasty edge-work, rotoscoping, and probably shaking a live chicken over the tablet about five minutes before delivery deadline.

Take lights, for example. In the real world, there is only one basic light type. All light sources fall into this one category and can be described using one set of rules. (Argue if you will; I'm not listening.) MAX, on the other hand, is equipped with a number of different light types. Each different light is characterized by specific light properties that may or may not exist in real lighting but have been designed to make your frames render much, much more quickly. None of the lights available in MAX behave exactly as real light does. Those brainiacs who have coded our lighting tools have split up various light properties into separate lighting instruments and controls, giving us the ability to create lighting looks without having to go through all the hassle of using real physics to render.

For example, in the real world, if you turn up the intensity of a light, the specular highlight and reflection on a surface will also increase. That is because they are all part of the same property. In the virtual world, however, these properties can all be manipulated individually, completely disobeying the law. Shame!

So to begin with, we are going to ignore physics except in our observations of real-world light. When it comes to lighting in the virtual world, we need to understand the laws so we can make something that *appears* to work like them, but we do not need to obey them. In this way, we are gods and make our own physical laws. Light behaves the way we desire it to in our virtual worlds because we wish it.

There, now don't you feel like tossing a lightning bolt or something?

Some Notes about Observation

Observation of the real world is the backbone upon which all the rest of your artwork, including lighting, rests. You will never, ever learn good lighting, animation, texturing, or much of anything else by simply sitting in front of a computer monitor clicking keys and scrolling your mouse wheel. If it is your desire to become a truly world-class artist, it is your obligation to yourself to get out there and study the world that you are striving to copy.

Painters perform many painting and drawing studies before attempting a large work. If they need to work out just how a human hand lies or just how cotton fabric crumples, they will draw hands in many different positions or they will get cotton and lay it out, drawing it over and over until they fully understand its properties and behaviors. Lighting is just like this.

If you expect to create realistic lighting, you absolutely must get out there and observe lighting conditions. See the properties of light and shadow under as many different environmental conditions as possible. Analyze and study both lighting and shadow. Understand how different textures react to specific lighting conditions. Know what a reflection is before you attempt to alter the reflectivity, specularity, and glossiness of a texture at the workstation. As a lighting artist, it is your duty to reach a Zen understanding of lighting. Be one with the light, young pixel samurai, and ye shall reap the rewards.

Rules of the Road

The first rule any artist learns is that there are no rules. This book will demonstrate how light works, how to look at it, and how certain tools in MAX's toolkit can be used to approximate or replicate it. There are also a number of lighting techniques covered, some of which are commonly used in film and television. These are not rules; they are principles and techniques. Once you understand lighting, you will discover that you do not need rules or techniques described for you, that you can create your own techniques, that you can make up your own rules. Simply put, you can light a scene any way you wish if it pleases you. Your best bet for learning how to gain complete control over your lights is to experiment, ignore standard practices, and investigate exactly how your lighting instruments perform and react. Anyone who tries to tell you about rules is mistaken.

What is "good lighting"? That's a loaded question. If I had to define it I would say "good lighting" is what occurs when the results are what the artists set out to create. I have met directors who believe that "good lighting" means everything in the scene is brightly lit so you can see every detail. What if the scene is in a dark alley at night with a couple of small overhead street lamps just barely bright enough to create two dim pools on the asphalt? Should I throw in a nice bright distant light at 100% so everything is brightly lit? Of course I shouldn't. This is a pretty obvious example but it demonstrates the point: Good lighting looks and feels right. Believe it or not, you are already an expert on what light should look like. You've been observing the effects and qualities of light since you first opened your eyes. Trust what your eyes tell you. My job is to dissect and define all those things you already know and present them to you in a way that will allow you to manipulate them like old, familiar hand tools.

A Note About Art: There is little that can replace a traditional art background. You have probably heard or read this a hundred times and rolled your eyes, but it remains fundamentally true. It is not about whether you can draw, paint, or sculpt but about learning how to look at your subject and dissect it into forms, colors, and intersections so they can be recreated on your own canvas, in this case your computer. If you do not have any art training, do not dismay; this book will still help you improve your lighting. I would be remiss, however, if I did not recommend that you take a couple of evenings a week and attend a class at your local arts institute. Most community centers have arts classes of some sort. If your desire is to become a world-class artist, you really should study art.

All right, enough of that soapbox.

Lighting, Both Beautiful and Accurate

Pleasing lighting is not mutually exclusive from accurate lighting.

This may seem to be an obvious statement, but you would be surprised how many artists throw lights into a scene to highlight an item when there is no lighting source to justify the illumination. Accuracy is key to good-looking lighting. If you really need to highlight something and there are no light sources to justify it, there are other steps you can take to achieve a good look. Altering the background is one such solution, although it's not always possible. Find a way to add a light source to justify the light you need. If nothing else works, at least try to make the offending effect subtle enough to pass notice.

You might even get away with making alterations to the subject or its textures. Creativity is not just about building, painting, and lighting. It is also about finding creative solutions to problems just like this that pop up every day. Part of your job is to fix them.

In your career as a lighting artist, you will probably encounter situations where you are ordered to highlight something and denied permission to make any alterations that will justify that highlight. This especially happens when the budget is tight, time is short, and/or the director or VFX supervisor is inexperienced. This is where the VFX supervisor has a tough job trying to coordinate between director, gaffer, and CG department to try to make the final composition seamless and real. You should try to argue your point, but sometimes they don't want to hear it. Just smile, nod, do the work, and don't put it on your reel. Sometimes you just have to walk away.

> **Note:** Some filmmakers are euphemistically referred to as "guerilla filmmakers." This evokes a mental image of hurried, hit-and-miss operations that spawn marginal results or failures. If you are very lucky, you will never end up trying to light shots for these "guerilla" filmmakers, whose favorite expression at the end of a long day seems to be "They'll fix it in post." Because visual effects shots seem to be left until the end of the day when everybody is very tired, working double-overtime, and anxious to get home, the work is hurried and sloppy. That means it is up to you and the rest of the VFX team to fix whatever mistakes these filmmakers can't be bothered to fix themselves. I have seen some pretty incredible expectations come from set regarding post fixes.
>
> - A chair is left in frame for a shot. Instead of reshooting, the crew wraps for the day and requires a compositor to paint out the chair.
> - A scene is in the can. Later the production team decides they don't like the round neckline on a dress. A compositor is ordered to make it square.

- Green-screen shots come back with completely improper lighting angles for the CG environment that is to be added by the VFX team. Green light spills all over the talent. Many hours of roto are required and the lighting must be altered to accommodate the plate.

  All of these are due to lack of planning, unrealistic time constraints, and laziness. Unfortunately, it adds a massive workload to the VFX department, which would like to be spending its time making the shots world class but instead spends time cleaning up other people's messes and does not then have enough time to properly finish its own shots.
  There are also many filmmakers who plan carefully and who care about the results.

If you are lucky, the shots are carefully planned, the CG department is included in the planning process, and the shots come back as expected. What is more likely is that one or all of these events will not occur. This is where your creativity is really going to come into play, where you will really need to know your lighting to pull off a miracle.

You will discover that there are many ways to skin a cat. Regardless of whether the shots you receive are manna from heaven or guerilla crap, you will find that stunning results can be achieved with the slightest planning.

About Trial and Error

Many CG artists rely on trial and error as a prime lighting technique. This is not the same as experimentation. Since rendering a frame is hardly real-time feedback, there will be some amount of tweaking and rendering to achieve the right levels, colors, and balance; however, most aspects of lighting do not, and should not, require trial and error. Properties such as instrument choice, position, direction, basic intensity, and color should require marginal adjustment, especially in visual effects shots where these properties have already been established by the film crew or where visual references are available in the plate and your job is simply to recreate the lighting environment. The VFX artist should be able to look at a plate; identify exactly how many light sources there are; identify roughly their position, direction, and colors and what light types are required; plan out a lighting kit; and then proceed with placement.

Designing your own lighting is a slightly different matter and may require more experimentation, especially considering this may be part of the creative process for some artists. This process, however, should not be mistaken for "trial and error." Trial and error is best illustrated by the artist who does not know what he wants, does not know exactly how to achieve it, and adds lights, colors, direction, and intensity in the hopes that sooner or later he will accidentally hit on a pleasing combination.

Once again, the artist should be able to look at the scenic requirements, plan out lighting type, placement, angle, and color, and then proceed with placement.

Visual Effects vs. CG Lighting Design

There are two main reasons to light a scene or an element in MAX. One reason is that you are adding a CG element to a background plate that has come from set. You usually have few options but to analyze and replicate the on-set lighting so that your element will blend into the plate. This is visual effects (VFX) lighting. The other reason is that you are working on an all-CG shot and you must create the whole lighting environment. This is CG lighting design.

The skill set required to accomplish competent visual effects lighting is primarily technical, requiring an understanding of the light sources and techniques used in the plate and how to replicate those sources and techniques using specific tools available in MAX. Lighting design also requires these technical skills and also calls on the artist's knowledge of such qualities as intensity, direction, color, shadow, and contrast. The artist is now making an artistic interpretation and converting that interpretation into a lighting environment. Do you want to know how to do this? All these things are covered in the pages that follow.

Part I

Lighting Theory

This first section will lay the groundwork you will need to become a successful lighting artist. Anyone who has studied drawing, painting, photography, or other visual arts designed to capture or replicate life will know that a solid understanding of the qualities and properties of real-world light is essential to the success of the artistic reproduction. This is as true in computer imaging as it was when Rembrandt began painting portraits in the 17th century.

Lighting cannot be learned at a computer terminal. It can, however, be learned by observing and understanding real light in a real environment. Expect to spend time outdoors examining the quality of a shadow from a nearby tree. Look not only at the color of the sunlight but at the hue of the shadow. Note how the colored light from one source mixes with the colored light from another source to produce an entirely new effect. See how the light color mixes with the surface attributes of the objects and materials around you. Notice how light colors and solid colors mix to create new variations.

To be a successful lighting artist, the properties of light must interest you enough to study them. This section will help you with that.

1

Properties of Light

This chapter deals with the properties of light in the real world, specifically intensity, color, direction, diffuseness, shadow, shape, contrast, movement, and size. By the time you finish this chapter you should be able to identify and explain each of these properties in a lighting environment.

Understanding light is not difficult. Just as an automobile mechanic understands how to build, repair, and operate a vehicle — not by seeing the vehicle as a single system but as a complex interaction of individual systems — understanding light is as simple as understanding each of the individual properties that are part of the whole. Once the following concepts are grasped, you will be able to look at any lighting situation and clearly identify the direction of the source, its intensity or luminosity, the light color, the diffuseness of the light, the movement (if any), the shadow qualities, the shape, and the contrast. Actually, you are already an expert in observing light. These terms and definitions will simply allow you to manipulate them effectively.

Intensity/Luminosity

Intensity and luminosity are similar concepts. The following two images illustrate the difference. Figure 1.1 shows intensity, while Figure 1.2 demonstrates luminosity.

Figure 1.1: Intensity refers to the brightness of a light source.

Figure 1.2: Luminosity refers to the brightness of a surface.

The difference is this: In CG art, we use *intensity* to refer to the brightness of a light source — an actual lighting instrument within the CG environment such as a spotlight, point light, or omni light. In other words, when we say intensity, we are talking about *direct* lighting from a hot lightbulb filament or a candle flame. When we say *luminosity*, we are talking about *indirect* lighting such as when direct light is diffused through a frosted glass bulb or the colored glass in a neon sign. MAX's radiosity allows us to make polygonal objects self-luminous. So if we model a frosted white lightbulb, we can have the actual polygons of the object emitting light without adding any lights to the scene. When object surfaces have a luminosity setting higher than 0%, they contribute light to the scene if radiosity is enabled. The higher the luminosity, the more light is emitted. So in the case of radiosity, luminosity means the same as intensity but refers to the light emission from materials as opposed to lights.

Take our lightbulb example. In the old days of CG, we would have to create the effect in MAX by putting an omni light in or near the lightbulb object and letting it shine its rays out into the scene. Nowadays, we have another option. Instead of adding an omni light, we can turn up the self-luminous value on the actual lightbulb material and enable radiosity. The render will take considerably longer, but the resulting light will be far more accurate. Most of the time, the easy method of adding an omni light will work fine, but sometimes detail is everything and nothing else will look as good.

Intensity or luminosity is one of the first things you may notice about a light source's quality. Is it very bright or very dim? Is it somewhere in the middle? Is it so blindingly bright that it can only be the sun or a nuclear blast? Or is it so gentle that it must be a candle? The intensity of a light source will often signal to the viewer what the light source is, even if the source itself is not visible in frame.

> **Note:** It is easy to let the audience know what and where your light source is without being obtrusive or obvious. As you read through these sections about light properties, imagine how you might use each one to let your audience know just how the scene is illuminated.

Color

Perhaps the second quality you may notice in a light source is the color. Take the sun, for example. On a midsummer's day, the sun can be very close to white and on the yellowish side. On an autumn afternoon, it can be a fiery orange. Look in the shadows on a clear, bright sunny day. Don't they look blue? What about the living room with the fireplace burning? Here you see orange, red, and yellow all spilling across the room. Or check out those mercury vapor lamps used for street lights. These are sort of a light orange.

Take a look at the following photograph for example:

Figure 1.3 (See color image.)

There are three main light sources in this shot, resulting in three distinct color ranges. In a few places, you can see direct sunlight, mainly along the top of the image and at the bottom right. The sun is the key light. It is nearly white, on the amber side of the spectrum. But the most obvious light sources and colors are the fill sources. On the left of the image, rock faces that angle upward are a deep blue. This is because they are facing the blue sky on a bright, sunny day. The sky is highly luminous and is emitting a blue-tinted diffuse light. On the right half of the image, the cliff face is undercut, making it face downward toward the road where sunlight is reflecting off the dirt and creating an amber fill.

> **Note:** This image is a great example not only of contrasting color in a lighting environment, but also of fill lighting and of diffuse lighting sources.

> **Note:** There has been heated debate in the CG community over the color of shadows on a sunny, clear, blue-skied day. Some argue that shadows have no color, being by nature the absence of light. On the other hand, it can be argued that on earth shadows are never completely devoid of light. I suppose for the picky physicists in the room, the question should be "What color of illumination fills the shadowed area?" I won't address the doubt, incredulity, debates, insults, or downright crying that was involved, and I stand by my analysis of the lighting conditions. I urge you, the incredulous reader, to simply go outside and do some careful, thoughtful observation. Come to your own conclusions.

There are as many colors for lights as there are colors in the visible spectrum. In fact, you can divide up the visible spectrum of light into many more wavelengths than can be discerned by the human eye. Your computer monitor is probably capable of displaying about 16 million colors, and that's only some of the available ones!

Color can be a visual key to what is going on in your scene. If you see a back alley scene, and there's a pink light source out of frame that's blinking on and off, you will subconsciously know that this probably represents a neon sign flashing "Tattoos" or something. If you want to create a somber, depressing mood, you might choose cool colors — steels and blues, colors that seem cold and dead. If you wish to make the viewer ill at ease, you may choose eerie, unnatural colors in the green portion of the spectrum. Or perhaps pinks and ambers may be your choice for a bright, happy setting. Keep in mind that these examples are merely the most common uses for these color ranges. Why are they common? Most people have specific emotional reactions to certain colors. You can use this knowledge to get your audience into a specific frame of mind.

> **Note:** My experience has shown that people are most comfortable with colors and brightness values that are most often found in nature. If I wish to create tension, I will use strange colors and unusual intensities. People know instinctively what lighting environment is natural. That is why most room lights are on the ceiling or above people's heads and are roughly the color of the sun. It is what humans have been accustomed to for millions of years.

Direction

Light direction is another powerful tool in establishing light source and setting. If the shot is outdoors and the angle is very steep, very bright, and amber-white, we might assume that the light source is the sun. If the shot is outdoors and the light is very bright, amber-white, and coming from below, we are certain that it cannot be the sun. It must be something else. Everything is the same except for the angle.

Let's say all the lights are out in a living room, but there is a light source out of frame. It is coming from floor level and is colored red, orange, and yellow. We guess this is a fireplace. If we look again and see by the angle of the shadows that the source is above us rather than below, we will probably think that the house is on fire.

Take the classic example of the spooky story told on a camping trip. The storyteller places a flashlight below the chin, causing deep, strange shadows that make the face appear frightening and unnatural. This is referred to as "dramatic lighting." The same flashlight pointed straight at the face or from above will elicit no such reaction.

From the earliest days when theater moved indoors, footlights were used to illuminate the stage. Why footlights? Well, the earliest lights were candles floating in a moat of water in front of the stage. These were followed by gas lights. The nature of these lights required them to be within easy access of the operators, especially considering how many theaters burned down while these technologies were in use. When electric lights were introduced, they were placed in footlight positions mainly due to tradition. The villains of the old melodramas made use of the footlights by leaning close over them, producing the same frightening and unnatural shadows of the campers telling the ghost story. Footlights can still be found in theatrical productions where a lighting designer seeks that melodramatic feeling of the old theater, or where strange, unnatural lighting effects are desired.

The following three images illustrate the use of direction in lighting a subject. Figure 1.4 uses a natural lighting angle high and to the subject's left. The lighting angle is similar to one that may be found on a sunny day. The subject appears normal and familiar. Figure 1.5 uses a low-angular direction. We still recognize the subject as familiar, but the lighting is obviously strange, especially considering the lack of a fill source. Figure 1.6 uses the "spooky flashlight" dramatic lighting effect. It makes the viewer ill at ease because of the subject's unnatural appearance.

Figure 1.4: A normal lighting angle like the sun or a ceiling light.

Figure 1.5: A side lighting angle. Unusual, but seen during sunrises and sunsets.

Figure 1.6: A low lighting angle. Very unnatural and strange.

Note: In the days of candles, sailors were hired to run the rigging and lighting in the theater. The man taking care of the candles often needed to remove one of the floating candles from the moat to repair its guttering or to relight one that had blown out. The sailor used a tool known as a "gaff" (a long metal hook used to retrieve wayward ropes on sailing ships) to pull the candles to the edge of the moat and to push them back out. Thereafter, the man taking care of the lighting came to be known as the gaffer. Strangely, as the technology in the theater advanced, the gaff was cast aside, except for those occasions when an actor needed to be violently removed from the stage with a hook, and the term "gaffer" fell into disuse. But somehow, the term survived in the film industry and today the head of the lighting department is known as the gaffer.

Diffuseness

In general, *diffuse light* is any light that has been scattered after leaving the light source, or any light source that has a varying area of luminosity or intensity. Scattering can be caused by atmospheric gases or by reflection, or bounce, off an uneven or rough surface. Any material that causes orderly light rays to be scattered, bent, or reflected into disorderly paths is creating diffuseness in the light.

See Figure 1.3 for an example of an image that is lit primarily by two diffuse light sources.

Here on earth, all light has some measure of diffuseness. This is because the light rays (or particles, or waves if you wish to be picky) pass through atmospheric gases, colliding with the gas molecules and shooting in all directions. The most obvious example of this is the sky. Blue light is scattered in the atmosphere much more than light at the red end of the spectrum. This is because blue light has a much shorter wavelength than red light and is, therefore, scattered throughout the atmosphere about ten times as much as red light. This scattering is what makes the sky appear blue. Subsequently, the scattered blue light continues omnidirectionally, some of which reaches the ground as diffuse light. This bluish, diffused light can be seen in shadows on clear days. Direct sunlight can also be diffused through clouds, colliding with water droplets and continuing omnidirectionally. Cloudy days provide an excellent example of white diffused light. All the shadows on cloudy days are soft and diffused. Only the deepest crevices are likely to be very dark since light is approaching from most directions but may not reach into them.

Diffuseness can tell us much about the light source and the environment. Direct light sources such as the sun, a candle flame, or a bare, clear lightbulb produce orderly light rays and harder shadows than diffused light sources. But put a curtain, a lampshade, or frosted glass in front of the source and the light becomes diffused, making shadows softer. Fluorescent sources are all diffused sources. They all have a wide area of luminosity that creates soft shadows because the light appears to "wrap around" objects, creating an area of shadow "falloff."

The following two images are the same except that one is directly lit and the other is diffusely lit. There is diffuse lighting in both images but direct lighting in only one of them.

Figure 1.7: Sharp shadows and higher contrast are visible in this image, which has both diffuse and direct lighting sources. The direct light is overpowering the diffuse light and diffused shadows.

Figure 1.8: This image is nearly identical to the previous one, except for the absence of direct lighting. As the contrast is lower, the softer illumination and softer shadows are clearly visible.

Shadow

Shadows are not technically a quality of light. While some may teach that lights cast shadows, in fact it is objects that cast shadows. A shadow is the absence of light and therefore cannot generally be considered a light quality. Rather we think of it as a "lighting" quality. In other words, shadows are one of the things we think about when creating our lighting, although it is not actually a part of light. How hard or soft the shadow edges become, and how shadow depth changes over the area of a shadow are a direct result of the properties of the light source, but shadows themselves occur because of objects lying in the path of the light emission.

The images shown in Figures 1.4, 1.5, and 1.6 demonstrate that shadow is linked to the direction of the light source. They help us see the subtleties of form in the subject, and can be used to evoke an emotional response from the viewer.

Shadows are as crucial to lighting as beer is to pizza. Without one, the other is rather plain. It is shadows that give all objects their subtle form and distinct shape. Shadows play a large part in helping us define what plane we are looking at when we see a wall or the ground. Look at a wall near you and notice the shadow gradient that occurs on the wall surfaces farther from the light source. Notice the intersection with the floor and see where the deepest shadows lie. Imagine if there were no shadows. In a white room with a white door frame and a white door, you would never be able to find the door. All that really defines the door and frame is the shadows around it.

We are all experts at seeing shadows. We have honed our expertise in this area our entire lives. It is because of this expertise that each of us can look at a visual effect or other computer-generated shot in a movie and know instantly that it is not real if the lighting is not quite right. We may not be able to verbalize exactly what the problem is or even that it is with the lighting, but nonetheless it will look wrong.

This is why shadow is one of the most subtle and most crucial of lighting qualities. As lighting artists, we must understand exactly what happens to create shadows of all types in all situations. Chapter 5 deals with shadows in detail, including different shadow types resulting from different light types. For now, suffice it to say that there are two main types of shadows: hard and soft. *Hard shadows* are the sort you see from small light sources like the sun or a clear, bare lightbulb. (I know the sun is very large, but it acts small most of the time as far as lighting is concerned, mainly because it is extremely far away and only a small amount of the sun's light reaches us. See Chapter 5.) *Soft shadows* are the kind you usually see in the absence of hard shadows. That is not to say that they cannot exist together; they usually do, but hard shadows are scene stealers. People tend not to notice the gentler soft shadows when the bully hard shadows are around — this is an important point. Because we live on a planet with a gaseous atmosphere, soft shadows are everywhere, under every lighting condition. Failing to add them to your scene is like forgetting the cheese on a pizza. Soft shadows exist in situations where there is a diffuse lighting source such as the sky, clouds, a computer monitor, or sunlight reflecting off a wall. In reality, there is always a diffuse lighting source.

Shape

Figure 1.9: Even if the wire fence were not visible in the scene, you would know the shape and proximity of the object casting the shadow on the child. Shape is a great tool for setting the scene.

The shape of a light can tell you a great deal about the light source. Shape is very similar to shadow in some ways. For example, the shadow cast by palm leaves may actually be palm leaves, or in the case of MAX, it may actually be geometry casting a shadow. Lighting designers long ago invented a device for changing the shape of the light before it leaves a lighting instrument so that you don't actually have to place a palm tree in front of the light in order to get the effect. Earlier, I mentioned that you don't always need to see the light source to know what it is. This is true of shadows as well. You don't need to see a palm tree to know it is casting the shadow. This shaping device is called a *gobo* or *lighting template*. Simply put, it is a small sheet of metal with a shape cut out. The sheet is placed at the focal point of the light, and the cut-out shape is projected. So if that shape were to be some palm leaves, then it might appear that the light source is the sun and that it is shining down through some palm leaves. Technically, the gobo is casting a shadow inside the lighting instrument, only allowing some of the light to shine through. That is what alters the shape of the light. There are also *moving gobos*, which can be as simple as a disc rotating in front of the light or as complex as a movie projector. Lighting designers also use shutters, barn doors, and flags to alter the shape of their lights. *Shutters* are metal plates, also at the focal point, that can be slid inward to create straight edges on the normally round beam of a spotlight. *Barn doors* are placed at the lens end of the light some distance past the focal point and are usually used to cut down on *spill* (undesirable light diffusing out of the lens housing in all directions), although they can also shape a light somewhat or assist in sharpening the gobo image. *Flags* are usually small, round discs used to carve out light from specific areas, but in reality can be any item of any shape, as long as it does the job. Tools that work like the virtual cousin to each of these are available in the MAX toolset, as we will discover in later chapters.

You see that shape and shadow are very similar. For the purposes of CG lighting, we will consider shadow to be cast by geometry in the scene and shape to be the light that is coming from the light source before touching any geometry.

Contrast

Contrast refers to the range of difference between the lightest parts of the image and the darkest parts. An image in which the lightest parts are much lighter than the darkest parts is considered to have high contrast. On the other hand, a frame in which the lightest parts and the darkest parts are similar is considered to have low contrast. For example, on a bright sunny day, the sunlight shines on a white table. It is nearly blinding to look at and the shadows below it seem to be pitch black. There is a great difference in illumination between the table and the shadow below. This is high contrast. If, on the other hand, it is a cloudy day and you look at the table, you will notice that the white of the table and the light gray of the concrete below do not seem to be so different. This is low contrast.

The following images demonstrate the difference between low-contrast and high-contrast imagery.

Figure 1.10: This image demonstrates low contrast. All the illumination and texture values fall within the middle range of grays.

Figure 1.11: This image demonstrates high contrast. All the illumination and texture values range from highest (white) to lowest (black).

Some of this effect is caused by the dilation of your pupils. When it is very bright outside, your pupils get smaller, blocking out much of the light and protecting the retina. When this happens, only the brightest light gets through. The concrete under the table is lit even more than it is on a cloudy, low-contrast day, but your eye is not registering the light because it has been filtered out by the pupil. This creates a high-contrast situation. When clouds obscure the sun, there is much less light available. The pupils dilate, allowing more light in. The concrete beneath the table becomes more easily visible and more similar in contrast to the table. Essentially what is happening is that as the pupil opens and closes, the eye's light *range* is changing. It is that light range that determines high or low contrast.

Why the anatomy lesson? It is important to understand not how the eye works, but what light is actually there and what situations create the lighting quality known as contrast so that these can be accurately recreated (or at least butchered, cheated, and faked) in a CG environment.

Movement

Movement may not be the first thing you consider when you think about light, but it is a powerful tool. Movement refers to the qualities of light that change over time. Take a fireplace, for example. Each bit of flame is a light source. As the fuel is spent, the flame rises and flickers, changing color and intensity. This is a moving light source. So often I have seen artists attempting to create realistic light from a flame by applying variations in intensity but not in motion or color. Motion, especially, is crucial to this look.

Check out the fireplace.max file on the companion CD. This gives a quick-and-dirty example of how you might set up fireplace lighting.

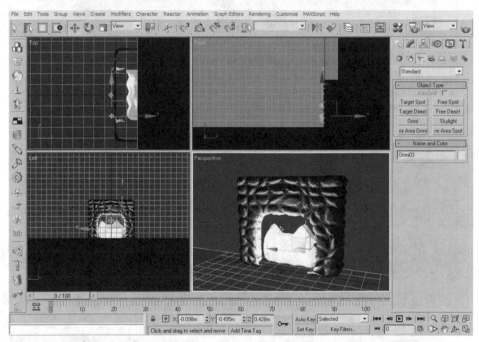

Figure 1.12: There are three simple omni lights in this scene, each with a different motion path, intensity variation, and red color channel variation. This took me about five minutes to set up. If you wanted to do a really beautiful, elaborate setup, it would probably only take a couple of hours.

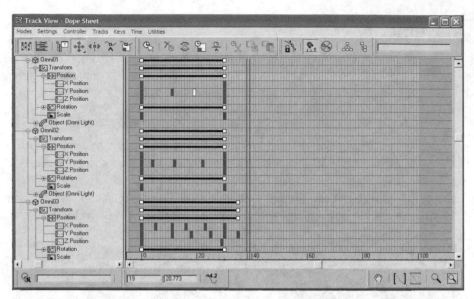

Figure 1.13: You can see in the Dope Sheet how the transform keyframes (the individual blocks on each of the X, Y, and Z position transforms) are irregularly spaced to create unique behaviors for each omni light. Each light is behaving as a spark or a lick of flame.

Similarly, the motion paths for intensity and color create great variation.

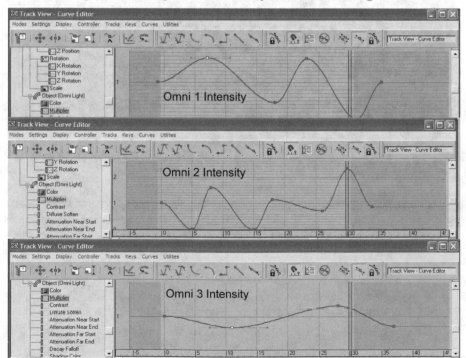

Figure 1.14: Intensity motion channels for all three lights in the Curve Editor

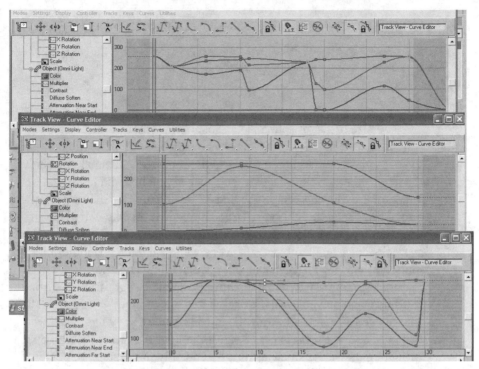

Figure 1.15: Color channels for all three lights in the Curve Editor. When you load up the example scene, you'll see the actual light color change in the animation in the Graph Editor as well.

There are many other examples of light in motion, such as a mirror ball in a club, headlights on a car, someone carrying a flashlight, or even the sun passing overhead. Movement can also apply to changes in the beam angle of a spotlight or changes in intensity or color. One could argue that a change over time of any of the other light qualities constitutes movement. Just imagine how you could use some of these moving qualities to help convey your intentions. Moving intensity might mean something is exploding or someone is turning down a gas lamp. Moving color might mean the sun is rising or a neon sign is flashing outside. Moving direction might mean a car headlight flashing by in the night or a spinning orange beacon on top of a construction vehicle. Moving diffuseness could show that a light source is getting closer or the sun is coming out from behind the clouds. Moving shadow might be palm leaves swaying in the breeze or it could be your shadow sweeping across the ground as car headlights flash past. Moving shape could be a film projection on a screen or window shutters being closed. Moving contrast could mean a supernova is occurring or a nearby rocket is blasting off. These examples came to mind in a moment. There are infinite other combinations that you can use to create a lighting environment that is true to the setting, conveys the mood you wish, and carries the desired emotional impact.

Size

Size matters.

The size of a light source, like most of the other properties, often will not matter in shots, but can occasionally be crucial to lending reality to your lighting environment. What difference does size make? Mainly the difference is in the shadows, specular highlights, and lighting wrap-around. Shadow shape and behavior will vary depending on the size of the light source. A very large source like the sky will result in hard shadows very close to the object and much softer shadows farther away. Specular highlights are also very wide and diffused, sometimes so much so that they are invisible, effectively killing any specularity in a texture. Also, a very large light source will tend to light from the front and sides, and maybe even the back if it is big enough. A very small light source such as a light-emitting diode will result in very hard shadows that only become soft very far away, if the light transmits that far. Specular highlights will be small and bright, and only the parts of the object directly facing the light source will be illuminated. The net effect is that tiny light sources appear to result exclusively in hard, deep shadows and high specular highlights.

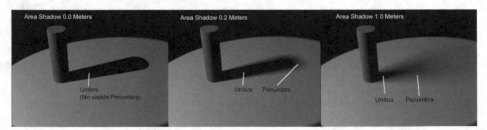

Figure 1.16: In these examples, a spotlight with area shadows has been used to demonstrate the varying size of a light source. Nothing is changed except the size of the area shadow. The size of the area shadow makes the spotlight behave as though it were a light with actual size, as though it were a true area light. A very small area light acts as though it were a point source, producing hard-edged shadows.

■ ■ ■

This chapter has demonstrated the basic properties of light. The physicists among you will, no doubt, care to argue the physical accuracy of several points; however, this is not a physics handbook. The understanding of the properties described here will enable you to light your scenes so they appear to obey the laws of physics (which is very important) without actually having to obey every principle and law (which is not very important).

The final render matters. Whether or not you obeyed the letter of physical law does not.

You should now be able to examine any lighting environment and define the properties of intensity, color, direction, diffuseness, shadow, shape, contrast, movement, and size.

Chapter 2

What, Where, When?

This chapter covers temporal and spatial issues that will hopefully provide clues as to what lighting setup to start with. By the time you have finished this chapter, you should be able to observe a lighting environment and define the time of day (if relevant), time of year (if relevant), atmospheric conditions (if relevant), and whether the environment is interior or exterior. You should be able to analyze a photograph's lighting (or the lighting outside your window, under your desk, or anywhere). You should also be able to start planning your own basic lighting setup based on the scenic information you observe about place, time, and atmospheric conditions.

It is always good to have a defined starting point for your lighting. Where do you begin? I begin lighting a scene by considering a number of questions that help me decide what lights to use, where to place them, how to color them, and what sort of intensity mixtures (or ratios) I will use. We begin with the largest, most obvious questions and move on to finer points. As in any analysis, "Start big, go small."

Interior or Exterior

Perhaps one of the first decisions you will have to make about your lighting is whether it is an interior or exterior shot. This is a basic and general question that will provide you with a great deal of information about your lighting setup. Perhaps the shot contains both interior and exterior elements, such as a room interior with a window through which the street outside is visible. Or it might be an exterior shot that includes someone leaning out a window and waving. There is interior lighting behind that person. It may be subtle, but illuminating that interior properly might make the difference between a shot that is believable to the audience and one that is not. The question is whether the camera is inside a building or out on the street. Interior and exterior light sources may both play a part in the shot, but the location of the camera dramatically changes how the sources will be handled and what the relative light intensities will be between interior and exterior.

Figure 2.1: An indoor lighting environment

Figure 2.2: An outdoor lighting environment

Interior and exterior light react and complement each other all the time, everywhere. Knowing how to create these complex interactions is as simple as identifying and simulating each individual source.

Interior light sources, for example, are usually incandescent or fluorescent. Exterior light sources are usually the sun, the sky, clouds, the moon, reflected sources, and reflected diffuse sources (technically, all these sources are the sun, but let's not wear our picky hats today). The sun's light, diffused through the air molecules in the sky, creates a global, diffused source. Or the sun may be occluded by clouds that block the direct rays from the sun, in which case the light is diffused among the water droplets in the clouds, creating yet another diffuse source. Direct sunlight may strike a wall or the ground, picking up the color of that wall or ground and reflecting it onto another surface. (Don't get all nitpicky about the actual physics of light reflection and radiosity yet. We'll discuss all that later.) Sunlight may reflect off the surface of a swimming pool, creating a hard reflection against the pool house. In each circumstance, the sun is the light source. All the other lighting events, with the exception of artificial light, are diffusions or reflections of that primary source.

While it is theoretically possible to create a global lighting environment with only one source and to provide diffusion and reflection events consistent with the real world, render times would probably be measured in weeks or months per frame. Instead of that, we have decided to make each diffusion and reflection event into a separate light source. Discreet, maker of 3ds max, has provided us with the tools to create these sources, and years of experimentation and research among the MAX community and, indeed the whole CG community, have provided us with innumerable methods for accurately capturing the correct look with the available tools. The basic lighting tools are not physically accurate but are close approximations. Some of the lighting tools reflect only a portion of the real properties of a light source. This makes render times manageable. In general, the closer a lighting tool is to physical accuracy, the exponentially longer it takes to render. The photometric tools, while physically accurate, are highly render intensive and constrain the artist in many ways. Photometric lights, for example, cannot be used with basic lights in MAX. It is, therefore, unlikely that an artist will use photometric lights unless the scene calls for extreme physical accuracy. We'll discuss photometric lights more in Chapter 9.

> **Note:** Bear in mind that it is the look, not the physical accuracy of the lighting model, that matters to producers, directors, and supervisors. The production reality is that any method you can use to create great lighting is valuable. If it is quicker to render and still looks as good, it is more valuable. There are many "tricks" to creating great lighting without the monstrous rendering times. Many of them are covered later in this book. But the main purpose here is to provide you with enough knowledge to create your own tricks that are most relevant to the job you are working on right now. Remember that not all techniques or methods are relevant to all lighting challenges.

Imagine a living room with a fireplace flickering brightly at one end. There is a soft, indirect incandescent source illuminating the pale yellow ceiling and casting a reflected diffuse light throughout the room. Halogen track lighting in the kitchen is spilling a crisp, sharp light from the pass-through into the dining area where it reflects off and refracts through the glass tabletop. The large glass windows reveal a wide cityscape many floors below and a moonlit sky twinkles above. In the distance, moonlight reflects off the Pacific Ocean.

Sound complex? This scene could be lit with as few as three lights. Why? That is how many light sources have been described and are acting on the foreground of the shot. Adding a few more lights to mimic some of the diffusion and reflection events, rather than calculating real reflections and diffusions, can dramatically improve render times.

3ds max is equipped with a robust and full-featured lighting toolkit to help you mimic all the lighting events in the scene without having to create a physically accurate lighting model which, while it may look marginally superior, will likely send render times through the roof.

One last note about interior and exterior lighting: When we talk about exterior sources, we are usually referring to "natural" sources such as the sun. While discussing interior sources, we are usually referring to "artificial" sources such as lightbulbs. Of course, sunlight can pass through a window into a room, and tiki lamps or neon signs are usually found outdoors, but don't be confused. Don't start arguments with your friends about the technical differences in definitions. I'd hate to be the cause of a lifelong friendship breaking up. Worry not! By the time you are finished with this book, you'll know how to create a neon source whether indoors or outdoors and how to create a sunny day whether on the beach or viewed through a tiny basement window. Just remember to think about whether your camera is interior or exterior, and the sources will fall into place.

Time of Day

Figure 2.3: A daytime lighting environment

Figure 2.4: A nighttime lighting environment

What time of day is it? Is it midday or sunset? Is it midnight or early morning? Each of these situations requires a completely different lighting solution. Midday might require a bright, hard-shadowed light source at a high angle to represent direct sunlight, while sunset might also require a hard-shadowed light source but with less intensity, more color

23

saturation, and a much more obtuse angle or direction. Early morning could mean the sun has not yet risen, so all the light in the scene is indirect, diffused, and colored according to atmospheric conditions. Midnight, on the other hand, might be lit by the moon, which acts as a direct lighting source although it is in fact a diffuse, reflected source and displays the properties of both. Finally, starlight may be the only source of illumination, or it could be light from a nearby window or a distant street lamp or neon sign. How do we deal with these? How do we balance the dim starlight with the bright neon sign and still tell our audience that it is nighttime?

So much depends on the time of day. Go out and look at lighting conditions around you at different times of the day. You will find infinite combinations of light sources and situations.

Time of Year

Time of year, while more subtle, is also valuable in establishing lighting conditions, mood, and setting in your scene, especially if the scene is outdoors. Imagine, for example, the kind of light you might see at 3 p.m. on a clear summer day. Contrast that with what the lighting might be like at 3 p.m. in the autumn or winter. The difference is the direction, intensity, and color of our light source (the sun). In the summer, the source is high, very bright, and very white, reaching a color temperature as high as 5800 degrees Kelvin, while autumn light is warmer and less intense, with a color temperature perhaps closer to 4500 degrees Kelvin.

> **Note:** See the sections on Kelvin temperatures in Chapters 12 and 16.

This change in color from summer to autumn occurs because of the ever-changing angle of the earth relative to the sun and what happens to the light rays as they diffuse through the atmosphere at a more obtuse angle. In the winter, the sunlight must actually pass through more atmosphere to reach the ground than it does in the summer. This is because half of the earth (the Northern Hemisphere in June and the Southern Hemisphere in December) is tilted toward the sun in summer, making the light rays reach the earth at an acute angle, which makes the sun appear higher in the sky and lets the sunlight take the most direct route through the atmosphere. In winter, the hemisphere is tilted away from the sun, making the sun appear lower in the sky and causing the light rays to reach the hemisphere at a lower, more obtuse angle. In this case, sunlight takes a longer path through the atmosphere.

Regardless of the calendar month or hemisphere, winter sunlight is always lower and closer to the horizon than summer sunlight, resulting in a lower average angle in winter and a higher average angle in summer. Spring and autumn light are phases between summer and winter, so the light source will be somewhere in between the extremes of summer sunlight and winter sunlight. If you plan on lighting a scene within one of the polar regions, perhaps it's best to go to the library and start studying geography!

> **Note:** Lest we confuse any readers, be it known that summer starts in June in the Northern Hemisphere and in December in the Southern Hemisphere.

Time of year may be a subtle consideration. It may not matter at all in many cases, but in some cases, illustrating the season can make the difference, giving the shot a temporal anchor.

Atmospheric Conditions

Not every day is sunny and clear. Changes in the weather make a dramatic difference in the way your scene is lit.

Take, for example, a clear sunny day and contrast that with a cloudy or a rainy day. Sunny days have a hard, bright, warm main or *key* source (the sun), complemented by a diffuse, cool secondary or *fill* source (the

Figure 2.5: A sunny day

Figure 2.6: A cloudy day

sky). On rainy days, however, the key source is usually the clouds —
most likely a grayscale diffuse source.

> **Note:** For more discussion on what constitutes key and fill sources,
> please see Chapter 6, "Principles of Lighting."

The eye can tell instantly, without seeing either the light source or the
sky, what the atmospheric conditions are outside by seeing the color and
diffuse qualities of the light. When you wake up in the morning and look
out the window, you don't need to look into the sky to see if the sun is
out or if it is raining. The signals are in the buildings and environment
around you, and in the shadows and the quality of the light.

Knowing how to identify and replicate atmospheric conditions is a
powerful tool in visual effects situations where the artist is required to
match lighting to a background plate. In design, it is crucial to delivering
not only the environmental message you wish but also the emotional
message.

How does a rainy, cloudy day make you feel? What about a bright,
sunny day with a few puffy clouds? How about a dry, hot afternoon with
dark, foreboding clouds hanging overhead? What about a foggy day, or a
deep red sunset where the red is not from clouds but from the massive
forest fire approaching your town? Think through all these examples and
pay attention to your own emotional reactions to each one.

Atmospheric conditions can send a scene down a desired emotional path, easily and unconsciously drawing the audience into a desired mindset.

You should now be able to view a scene or photograph and understand that atmospheric conditions play an important part in many cases, primarily outdoors. But don't forget the smoky room or the steamy shower. These are also atmospheric conditions that play a part in how you will light your scene. Lights interact with these elements, creating an effect known as volumetric lighting in which the light beams become visible due to their interaction with the atmospheric particles of smoke or steam. In MAX, such effects are dealt with using volume lights under Atmosphere & Effects. Volume lights are covered in Chapter 10, "Other Lighting in MAX."

■ ■ ■

Let's sum up the questions we ask when examining a scene for lighting.

- Is the scene interior or exterior (or both)?
- What time of day is depicted in the scene?
- What season of the year is depicted in the scene?
- What are the atmospheric conditions present in the scene?

If you remember these four areas of consideration, you should have no trouble in identifying just what the lighting conditions are in your scene.

Hopefully by now you are able to define the temporal and spatial issues that are present in various lighting environments. You should be able to observe a lighting environment and define the time of day (if relevant), season (if relevant), atmospheric condition (if relevant), and whether the environment is interior or exterior.

Chapter 3

Light Sources

This chapter will help you understand some specific types of light sources. There are many different sources of light in the world. Each has similarities and differences and must be handled appropriately in MAX. Once you understand these specific light sources, you should be able to look at any light source and understand its properties.

In the real world, a light source is defined as the direct source of illumination. The sun is a light source, as are a fluorescent tube, a lightbulb, a candle, and a tiki lamp. Described another way, physicists consider light sources to be events in which energy is spent, resulting in the emission of photons. Since this is not a physics manual, we will ignore that particular law. Apologies to physicists everywhere.

For the purposes of this book and CG lighting in general, a light source is also defined as an indirect source of illumination such as diffuse or reflected light. The sky, for example, is considered a diffuse light source, although all of its light comes indirectly from the sun. Reflected light such as light from a mirror and diffuse reflected light, also known as *radiosity*, is considered a light source in the CG world.

There is a good reason for this. Rather than create a physically accurate lighting environment in which diffuse light sources are actually diffused from the direct source, and in which reflected light is actually reflected 20, 30, or 100 (or infinite!) times, bouncing around the environment, we use cheats and tricks to create these effects. Why? There isn't enough rendering time. Computers are not fast enough. Deadlines must be met. Rendering diffuse and reflecting light sources accurately is very CPU intensive and takes a great deal of time. So instead of actually diffusing the light from the sun by creating a physically accurate diffusion event the size of the earth's atmosphere, we add a local diffuse light source that only affects the area within view of the camera. Instead of actually reflecting the light from the sun, we use no reflection but instead add a light source at the reflection point to simulate the effect. Usually the results are acceptable and save us hours per frame of rendering time.

What's the big deal about rendering time if the final render looks great? You're right. If you're working on a personal project at home and you want to leave your dual proc machine rendering for six weeks to get a great four-second shot, go for it. But if you are working in a production environment, you are probably not the only artist trying to get frames rendered. If you hog the render farm with frames that take an unreasonable amount of time to render, you risk missing your deadline (and incurring the wrath of the other artists). Trust me on this — CG artists can be very creative with their punishment. Many tricks and tips are covered in this book to help you create the best "bang for your buck." These tricks do not work for every situation, but you will find that most cases do not require the long render times, and you won't have to find out what punishments are inflicted on "render hogs."

Sunlight

Intensity	High to medium
Color	Warm
Direction	Side to top
Diffuseness	Low
Shadow	Usually very hard to soft
Shape	Usually omni
Contrast	High
Movement	Usually imperceptible
Size	Medium or small

The first and most common light source in the world is the sun. It is the source of almost all light on our planet, actually. All the photochemical or electromagnetic energy in the world originates with radiations from the sun. As a lighting artist you are most certainly going to run into situations where you will have to create sunlight for your scene.

This section deals only with direct sunlight — the stuff you see when the sun is visible in the sky, the stuff that gives you a sunburn, the bright light that blows out your photos and makes you squint, the stuff your mother told you not to look at during a solar eclipse.

A very simplistic description of sunlight may refer to it as a distant light source in which all the light rays are parallel and all the shadows are hard. The parallel light rays mean that objects in the path of the sunlight will cast shadows that are exactly the same size as the object itself. Some describe the sun as a point source that emits light omnidirectionally and is so distant that the light rays reaching the earth merely appear to be parallel because the angle is so negligible as to be imperceptible.

Some see the sun as an area source. In other words, they see the sun as a flat disc in space, the whole surface of which is emitting light omnidirectionally. Area sources behave as diffused sources and therefore result in soft shadows. In truth, all these descriptions are elements of how sunlight behaves.

Figure 3.1: A direct light with parallel rays and hard, raytraced shadows

Figure 3.2: An omni source with omnidirectional rays and hard, raytraced shadows

Figure 3.3: A spotlight with area shadows, behaving very much like a real area light

Before we deal with lighting types used in CG, let's discuss reality. In the real world, all light sources are omnidirectional area or volume sources. In reality, there are no omni lights, spotlights, or direct lights like the tools we use in MAX. This is because 1) all light sources have dimension and volume and cannot, therefore, be nondimensional point sources, 2) all light sources have limited dimension and cannot, therefore emit the same parallel beams in the same direction regardless of your position in space, and 3) no light sources emit only parallel light rays.

"But wait," you say, "a candle is a point source and so is an LED."

Actually, no. Candles and LEDs are small area sources, to be sure, but a point source, like an omni light in MAX, by definition emits all light omnidirectionally from a single nondimensional point in space. There are no such light sources in existence. Candle flames have dimension; so do lightbulb filaments. This means that every nondimensional spatial point within the shape of the flame and on the filament is emitting light in every direction, producing not only an area source but a diffused result.

"Who cares?" you say. "If you can't tell, what's the difference?" Well, that's a good point — and one worth remembering when you're on a production deadline.

The difference is in the details. But it is true that often you can get away with using a direct light or an omni light to simulate the sun.

The sun is larger than the earth. This means that there are light rays running exactly parallel to each other that cover the entire sunward face of our planet.

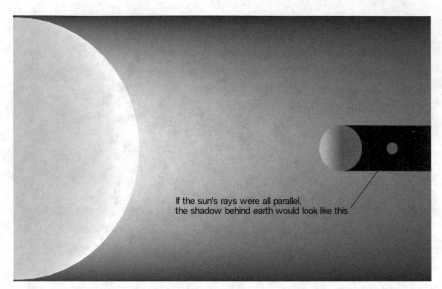

If the sun's rays were all parallel,
the shadow behind earth would look like this

Figure 3.4: If the sun's rays were all parallel, all shadows would behave the way those in this image are behaving — all parallel and hard edged — and the shadow would remain exactly the same size as the object that cast it. (See color image.)

In addition to these parallel rays, there are nonparallel light rays coming from the entire earthward face of the sun in every direction, some of which reach the earth.

Of those light rays that reach the earth, some come from near the edge of the sun's disc, some come from the middle, some come from everywhere on the sun. Since the sun is larger than the earth, some rays will angle behind the earth while rays originating near the center of the disc will either hit the earth or angle away from the earth after they pass it. A lunar eclipse is a good example of this effect.

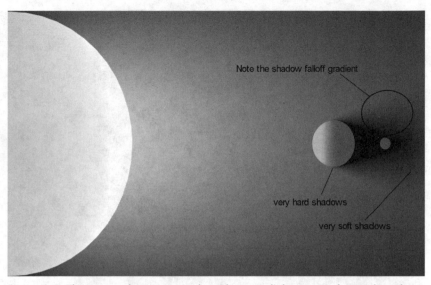

Figure 3.5: This image demonstrates how the sun's light acts on the earth and especially how sunlight gets behind the earth. Note that as less of the sun's surface is visible behind the earth, the light intensity falls off. Note how the area of falloff is very narrow nearest the earth and grows larger the farther from the earth you look. Effectively, since the earth is the shadow-casting object, it is the focal point of the shadow, which grows softer as you get farther away. *Remember this. It is crucial!*

Sunlight acts this way on every object on the earth but on a smaller local scale. The *penumbra* is the area behind the earth — or building or chair or anything on earth — where there is partial shadow. It is partial shadow because while some sunlight is blocked out, the sun is so large that some of the light still reaches that area behind the object. The *umbra* is the area behind the earth — or building or chair — where there is no sunlight at all and the shadow is complete. This is why you can look at a chair leg with sunlight shining on it and see near the leg that the shadows are dark and hard-edged. But the farther away you move from the leg, the softer and lighter the shadows become. It is because the sun is so much larger than the chair leg that some of the light manages to reach those areas behind the leg.

Figure 3.6: This image uses a spotlight with area
shadows. The spotlight is far enough away and the area
shadow size is small enough to create natural hard
shadows near the stool and natural soft shadows
farther away. This is a relatively close simulation of the
way sunlight acts on an object here on earth.

Note: We could also use a mental ray area light to create this
effect, with similar results. Mental ray and area lights will be discussed
more later in the book.

So hopefully you now grasp how the sun emits parallel rays similar to a
direct light in MAX, emits omnidirectional light similar to an omni light
in MAX, and emits light over an area similar to an area light (or a light
with area shadows) in MAX. Area lights are closest, but they, too, fall
short since they are planar and the sun is a volume; however, this physical inaccuracy will almost never be an issue.

"OK," you say, "if sunlight doesn't work exactly like direct, omni, or
area lights in MAX, then why do we have these types of lights in MAX?"

The answer is that these lights calculate much more quickly than a
physically perfect model, and that often, the precise physical accuracy
may be unimportant or unnoticeable. The camera may be framed on an
area very close to the object so that only the hard shadows are visible
and the more distant softening shadows are out of frame. In this
instance, you could use a direct light or even an omni light or a spotlight
to create the bright light and hard shadows needed to simulate sunlight.
Or there could be enough motion in the shot that physically precise
shadows would never be noticed.

Now that you understand how sunlight really acts on objects, you
will have to look at the requirements of your shot and decide how far to

take it and how far to fake it. The trade-off is that the most physically accurate solutions generally take longer to render. If the final render is no different whether you use a direct light or an area light, then there is no point in using the area light. Do the quick renders. Make the boss smile.

Skylight

Intensity	Medium to low
Color	Cool spectrum
Direction	Omni
Diffuseness	High
Shadow	Soft
Shape	Usually none
Contrast	Low
Movement	Usually none
Size	Very large

Skylight is the ultimate filler when it comes to lighting. Whether it is bright, blue sky or dark, gray clouds, skylight is a diffuse source that epitomizes the expression "global illumination." This is because skylight is global. It is a big ball around the earth that emits light omnidirectionally during the day. It is a gigantic, spherical area light. It is a luminous ball turned inward. Surprise! I have just described three different ways in which skylight can be simulated with MAX.

Skylight produces only soft shadows, yet it is remarkably similar to sunlight. Skylight is sunlight that has been diffused and spread around randomly in many directions. There are two primary differences between skylight and sunlight. First, sunlight appears mainly unidirectional, or traveling all in parallel rays, creating hard shadows. (I know we just spent a whole section describing how sunlight is omnidirectional, but compared to how random skylight is, sunlight appears relatively uniform.) The sky's light is omnidirectional relative to any place on the earth's surface, except where it is occluded by the earth, so it causes only soft shadows. Look at the underside of your chair outside on a cloudy day. See the shadows? Recall that objects cast shadows. What object is casting that shadow? Is it the chair? Partly. Mostly, however, it is the planet beneath your feet. Think of it this way: The sky is a big, luminous globe. You can't see most of it because the planet is in the way. If the whole ball of sky were not occluded by the planet (in other words, if you were just floating in a giant ball of luminous atmosphere with no planet), then everything would be lit from all angles. The reason most objects on the earth are dark on the bottom is because the earth is getting in the way and creating a shadow. Think also of nighttime. Night occurs because the earth is casting a big shadow and half the planet is sitting in it. This is an important consideration when building a diffuse global lighting solution. The earth is a big, fat shadow-caster. Don't forget it. Let's look at our stool again and see what a global light source like the sky will do to the shadows.

Figure 3.7: You can see in this image that there are no dark, "umbra" type shadows. The area under the stool does have a soft shadow because some of the light is occluded by the stool, but some amount of light appears to reach everywhere. The one disadvantage to using a directional light like a spotlight with area shadows is that, while the shadows behave correctly, the light is still coming from a single point. In this image, for example, light from a real area light would be wrapping around the object instead of leaving much of it in complete darkness.

Whereas the sun's light comes from one general direction and causes shadows on the opposite side of the object, skylight comes from all directions. There is no complete shadow from any direction as long as a line can be drawn between that point and any portion of the sky. This means that under skylight, most of the shadows are of the penumbra type. This is also known as "accessibility" lighting. If any part of the light source has "access" to any part of a surface, then there is some light. If a great deal of the light source has access to the surface, there is a great deal of light. If very little of the light source has access to the surface, there is very little light.

Incandescent Light

Intensity	Variable
Color	Warm spectrum (can be altered)
Direction	Any
Diffuseness	Usually low
Shadow	Very hard to soft
Shape	Any
Contrast	High to medium
Movement	Any
Size	Any

Incandescent light sources can be as simple as a frosted household lightbulb or a tiny halogen lamp. They can also be a burning fireplace, a candle, a stove element, an electric heater, or even a tiny LED. Incandescence involves the expenditure of energy at high temperature, resulting in light. So anything that is so hot it emits light can be said to be incandescent. For example, lava flows, fire embers, and a lit cigarette are all incandescent. Fireflies are not.

> **Note:** Some organisms emit light through photoluminescence. This happens because the organisms absorb infrared or ultraviolet radiation from sunlight during the day and then emit it when they move. We're not going to deal with the science of photo or chemical luminescence. Suffice it to say that by the time you finish this book, you will be able to look at any light source, identify its properties, and simulate it in MAX.

Because incandescence is caused by high heat, most incandescent light is on the warm or red side of the spectrum. Of course, clever stage and film lighting designers alter the color of incandescent light by placing a colored filter in front, which means you can get blue light out of an incandescent light source. Bear in mind that larger incandescent sources are likely to cause softer shadows, while smaller incandescent sources usually cause harder shadows.

Fluorescent Light

Intensity	Medium to low
Color	Cool spectrum (can be altered)
Direction	Any
Diffuseness	High to medium
Shadow	Usually soft
Shape	Usually none
Contrast	Usually medium to low
Movement	Usually none
Size	Usually medium to small

Fluorescent sources include, naturally, fluorescent lamps, neon lamps, computer monitors, televisions, and any other sources created by making a phosphor glow due to particle bombardment or electrical excitation. Technically, only lights containing fluorine are fluorescent. While neon lights, monitors, and fluorescents are technically different from each other, for the purpose of CG lighting their properties are similar enough that they will be dealt with pretty much identically, except for color and shape. For brevity we will refer to all such sources as "fluorescent" sources.

The primary difference between incandescent and fluorescent light, as far as we are concerned, is that incandescent sources are considered direct light sources and usually result in hard shadows, while fluorescent sources are considered diffused light and usually result in soft shadows.

> **Note:** *Hard shadows* refers to hard-edged or "sharp" shadows, while *soft shadows* refers to fuzzy, unclear edges on the shadows.

Reflected Light

Intensity	Any (depends on physical source)
Color	Any
Direction	Any
Diffuseness	Usually low
Shadow	Usually hard
Shape	Any
Contrast	Usually high
Movement	Any
Size	Any

Reflected light sources have distinct differences from other sources. Light reflected from a mirror, a water surface, a window, or other highly reflective surface displays many of the properties of the original light source. For example, sunlight reflecting off a pool onto a wall will retain most of the hard-edged properties as well as a good portion of the intensity, color, shape, and contrast. Skylight reflecting off the pool will retain all its diffuse properties as well. But adding light-reflective properties (called *caustics*) to a surface means a huge increase in rendering time. It is often simpler and quicker to place a new light at the place where the reflection would occur, replicate the properties of the original source (except for direction), and aim it in the direction that the reflected light would go.

Diffuse Reflected Light

Intensity	Any (depends on physical source)
Color	Any
Direction	Any
Diffuseness	High
Shadow	Soft
Shape	Usually none
Contrast	Usually low
Movement	Any
Size	Usually large

Diffuse reflected light is referred to in CG terminology as *radiosity*. What this means is that light coming from any source will touch a surface of some kind, then part of that light will reflect away, perhaps touching another surface and reflecting again. Radiosity reflections can continue infinitely until all photonic energy has been spent.

As with all reflections, the angle of incidence (the angle at which the light reaches the surface) must be equal to the angle of reflection. In the case of diffuse reflection, the surface is usually uneven or rough, causing the light rays to reflect away in numerous directions and effectively diffusing the reflected light.

A good example is that of sunlight illuminating the pavement in front of a wall. There is no direct lighting on the wall, and it is shaded by an overhanging roof. Blue skylight is filling in and lighting the wall, but there is a brighter, more yellow light on the wall coming from below. This is the light reflecting off the pavement and up onto the wall. The pavement is very uneven and so the light reflection is very diffuse. This is the most common form of lighting in nature. More than sunlight or skylight, the world is illuminated by this type of lighting. The light rays in nature can reflect from surface to surface an infinite number of times, radiating from pavement to wall, back to pavement, to nearby fences, trees, or whatever. Each time the sunlight strikes a surface, it diffuses into many new directions, so the more reflections that occur, the lower the overall intensity of the reflection becomes. As a lighting artist, you will learn to have a love/hate relationship with radiosity. On one hand, it adds a realism to MAX's renders that no other tool can match. On the other hand, the render times can become galactic very quickly, sometimes making radiosity impractical. We will spend some time later on discussing how best to fake radiosity and when it is best to use the real deal.

A Note about Proportion and Scale

These light sources have all been described according to their normal world scale, that is, as though you were the viewer standing there, looking at them. But the camera often sees things differently. What if, for example, there was a close-up of a candle? Well then, that incandescent source would not be tiny. It would be a major (and large) consideration in your lighting setup. What about the skylight? It is global and very large, unless you can only see a small square of it through a skylight. So in many ways the properties we have assigned to these light types are highly variable and will depend on the situation. Don't get stuck into one way of thinking about a light type or its properties. Infinite possibilities exist. Be prepared to create a technique never before tried for a situation never before seen. There are no rules. Look at the situation, analyze the light sources and their properties, and then proceed.

■ ■ ■

By now, it is probably becoming obvious to you that many different light sources can behave in many different ways and can display a number of variable properties. Just like the analogy of the auto mechanic who knows everything about the car but only thinks about fixing one system at a time, if you take each light source one at a time and analyze its particular properties and behaviors in a photograph, you should have enough information to understand what properties are present and you'll be able to add each light source, one at a time, into your scene. Later in this book, we discuss the tools we can use to simulate each of the many properties that we've discussed.

In this chapter, we have covered the properties of a number of specific real-world light sources. Hopefully by now you can analyze each light source type and recognize them in a photograph.

Chapter 4

Basic Material Considerations

Your job as a lighting artist is to light objects. These objects are textured with materials. In order to enable your lights to interact properly with your materials, you will need to understand some material properties that pertain to lighting. This is, by no means, a definitive guide to texturing. There are a number of great texturing books out there. I recommend you go and find some unless you are already a texturing guru. This chapter covers some of the basic material properties you need to consider when building your lighting environment, since the look of light and your texture properties are so closely interrelated. By the time you finish this chapter you should have a basic understanding of how color, specularity and glossiness, reflectivity, diffuseness, and luminosity affect your textures and your lighting.

Color in the Real World

The first and most significant property we discuss is color. We get into the dark art of color mixing in Chapter 20, but for now, suffice it to say that in the real world, the solid colors found on surfaces interact differently with colored light than they do by mixing other color into the surface. For example, if you mix paint colors of primary red, primary blue, and primary yellow, you will, theoretically, get black paint. However, if you mix light colors of primary red, primary green, and primary blue, you will, theoretically, get white light.

> **Note:** The reality of paint and light in the real world is that it is practically impossible to create true primary colors. A primary color is one that contains only a single wavelength. While it is possible to create this digitally, it is very difficult in the world of chemicals and pigments. So in reality, if you were to mix together paints labeled primary red, yellow, and blue, you will probably get a brownish gray. Keep this in mind when painting textures digitally, especially if you are trying to make it look photo-real.

The most obvious difference between solid pigment colors and lighting colors is that the primaries are different. For solids, it is red, yellow, and blue. For light, it is red, green, and blue. We deal with the reasons for this in Chapter 20, which covers color in depth.

Color is measured in wavelength. If we look at a spectrum of visible light, we see red colors at one end and blue colors at the other end. Blue and violet have the shortest wavelengths, while the red end has the longest wavelengths. Our eyes perceive these wavelengths and translate them into different colors. Various surfaces and materials in the real world will either absorb or reflect certain wavelengths based on the surfaces' own physical properties. A surface that absorbs only red and green wavelengths of light, for example, will appear mostly blue because it is reflecting the blue part of the spectrum. Furthermore, the reflected blue wavelengths will then reflect on other nearby surfaces. This is why if you put two objects of different colors near each other in bright light, they appear to gain some of the reflected color of each other. In the world of CG, this effect is called radiosity, or diffuse reflection.

> **Note:** It's the old trick of putting a buttercup under the chin to see if the yellow light reflects on the underside of the chin. OK, maybe you didn't do that as a child, but I did. The trick was that if you saw yellow light reflected under the chin, it meant you liked butter. Hey, it makes sense when you're six.

Be aware that if you shine a yellow light onto a blue surface, there will be little reflected light because the incoming wavelengths are opposite the surface wavelengths on a color wheel. This means that the yellow light is in the range most likely to be absorbed by the blue surface. Yellow light is yellow because it is missing most of the blue wavelengths, so there is little light left for the blue surface to reflect. More detail on color wheels, mixing, and the behavior of colors is in Chapter 20. Understanding the difference and interactions between solid colors and lighting colors can be confusing at first. This is all covered in Chapter 20 as well.

Specularity and Glossiness

If you were a physicist, you might comment that the reflectivity of a surface is based on its specularity. In the real world, *specularity* refers to the surface properties of an object that cause light to reflect in a directed manner, as from a smooth, polished surface, so that parallel light rays reaching the surface will still all be parallel light rays when reflected. In the real world, high specularity usually refers to mirror-like and other highly reflective surfaces.

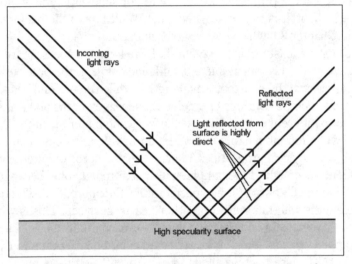

Figure 4.1: This image demonstrates how a very smooth surface reflects light information. The light information retains its original form and is therefore still easy to identify as an image. This is what occurs in a mirror. In the real world, shininess (or glossiness), reflectivity, and specularity are the same thing.

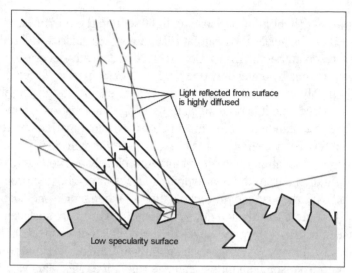

Figure 4.2: This image demonstrates how a rough surface reflects light information. The light information does not retain its original form and is scattered. The light information is no longer identifiable as the original light information. This occurs on any rough surface such as a sheet of paper or a wall painted with matte paint.

In MAX, however, specularity and reflectivity are two entirely different animals.

> **Note:** Specular Level and Glossiness in the Material Editor are misnomers. The control we know as Specular Level really should be called "Specular Intensity" because it refers to the illumination intensity of the specular highlight, or how bright it is. In other words, it's like having a brightness control over *just* the area of specular highlight. Glossiness, on the other hand, should actually be called "Specularity," because a high glossiness is a smaller, sharper, more defined specular highlight, indicating a smoother surface, while a low glossiness is a larger, softer, more diffused specular highlight, which indicates a rougher surface texture. Since real specularity refers to the roughness or smoothness of a surface (and therefore how "glossy" it appears), MAX's Glossiness control is real specular control. The Specular Level control in MAX actually is like a light intensity control that only affects the intensity of the specular highlight but not the illumination value.

Specular Level in MAX refers to the "shininess" of a surface. It's like that bright, white highlight you see on a polished apple. It refers to how much "brightness" or "lighting" information is reflected. But specularity in MAX does not include reflective image information. *Reflectivity*, on the other hand, refers to how much focused image information is reflected. In the real world, these two are inextricably tied together because image information *is* light information. The light seen in the mirror has reflected off the surface. One great reason why specularity and reflectivity are separate in MAX is that you can dramatically decrease rendering times by using only one or the other. A marble, for example, is usually highly specular. This means that there's a nice bright highlight on the surface, and it is reflecting all the image information around it. But if you are standing in a room and there are a few marbles on the floor ten feet away from you, it is unlikely that you will clearly see any of the image information unless you look very closely. All you can see is bright highlights from the nearby light sources or brightly colored objects. Why, then, spend time calculating it, when a nice specular light hit will complete the illusion quite adequately? For many surfaces, you will use specularity only and never turn on reflectivity, especially for surfaces with low specularity such as rough plastic or perhaps even skin. They both have some shininess, but the reflective (specular) value is so low and the reflected image so diffused by the rough surface that you will never really see an image reflected. You can save a good deal of render time by simply not calculating the reflections.

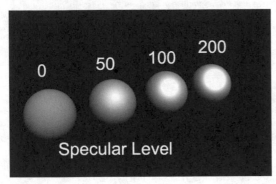

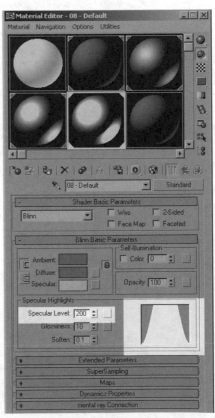

Figure 4.3: This image displays various specular levels. The Specular Level setting in the Material Editor determines the brightness or intensity of the specular highlight and really should, therefore, be named "Specular Intensity."

Figure 4.4: Specular Level can be set in your Material Editor. Press "m" to bring up the editor.

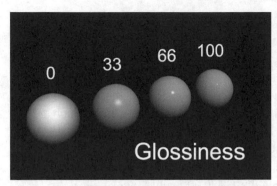

Figure 4.5: This image displays various levels of glossiness. The Glossiness setting in the Material Editor determines smoothness (or specularity) of the surface and really should, therefore, be named "Specularity." Note that the lower the Glossiness setting, the more spread out the specular highlight becomes. Wider specular highlights indicate a surface that is rough and is diffusing the light information more.

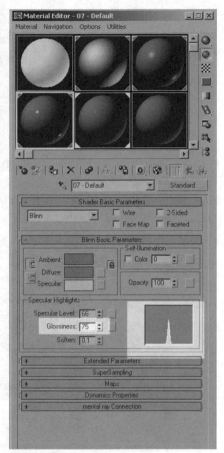

Figure 4.6: Glossiness can also be set in your Material Editor.

Reflectivity

Reflectivity in the real world refers to how much light is not absorbed by a material. For example, coal is not very reflective, but snow is highly reflective. A mirror is highly reflective, but a cast-iron frying pan is not.

Colloquially, however, we think of reflectivity as meaning how well you can see the reflection of an image in a surface. We think that a mirror is highly reflective, but a white wall is not. In truth, both the mirror and the white wall are highly reflective. The difference is that one material diffuses the light that it reflects, and the other does not. If you go back and look at the images in the previous section of this chapter, you will understand that the white wall has a very rough surface at the microscopic level, and so the image information is scattered so widely that we can no longer discern any image information in the reflection.

However, a mirror's surface is so smooth that the image information is not scattered at all and the reflected light is in almost the same form as it was before striking the mirror's surface; therefore, we can see the image information clearly.

In MAX, however, reflectivity refers only to image reflection and has nothing to do with diffuseness, specularity, or glossiness, all of which are separate controls in the MAX Material Editor panel.

So this means that you use the Reflection setting if you specifically want to reflect the surrounding environment in your object's surface, such as a mirror, a glass, or a shiny marble floor, but you can leave it off for diffuse surfaces that don't reflect images. For the purposes of this discussion, we'll use raytraced reflections because they look better.

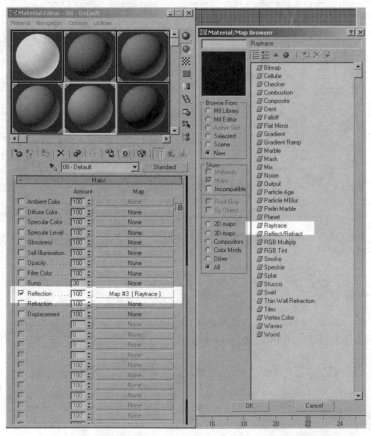

Figure 4.7: For raytraced reflections to work, you must have a reflection map added to the material with the map type set to Raytrace.

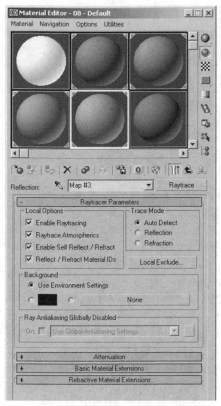

Figure 4.8: You will then have access to the Raytracer Parameters panel.

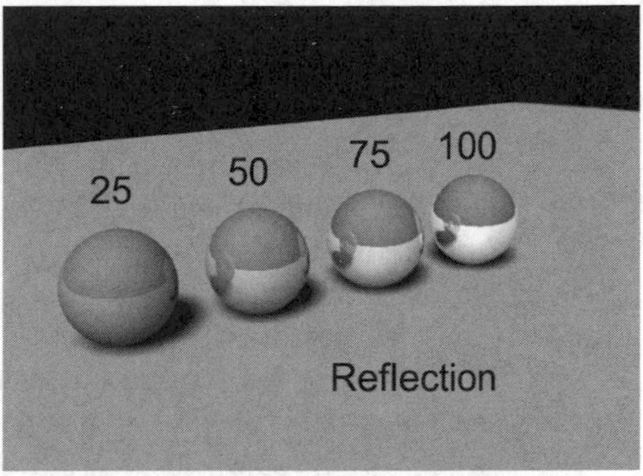

Figure 4.9: This image demonstrates the Reflection value at different levels. The higher the value, the more image information is reflected in the texture. Very simple.

Diffuse Color

In MAX, Diffuse Color is a single setting that defines two properties. The first and most obvious property is the material's color. When you click on the Diffuse button in the Material Editor, you are presented with the Color Selector. The second and less obvious property refers to the diffuse *value* (or diffuse *level*); in other words, how bright or dark the material is, or how much light it absorbs and how much it diffuses or reflects. For example, a beach ball has a high diffuse value regardless of its color. When light hits it, you can see that it is brightly lit and easily visible. Technically, we are saying that because light hits the object and is widely diffused, or dispersed, the object is easy to see from any direction because a great deal of light is reflecting from its surface in all directions. As another example, a mirror has a very low diffuse value. While it does reflect all the light away, it is not diffused. The reflections are direct. All you see is a reflection of whatever image is before the mirror. It is technically possible in the real world for a material to have no reflectivity and no diffuseness. A material such as this would be invisible because no light is reflected or diffused from its surfaces. The only item known to have these texture properties is a black hole, which does not reflect or diffuse light from its surface. But this is mainly due to gravity rather than surface properties. If black holes did not have the immense gravity necessary to suck in light, then they would be visible because all surfaces have some measure of diffuse value. Even the surface of the sun has a diffuse value, but it is completely overwhelmed by the luminosity of the sun.

In MAX, if you wished to remove shadows from an object's surface, you could accomplish this by lowering the Diffuse Level value of the surface and increasing the Self-Illumination value. Or if you want to look at it another way, in the real world, a white surface like a piece of paper has a high diffuse value because it diffuses a great deal of light and is, therefore, highly visible. A black surface, on the other hand, has a low diffuse value because it diffuses very little light. The easiest way to envision this is by imagining driving down a dark road at night. If a person is wearing all white clothes, your car headlights will pick him up sooner and he will be visible much farther away because his clothes have a high diffuse value. Someone dressed entirely in black might not be seen until you are very close, because very little light is being diffused back toward you, and therefore there is very little light information entering your eyes. The person is very difficult to see.

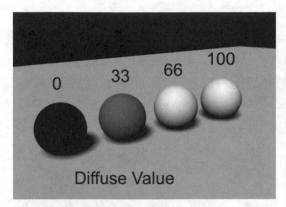

Figure 4.10: The texture settings on all four balls are exactly the same except for the Diffuse Level value. In MAX, Diffuse Level is defined in the Color Selector as the Whiteness value. Diffuse Level indicates how much of the light received by the surface is reflected back. A low diffuse value means very little light is reflected, while a high diffuse value means a great deal of light is reflected. The more visible light reflected by the surface, the more visible it is to the human eye. So remember that diffuse is about more than just the color; it is also about diffuse reflection of light.

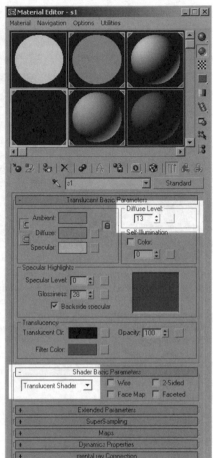

Figure 4.11: Pure diffuse value can be seen in the basic parameters of the Translucent Shader.

Luminosity

Some objects in your shot will have surfaces that emit light. These surfaces are said to be "self-illuminating." In other words, they display the property of *luminosity*. The surface of a lightbulb, for example, has a pretty high luminosity value. So does a computer monitor. Any surface that emits light can be said to be luminous. Discreet, the makers of MAX, has provided us with some great tools to simulate the luminosity of a surface. One is the Self-Illumination value found in the Material Editor. This value brightens the surface, eliminating shadows as though the brightness were overpowering any shadows. This value, however, does not actually emit light. It does not actually transmit illumination to nearby surfaces unless you turn on MAX's radiosity. In this case, the luminous surface does emit light to nearby surfaces.

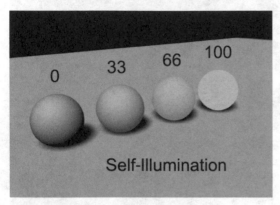

Figure 4.12: In this image, the texture values are the same for all four balls, except for luminosity. The higher the Self-Illumination value, the more light a surface is apparently emitting. A lightbulb, for example, has a low Self-Illumination value when it is turned off, but a high Self-Illumination value when it is turned on. Note how, as the luminosity increases, the shadows are filled in.

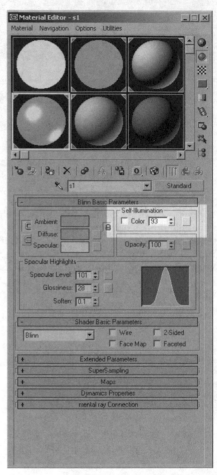

Figure 4.13: Self-Illumination is also accessed in the Material Editor under most Basic Parameters panels.

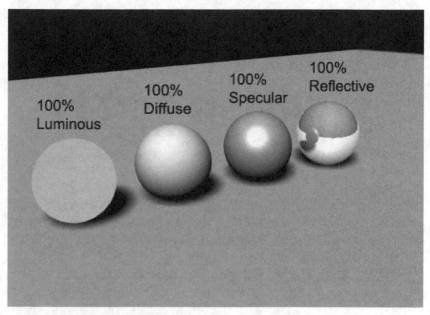

Figure 4.14: This image demonstrates the use of luminosity, diffuseness, specularity, and reflectivity. All other settings are at 0%.

■ ■ ■

I hope this chapter has helped you understand some of the surface properties we deal with when lighting our scenes. Lighting is only half about the lights we use and how we use them. The other half of lighting is about the surfaces that we light. The surface properties have a direct effect on how the light looks when it reaches them.

Chapter 5

Studying Light

This chapter deals with the observation of light in the real world. By the time you have finished this chapter, you should be able to observe and identify the light properties specific to various types of natural and artificial light sources and to shadows.

Being a great lighting artist is all about understanding how real light works so that you can recreate it in your virtual environment. The only way to really understand the nature of light and shadows is to study it.

Studying light is really as simple as it sounds. As an artist, you wish to recreate something in the medium of your choice. If you are a painter, you might wish to paint a portrait. This requires you to understand human skeletal and muscular structures, the behavior of fabrics, the visible properties of skin, iris, lens, and hair. Perhaps there is a chair in the portrait. You must understand the grain of the wood and the properties of the velvet or leather upholstery. You must understand how the light will play off each surface, how the specular highlights and reflections should look, how shadows are formed and where, what the diffuse reflected light will do to the underside of the chin and the nose, how back-lit cotton will react translucently, and so on.

Studying to be an artist means studying the art of the masters. It also means studying the natural elements that come together to create an image. In this case, the element we are talking about is light. Light deserves as much study as any other element of your composition — perhaps even more. In the world of CG, your lighting is mission critical to making your shot look real. So start by spending some time just looking around. You don't have to go to a gallery. Light is everywhere, in every form. A trick used by many lighting designers is to hold up one hand or a piece of paper and stare at it, turning it over and around to see how the light plays across it. Look at the shadows and where they are, what color they are, and what sort of light is filling the shadows. Check out the contrast, the shape and softness of the shadows, and the direction of the light source. Can you identify all the light sources around just by looking at your hand? You should be able to, but if you can't, don't worry — you will be by the time you've finished this book!

Some artists like to put a white or gray ball in an environment to study the lighting. This works, but I find it sterile. A hand is a much more interesting shape and will provide much more information. That's not to disparage the white or gray ball. If you can get the VFX supervisor to stick a ball (especially a reflective ball!) on the set and take a photo or provide some extra footage from the plate, it will provide valuable information for matching the shot's lighting.

> **Note:** Reflective balls and 18% gray balls are commonly used as lighting references on the set. A good VFX supervisor will be sure to provide these references to the visual effects department where the CG lighting will take place. The gray ball shows general light effects on a diffuse, round shape, while the reflective ball works like a 180 degree mirror, showing you the precise position and color of the light sources and giving you a rough approximation of the intensity ratio between light sources.

Here are some of the light types you may encounter, along with some suggestions on how to start looking at them.

Natural Light

Natural light refers to the light we find in nature — light that is not made by people. I am going to tell you many times in this section that the best way to really understand these light types is to go out and study them. No book, no video, and no plug into your brain will take the place of observing, experiencing, and understanding for yourself the way real-world light interacts with things in your environment.

Sunlight

The most obvious natural light source is the sun. Understanding how sunlight reaches the earth and how it lights objects in your environment is important to creating realistic sunlight in your CG scene. A common misconception is that the sun is equivalent to a point source with light rays radiating outward omnidirectionally. Another misconception is that the sun is a distant light that is so far away that all its rays are parallel by the time they reach the earth. The fact is that these are both true in part, but there are more qualities not yet discussed.

The sun is about 149,597,890 kilometers away from the earth and its diameter is about 100 times that of the earth. The entire surface of the sun is radiating light in every direction at once. This means that over the width of the sun's disc as viewed from the earth, parallel rays of light are approaching the earth. There are also rays of light spreading out in all directions from every point on the surface of the sun and rays of light converging on the earth and all things on it from many directions. The result of the size differential between the sun and the earth can be observed during a lunar eclipse when the earth passes directly between the sun and the moon. The moon first passes into the penumbra, that area behind the earth where the sun's light is partially obscured. The sun is so much larger than the earth that some of the sun's light manages to reach behind the earth, creating a partial shadow. The moon then passes into the umbra, that area where there is no direct sunlight at all.

Let's look at an illustration of a lunar eclipse to describe this phenomenon.

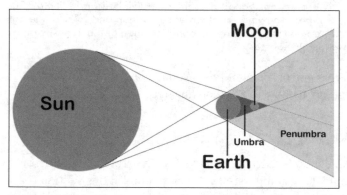

Figure 5.1: This effect occurs for every object lit by direct sunlight, but the angles are usually so slight as to be imperceptible. The light rays often appear to be parallel. In many cases, this effect will not need to be addressed in CG lighting. Sometimes, however, understanding this effect is critical to your lighting.

If you place a chair in the sunlight, you will notice that the shadow cast by the chair is sharpest near where the chair is touching the ground and becomes fuzzier with distance. This is the same effect that is found in the lunar eclipse. In the case of our chair, the sun is much larger than the chair, so the converging light rays are able to reach around behind it, "softening" the shadow.

Skylight

When we say "skylight" we are usually referring to a clear, blue sky. When the sky is blue, you will notice that shadows have a bluish tint to them. It does not seem obvious at first, but look closely. If you look outside on a snowy day, it is very obvious. Skylight is a global light source that has several immediately obvious effects.

> **Note:** In my discussions with lighting artists of varying experience and skill, this, more than any other topic, has become one of debate. Some artists outright refuse to believe that the blue sky illuminates and fills in the shadows cast by objects on a clear, sunny day. Some insist that shadows are the absence of light and, therefore, contain no illumination at all (even though they admit they can see into those shaded areas). Others, recognizing that there is some light in the shadowed area, insist that the shadows must be gray because, well, isn't it just lit at a lower intensity? To address these directly, lest you become befuddled by these non-thinkers, a shadow on earth is not the absence of light. It is the absence of *some* light or the absence of light from a particular light source, but not the absence of all light, because light is always reflecting and refracting around the atmosphere. As for gray shadows, if the sky is blue, and the sky is filling in the shadowed area, then the shadowed area must be blue...just as blue as it would be if you were shining a flashlight with a blue filter in front of it. The problem seems to be that people let their eyes be fooled by their preconceptions. If the tablecloth is white, and it is less lit in one area than another, then it must be gray in that area, not blue. Read on, though. If this is not yet clear, it will become so in the following pages.

Skylight fills the shadows with a blue, low-intensity light. It illuminates almost every surface except the most obscurely hidden. Skylight is most visible in areas where direct sunlight does not reach. That's one of the main reasons you can see down a narrow back alley between two tall buildings even if it is not directly lit by sunlight.

Skylight, which seems relatively dim in broad daylight, can seem blinding if you are indoors. (Ever leave a movie theater on a bright but cloudy day?) Skylight can also be orange, red, or yellow if it is sunset or sunrise. It can even have a greenish tint under some strange atmospheric conditions. Keep in mind that a surface lit by direct sunlight is also additively lit by the sky. In other words, on a clear, sunny day, both skylight and sunlight are illuminating most surfaces outside. There are two light sources, two colors, two completely different sets of properties at work on that surface. The reason that light on a surface looks whiter than the sun is that the relatively yellow light of the sun is being mixed with the blue skylight. This phenomenon pushes the final, mixed color much closer to white than either skylight or sunlight emissions. Go out and observe. Record your findings. Get to know the sky.

> **Note:** To clarify, the apparent light from the sun appears more yellow because some of the blue light is absorbed and re-emitted by the atmosphere (which is why the sky is blue), leaving less blue in the sunlight that is finally transmitted to us down here on the surface of the earth. When the blue skylight and the yellow sunlight mix together again on a surface, the final mix is closer to the actual color of sunlight than either earthly skylight or earthly sunlight on its own.

Cloudy Day

A cloudy sky can throw some pretty wild changes into an otherwise simple lighting situation. While a cloudy day still provides a global illumination (or "sky dome") scenario, there can be several key differences. First, there is usually little or no direct sunlight, meaning the skylight becomes the key source of light. Second, clouds can range from white to dark gray, pink, red, orange, or even greenish. This means variations in color and intensity. Third, there are unlikely to be any hard shadows. Fourth, these factors will often change more rapidly than on a clear, sunny day (depending on your weatherman). Check out your next cloudy day. Imagine what tools in MAX you might use to simulate the soft lighting environment you see outside on a cloudy day.

Moonlight

Moonlight is very interesting. Because it is 100% reflected light, it comes to earth roughly the color of the moon, which appears far more white than sunlight. Sometimes moonlight is perceived as blue light and is often simulated this way on set. The human eye is accustomed to a more yellowish light from the sun, but the relative whiteness of the moonlight is closer to the blue end of the visible spectrum. This relative color shift is often misinterpreted as blue light. Also, the blueness of moonlight is simply near-white reflected moonlight that has been diffused through the atmosphere. Just as daytime skylight is blue, nighttime skylight is also blue but at a much lower intensity. The mix of white moonlight and blue nighttime skylight gives the real impression of blue-tinted light. The moonlight is reflecting from a highly diffuse surface, but the light comes so far that most of it is lost in directions away from the earth. We actually receive only a tiny fraction of the light that hits the moon, just as we receive only a tiny fraction of the light that leaves the sun.

A night lit by a full moon can seem quite bright when it is, in fact, only slightly lighter than pitch black. The key to understanding moonlight and how to simulate it is in knowing how the human eye reacts to low-light situations. The eye is far more sensitive than a computer monitor, a painter's canvas, or a photograph. The iris will dilate to let in more light when it is dark and will contract to let in less light when it is very bright. This keeps the illuminated world within a range that is comfortable and understandable to the light receptors in the eye. So while a moonlit night is much darker than a sky-lit shadow on a bright sunny day, the eye may be able to see clear details in the moonlight but almost no details in the shadows on a sunny day, perceiving those shadows to be nearly black. This is because the eye has adjusted. It all comes down to these three words: "It's all relative."

> **Note:**   To demonstrate this "relative" effect, my college stage lighting class once aimed all the lights in the theater at a single spot on the stage floor. It was a blinding 200,000 watts of light. Nobody in the class was capable of standing in the lit spot and looking up at the lights. At about 3 p.m., the sun would pass by an open shutter, allowing the sunlight to shine on that same spot. The sunlight cut through the stage lights like a hot knife through butter.

Starlight

Starlight is very similar to moonlight except that it is usually lower intensity, it is usually either white or a steel blue in color, and it does not cast hard shadows being, by nature, a rather omnidirectional source. The best way to understand starlight (or any light) is to go out into it and look around. You'll see soft shadows and gentle, very low illumination.

Starlight behaves exactly the same as skylight, but at a much lower intensity level and a much more saturated color.

Artificial Light

Artificial light refers to light emitted by manufactured devices. This usually means electric light, but one can also argue that torches, lighters, fireplaces, rocket engines, lasers, gasoline fires, and H-bomb explosions belong in this category. Let's not be nitpicky.

Incandescent Sources

Incandescent sources usually mean light sources that emit light by the conversion of electricity to heat, such as common household lightbulbs. We can also include flame sources such as candles, fireplaces, or torches that do not use electricity but emit light through the production of high heat through a chemical conversion (burning or rapid oxidation). We generally consider flame sources to be incandescent because the color temperature of these processes falls into the same range as those of electric incandescent light sources.

Diffuse Sources

Diffuse incandescent sources are very common. A frosted lightbulb, for example, is a diffuse incandescent source. Notice how much like the sun these lights behave. Shadows are sharpest near the object and become softer farther away. This is because the area of light emission is relatively large, causing the shadow falloff or "penumbra" gradient-like effect. They are just a much smaller-scale version of the same type of light.

Point Sources

Point light sources are represented in MAX as omni lights. Incandescent point sources include light-emitting diodes, small candle flames, and tiny lightbulbs. In truth, none of these are technically point sources because a point source should, by strict physical definition, have no dimension or measurable size in any direction (that is how omni lights behave inside MAX). But these examples are usually small enough to qualify for "point source" status in the CG world. In some cases, the sun can be considered a point or omni source for CG purposes because it is so far away that it may seem small. You can get away with it under the right conditions. Point light sources, whether in the real world or in CG, result in hard, diverging shadows. Point sources are always smaller than the objects they illuminate; therefore, the shadows from omni sources are always diverging (getting larger with distance). Since these sources are usually physically small, they are also usually appropriately less intense. But that doesn't mean you can't think up some completely strange and unique use for a point source that follows none of the normal properties.

Fluorescent Sources

Fluorescent sources refer to lights such as neon or fluorescent fixtures where illumination is achieved by bombarding "phosphors" with electrons. These light sources are always diffuse since the illumination occurs over a relatively large area. Take a neon sign or a fluorescent tube, for example. Look at the type of light cast by these fixtures. Examine the shadows. They are soft because of the wide area of light emission. Note that neon lights also come in a wide range of colors, shapes, and sizes, far more variable than any natural source.

Shadow

Perhaps the most common misconception about shadows is that they are an effect created by a light source. Some say lights cast shadows. If you take a moment to think about this, it is obvious that lights do not cast shadows. Shadows are cast by objects that are being illuminated by the light. Shadows are the absence of light from a particular source. Shadows are the space behind an object where the light cannot reach. This is not to say that all shadows are completely void of light. In fact, almost all shadows have some visible light spilling into them from other sources. Shadows occur where some or all of the light sources are completely or partially occluded. Normally, the most obvious shadow cast by an object is the area where the key, or main, light does not reach.

Figure 5.2: In this image, the shadow is cast by the railing. Its position is exactly opposite the sun relative to the railing. Some detail is still visible inside the shadow though. This is because while skylight is present everywhere in this image, the sunlight is partly occluded by the rail.

Shadows are critical in our everyday life. They allow our visual systems to understand where a stair ends or where the curb edge is on the sidewalk. Without shadows we would constantly be tripping over and bumping into things. When you walk through a doorway into a room beyond, one of the main identifiers of that doorway is the difference in lighting between one room and the next or of the shadows defining the

61

shape of the door or the molding around the doorway. If all surfaces were
evenly lit and without shadow, the only differentiation between the surfaces would be color. What if you are trying to find a white door in a
white wall? It would be impossible without some lighting differentiation,
that is, shadows of some sort. Look around you and find a door. If it is
the same color as the wall, then the only reason you can see it is
because of the shadows that give it form.

The qualities of shadows can provide a great deal of information
about the lighting environment. Are the shadows hard or soft? Are they
deep or subtle? Are they long or short? What colors fill the shadow, if
any? What shapes do we see within the shadow or outlining the shadow?
Is it only the shape of the object casting the shadow, or are there other
shapes? What causes the other shapes? Shadow shows the direction of
the light source. Do the shadows demonstrate a natural light source or a
strange, unusual one? Are the shadows uniform, or does light and darkness vary over the surface of the shadow? What causes the variations?

Shadows come in infinite shape, size, and quality. Pay special attention to what the shadow qualities are for your particular light source.
Hard shadows, for example, are actually pretty uncommon in the real
world. They are created by point sources or any source that does not
have an area of illumination. In the real world, there is no such source,
but in the CG world, omni lights and direct lights with raytracing create
hard shadows. We will get into the reasons for this later on. For now, suffice it to say that even though the shadows are physically incorrect,
these lights are not useless. They are very useful indeed, but must be
used judiciously (and cleverly) to accomplish a realistic simulation of
real-world lighting.

In the real world, both diffuse reflection and area source lights create soft shadows. Fortunately, MAX's shadow maps are soft by default, if
not exactly physically accurate. And there are plenty of other options for
soft shadows too. For more on spotlights, see Chapter 7.

Most real-world shadows will be filled with a secondary light source.
This secondary light source is likely to be a global source such as sky or
cloud or a diffuse reflected source such as the light bounced off a road or
wall. Most likely, the secondary or "fill" source is colored, either because
the sky is blue or because the wall is yellow or whatnot. Either way, the
fill source is probably colored, which means the shadow is colored. We
take note of these real-world lighting properties and recreate them in
MAX. For more on key and fill lighting, see Chapter 6.

Light Color

We should begin here with a short discussion of "color" versus "color temperature." Colors in the red side of the spectrum (including orange and yellow) are considered to be "warm" colors because they remind us of fire and heat, while colors in the blue side of the spectrum are considered to be "cool" because they remind us of ice and snow.

The reality is that when a chunk of metal is heated up, it begins with a red glow, and as it gets hotter it goes to orange, yellow white, and even blue, provided it hasn't melted already. This is where the term "color temperature" comes from. The higher color temperatures are closer to the so-called "cool" end of the color spectrum, while the lower color temperatures are closer to the so-called "warm" end of the color spectrum. In astronomy, red giants are considered relatively cool (temperature-wise) while blue dwarfs are considered to be extremely hot stars. Confusing enough? We use both terms in this book, but for convention's sake, a color that is described as "cool" will be in the blue end of the color spectrum and a color described as "warm" will be in the red end. If I want to talk about color temperature, I will specify it as "color temperature." Don't worry if you don't have a handle on this yet; we cover color and color temperature in the "Kelvin" section of Chapter 12.

■ ■ ■

Hopefully, this chapter has provided you with a place to start observing light in your world. Observation and understanding are absolutely essential to creating believable lighting in your CG work. There will be examples later in the book to help you understand exactly how to replicate the light you see around you once you understand it.

By now, you should be able to observe and identify the light properties specific to various types of natural and artificial light sources and to shadows. Whether it is sunlight, neon lights, or a ball of flame, you should have a good idea about what differentiates one set of light properties from another.

Chapter 6

Principles of Lighting

This chapter covers basic lighting principles including concepts such as the key light, the fill light, the highlight (or rim light), three- and four-point lighting, basic coloring, intensity ratios, and a little history discussing how lighting became what it is. By the end of this chapter, you should have a grasp of these basic concepts and how they relate to not only photographic lighting but also light in the real world.

Lighting has four primary purposes. First, we light a scene to illuminate the subject, to make it visible. Second, we try to focus the viewer's attention on specific areas of the shot and to subtly make other areas less prominent. Third, we give form or shape to the subjects, the set, and other elements in frame so they don't seem flat and unreal. And fourth, we wish to build an emotional framework for the scene so that our viewers will follow along with the story just as we wish.

As with any other visual element, there are certain principles that apply to most lighting situations. I hesitate to call any of these rules, since this is art and artists tend to make hamburger out of anything they are told is a rule. So consider these principles a starting point. Once you have fully grasped the principles, do with them as you will. Please don't misinterpret that statement as meaning that the principles in this chapter are not important. They are crucial in being able to move on to more advanced lighting concepts, just as when learning to play a piano, the pianist must first learn which key is middle C, what a scale is, and what keys are. The pianist later forgets about these things. They simply become second nature to the pianist, but they remain there in the subconscious, the absolute core of knowledge that allows the pianist to play the piano. In the same way, these principles will become your keys, scales, and "middle C." You must know them so well that you can forget about them and carry on playing and composing.

The Key Light

The *key light* in a scene is the primary source of light. It can be any light source from any angle. It is the light that provides primary illumination. Sunlight is an easy example. On a sunny day, sunlight is the key source. There are no brighter lights on earth that you are likely to see in your shot. Make it a cloudy day and the sky becomes the key light because it is now the primary source of illumination. (Yes, the clouds are luminous because they absorb and diffuse the sunlight, re-emitting it toward us.) This is an entirely different type of source, but in this situation, the clouds become the key light. In your living room, a floor lamp may be the key, or the fireplace could be the key if the electric lights are all off. It's a simple concept.

Figure 6.1: This image demonstrates a single key light alone on a chair.

The Fill Light

Look at any shadow in front of you. There it is — the *fill light*. Fill light does two main things. Most obviously, it illuminates areas that are shadowed from the key light. It also usually illuminates all the areas that are lit by the key light, or at least some of them where the key light and fill light overlap on a surface. In other words, in a situation with a key light and fill light, the shadows are illuminated by the fill light and the unshadowed areas are illuminated by the key light and the fill light wherever they overlap.

If there were no fill light, shadows would be pitch black and you would see no details inside them. This is not likely to happen on or near our planet, although there is a good deal less fill light available in space, since there is little or no atmospheric diffusion going on.

Fill light can be created by any secondary source. Usually, however, it is either a global source like skylight and cloud light or it is a diffuse reflection (radiosity). But since fill light is simply a lower-intensity light filling up the shadows, you can use any tool in your CG arsenal to create this illumination. For a skylight fill, for example, I would probably choose an area light as my first choice for accuracy and speed. My second choice might be global illumination. My third choice would probably be a spotlight with high shadow fuzziness. These are all covered in detail later. Suffice it to say that the fill light mainly "fills" the shadowy spaces left over by the key light.

Figure 6.2: This image includes both a key light and a fill light. Note the soft shadows beneath the chair created by the area light that I used for the fill.

The Highlight

The *highlight* is also known as the top light, the back light, the tip light, and the rim light, depending on where you learned your lighting. Its primary purpose is to make an object stand out from its background, to help define the shape, and to provide a nice, defined edge for those nasty green-screen or blue-screen shots.

Figure 6.3: This image demonstrates the concept of a highlight or "rim" light. The top edges are clearly outlined by a specular hit and heightened illumination. This makes the object stand out sharply from the background.

Figure 6.4: Here is a good example of a highlight in nature. In this example one could argue that the key light is the highlight or rim light. Others may say there is no key, just a fill and a rim. (See color image.)

Some artists go pretty wild with highlighting, adding a rim light for every shot. But like all other light sources in your shot, there had better be some motivation for the light.

Note: The rim light is the most overused light in the CG world. It has become almost a joke to see an animated CG film in which every character has a strong rim light in every shot from every angle, regardless of the lighting environment around them. It's getting downright cheesy. Please, I beg you, as up-and-coming lighting artists, for the love of all that's good, break the "cheese" barrier and start using rim lights judiciously and subtly!

Note: Sometimes what appears to be a rim light on a texture is really a texture shader that makes the surface luminosity change based on its angle to the camera. So lights are not always to blame, but the result, effect, and "cheese factor" are still the same.

If, for example, a person is sitting in a small room and the only light is from a window to the subject's left, there had better not be a rim light making a nice halo over the subject's hair. There is no light source to justify it. It will definitely look very wrong. If you really want or need this nice rim, find a way to create a justification or find another solution. Don't add lights that have no source in the "real" world.

McCandless Lighting

Once upon a time, a lighting designer named Stanley McCandless observed the natural interaction between key and fill lighting and desired to recreate this effect for the stage. McCandless observed that a very bright, very large light source (the sun) approached the subject from one angle. He thought to recreate this using a large array of "key" lights all pointing in the same direction. He also observed a secondary, very uniform source (the sky) filling in all the shadows. He sought to recreate this using a large array of "fill" lights, also all pointing in the same direction but opposite the key array. Thus, the McCandless lighting system was born. Each area on the stage (of which there were usually six or nine) was lit with two spotlights, one 45 degrees to the left and one 45 degrees to the right. Both lights came from 45 degrees above. One set of lights was the key light and the other was the fill light. Usually the key was colored warm and the fill was cool.

Note: Of course for a nighttime scene, one might have both the key and fill on the cool side of the spectrum. For a very hot summer day in a desert, one might make both key and fill on the warm side. Much depends on individual taste, style, and desired emotional impact.

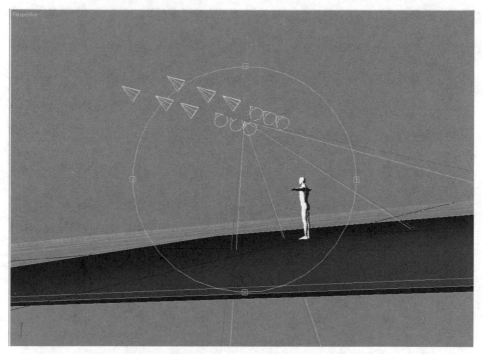

Figure 6.5: This illustration shows a basic McCandless lighting setup.

Try a render using two plain spotlights in the McCandless setup, 45 degrees to either side of the subject and 45 degrees above. Make one slightly amber and the other steel (faint) blue. Light any subject you wish; it doesn't matter. You should get an image something like this:

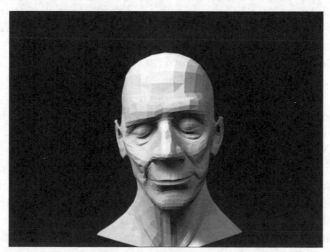

Figure 6.6: McCandless lighting (See color image.)

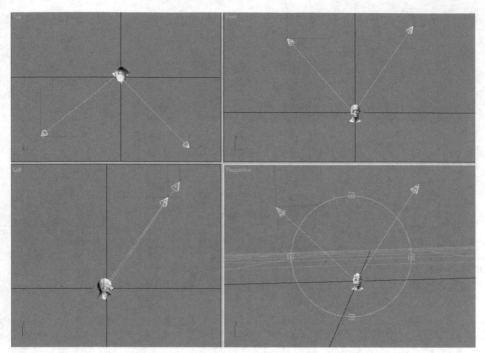

Figure 6.7: You've just created a key/fill lighting setup. Hold onto it. We'll be adding more light.

Key/Fill Lighting

Key/fill lighting is McCandless lighting boiled down to its most basic principles. It doesn't require the formal rules or rigidity of the original theatrical system that defined specific lighting angles relative to the audience or viewer. In a theater, the audience sits in a specific spot relative to the action and to the lighting. In film, the camera has the advantage of taking any point of view (POV), even if it is from within a mouse hole or atop a giant chandelier. This means the lighting designer must be much more flexible in planning than Stanley McCandless had to be. In the world of CG, the camera can even be placed within or behind light sources — something that is not possible in the real world.

Observe key/fill lighting in the world around you. You can see that the lighting angles, colors, shapes, sizes, and source types combine into infinite variety. In some cases, the key light may also act as a highlight. In other cases, the key and fill light are the same source. Sometimes the key is cool and the fill is warm. Sometimes both are cool or both are warm. Sometimes the fill light is also the rim light, or the rim light could be the key. The primary source does not necessarily have to be the light that presents the most illumination toward the camera.

It comes down to this: You have a key light shining on an object. Whatever light is illuminating the shadows is the fill light. Any angle, any light source, any property is allowed. The key light illuminates; the fill light shapes.

Three-Point Lighting

Yet another step beyond key/fill lighting, three-point lighting is a key light, a fill light, and a highlight (or rim light). It is a simple combination that provides illumination, form, and dimension. Three-point lighting is, perhaps, one of the best-known, most used, and most misused lighting setups known. Although it is a very functional setup, it is often used in completely inappropriate environments. Remember: Every light must be justified.

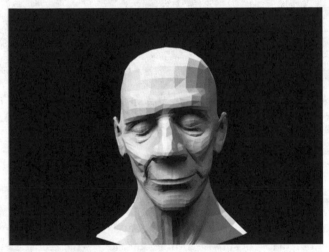

Figure 6.8: Three-point lighting (See color image.)

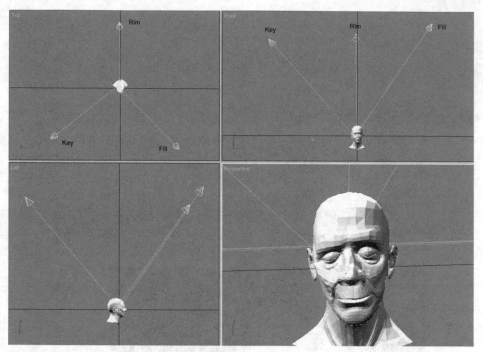

Figure 6.9: This render demonstrates a typical three-point light setup. Here we have a key light as the primary illumination, a fill light providing secondary illumination within the shadows, and a highlight giving a sharp outline to the subject.

Simple, right? Now you are a studio lighting god.

What Is Great about Three-Point Lighting

Three-point lighting is a simple, versatile, and powerful method of providing an immediate "beauty" lighting scenario in which most elements are likely to be visible and attractively lit. The key light provides primary illumination, the fill light provides form and shadow fill, and the highlight provides dimension.

Three-point lighting using spotlights is also extremely fast to render with shadow maps.

No scene or lighting analysis is necessary, and the artist can import a generic three-point lighting rig from a prepared scene any time, scale the rig, and start a render.

What Is Not So Great about Three-Point Lighting

Three-point lighting is probably the most grossly overused and most inappropriately used lighting setup in the world of CG. Mostly this is because artists know it is a rig that will make their 3D objects look attractive without having to learn anything about lighting. Consequently, CG artwork from animated TV series to feature visual effects is lit using this technique with little consideration for whether or not it is appropriate to the shot. It's a travesty that so many scenes that call for great, creative lighting are shortchanged by artists who don't wish to take the time to learn how to provide really good lighting or by those who think they know how to light, simply because they have been pointing lights from a computer terminal for years. Make no mistake about this: You cannot learn lighting by sitting at a computer monitor with 3D software in front of you, no matter how many hours a day, no matter how many years you have been doing it. An experienced lighting artist will see a shot with three-point lighting at the movie theater and will shrug and wonder sadly why there weren't any real lighting artists available at the time.

Four-Point Lighting

Just to add another monkey wrench to the works, I'm going to include one of my favorite "beauty" techniques. It's a variation on the age-old three-point technique. One of the limitations of three-point lighting is that it doesn't account for any "bounce" source reflected from the ground in front of objects. Key, fill, and rim light all come from above, leaving any underside surfaces in the dark. Bounce light is often forgotten simply because it is a subtle and usually low-intensity light source in the scene, but adding this one light to create a four-point rig can really make a big difference.

> **Note:** There are some, but few, instances in which ambient intensity is appropriate for use in your CG artwork. The main reason it is so infrequently used is that ambient intensity simply adds an even illumination to every surface regardless of light direction or intensity. This has the effect of "flattening out" your beautiful 3D work. That doesn't mean we never use it, just rarely in photoreal VFX work.

Figure 6.10: In this image, the "bounce" light behaves like radiosity reflected from the floor or road in front of the man, also filling in where lesser experienced lighting artists might be tempted to use ambient intensity—a big no-no in most cases. (See color image.)

Other Lighting Angles

Lighting designers in film, TV, and especially in theater are constrained to the physical and technical requirements of their lighting instruments. A light must be placed where it has access to electricity, where an operator can reach it if necessary, and where it is not in the way of the camera or the audience. In the beautiful, versatile world of CG, we have no such constraints. We can place any light anywhere at any angle, even directly in front of the camera. Let your imagination go wild. Play with lighting angles and see what they do.

In addition to key, fill, and highlight angles, two of the most common additional angles used are sidelight and footlight. Sidelight is a valuable tool for its ability to punctuate an object's form using a slightly dramatic angle. This usually results in a strong emotional response from the viewer.

Figure 6.11: Sidelight (See color image.)

The term "footlight" derives from the early days of the stage when candles, gas lights, or early electric lights were placed at the front of the stage on the floor (where actors often kicked them). These days, this lighting angle is more often referred to as "dramatic" lighting, due to the dramatic effect achieved by this angle.

Figure 6.12: Footlight (See color image.)

We know from our childhood that a flashlight under the chin is a great effect when telling spooky stories. But why? Simply put, the lighting angle is very strange and unnatural. Natural light almost always comes from above. Millions of years of living in nature has taught animals (including us) what feels right and what feels wrong as far as lighting angles are concerned. Here's an important tip: If you want your scene to feel strange, try unusual lighting angles.

Coloring Your Light

We have dealt with a few coloring issues. Key light, for example, will be warm if it is the sun, a candle, flashlight, household bulb, or red neon lamp. Fill light will be cool if it is the sky. Natural lighting generally falls within the Kelvin scale of color temperature, although natural lighting on Mars or beneath the ocean's surface may be radically different from natural lighting in downtown Vancouver. Artificial lighting has a color range as wide as the visible spectrum.

Regardless of what colors you choose for your lighting palette, chances are you will have at least one key source and at least one fill source. We differentiate between key and fill not only by angle and intensity but also by color. The fill color is almost always different from the key color, even if it is on the same side of the color spectrum.

Complementary Tint

A key/fill lighting setup in which the key and fill colors come from opposite sides of the color spectrum or color wheel is said to be complementary. In other words, a red key with a blue fill is complementary. So is a blue key with an amber fill, or a purple key with a yellow fill.

Daylight is a typical example of basic complementary key/fill coloring. The sun is a warm key and the skylight provides a cool fill.

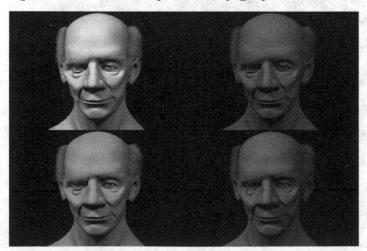

Figure 6.13: Complementary tint (See color image.)

Related Tint

Related tint also employs a basic key/fill setup; however, this method uses colors that come from the same side of the color spectrum. An amber key with a yellow fill would fall into this category, as would a light blue key with a dark blue fill.

You may find a related tint key/fill scenario where the primary source is warm, such as a lightbulb, and the fill light is diffuse reflected light from a warm-colored wall.

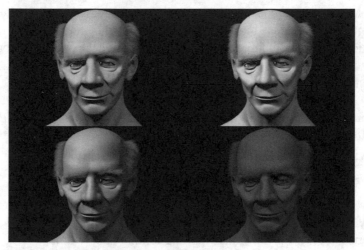

Figure 6.14: Related tint (See color image.)

Intensity Ratios

Just as important as the key/fill color selection is the key/fill intensity ratio, and the ratio between these two lights and any other light sources in the scene.

As a rule of thumb, you can start by considering that the fill light should be about 60% of the intensity of the key light. Why is this? If both the key and the fill light were the same intensities, there would be no distinction between the two. Also, the fill light is distinguished by its lower intensity and tendency to "fill" shadowed areas left over by the key. If the fill were the same intensity as the key, there would be few shadowed areas left and the lighting would become flat.

The rim will generally be about the same value as the key intensity plus the fill intensity. For example, if you have a key light at 150% and a fill light at 90%, then you'd want to start your rim light at about 240%. Why so high? Well, the rim light isn't there to illuminate anything; it's there to provide a bright "halo" around the exterior shape of the object. If the rim light isn't brighter than the key and the fill, you won't see it at all.

The bounce light, being a diffuse, reflected light source, will usually be the most subtle of all light sources and is likely to be lower in intensity than the fill light. I'd be inclined to start around the 40% range.

Of course, these values are just a starting place and might not be appropriate for your scene. As a matter of fact, you might find that your scene calls for completely different intensity ratios. Just bear in mind that certain light types have certain intensities relative to the other lights, and that these intensities are determined by the light type, properties, and environment. There's a very good reason for them. Analyze your scene, find out what they are, and proceed with your lighting levels appropriately.

Intensity ratios are used throughout the book. Watch for differences in intensity between key, fill, and other lights and see if you can detect a pattern.

Options in Lighting a Scene

If you start thinking about all the options and using these few simple principles, the possibilities are mind-boggling. Infinite angles and colors alone should keep you experimenting for quite some time.

■ ■ ■

Now that we have covered some of the basic principles used for lighting a scene, you should start seeing how you can alter, mangle, and even completely ignore much of what has been discussed here. Now that you understand why key and fill light are used and why the three-point technique was invented, you should start seeing how you can develop your own techniques to illuminate a scene and to focus the viewer's attention while helping to shape the subjects and convey an emotional framework for the scene.

You should now have a grasp of these basic lighting principles and concepts. The key light, the fill light, the highlight (or rim light), three- and four-point lighting, basic coloring, and intensity ratios are used in lighting every day, so it is important that you clearly understand them. If you don't, go back over the chapter, as these concepts will form the underpinning of any lighting work you do.

Part II

3ds max Lighting Tools

If you have read through and studied the first section of this book, you should have a reasonably good understanding of the qualities and properties of light and shadow in the real world. By now you should have spent some time observing real-world light and shadow and identifying and analyzing natural and artificial light sources and the nature of shadows caused by light sources of different properties. This is the first major key to your ability to create realistic and efficient lighting in MAX.

The second major key is the understanding of all the available tools. In this case, we'll be discussing the tools that arrive with MAX fresh out of the box. Start out by learning MAX's basic toolkit, but remember that there are many plug-ins available out there on the web—tools that will extend your capabilities and should be learned at some point. Prices range from free to very expensive indeed. High-priced plug-ins are usually intended for the professional production market. Some of these have demos available and some do not. If you are considering purchasing a plug-in but can't decide whether or not to make the cash outlay, I'll say this: If you have a project where you need the plug-in, factor it into your budget. If the project can pay for it, then by all means get it. If, on the other hand, your own work won't support either the need or the expense, then find another way. There's always another way.

Hopefully, by the end of this section, you will have a reasonably full understanding of MAX's lighting toolkit. This section presents the tools, but does not teach their use much. See Chapters 24 and 25 for tutorials. Better yet, buckle down and start using the tools, go through the MAX manuals, and spend some time searching online for tutorials on their use. There are tons of tutorials out there. You will become familiar with all the tools soon enough.

Chapter 7

Standard Lights and Typical Uses

This section of the book deals specifically with the 3ds max toolset, and this chapter specifically with the standard lights of the toolset. Rather than just regurgitating what can be found in the manuals, this section will attempt to demonstrate some typical real-world uses and examples for the tools. There is certain to be information here that is also found in the manual, but in writing this chapter I decided it would be easier for the reader to have the information right at hand rather than flipping back and forth between this book and the manual. There is practical, production-based information found in this book — and in this chapter in particular — that is not available in the manual. Furthermore, there is a great deal of information in the manual on a wide variety of subjects that is not covered in this book. I strongly urge you to take a serious look through the manual, not just when you need some specific information. I have discovered many gems of information by casually flipping through the manual.

This chapter is designed to expand on the manual by providing a production-based context for each of the tools. Certainly, many of the tools in MAX have been used for many other purposes than those for which they were originally intended by the authors.

By the time you have finished this chapter, you should have a good understanding of the different standard light types available, what each does, and some ideas on how best to use each of the various light types in different lighting situations.

Default Light

Very handy and much more useful than simple ambient light, default lights appear automatically whenever there are no other lights in the scene. They are two omni lights, one from above and to the left, the other from below and to the right. The default lighting disappears as soon as you put in any light and reappears if you delete all your lights.

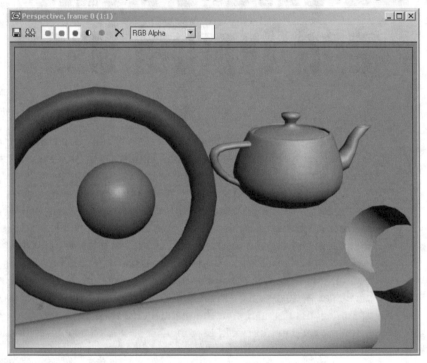

Figure 7.1: Some simple geometry rendered with default light

Default light can be very handy for quick renders or test renders where you want to check geometry or textures, but don't want to wait for expensive lighting. Default light, however, has no practical value when it comes to lighting renders of any kind.

Ambient Light

Ambient light doesn't exist in the real world, although it is meant to approximate some lighting behavior we see every day. In the real world, light reflects from one surface to the next over and over, perhaps millions of times, until all the light energy has been absorbed. This is known as *radiosity*. Radiosity has the effect of giving an overall brighter appearance to any environment and occurs everywhere all the time. Radiosity illumination is based on incidence and reflection angles, accessibility to cracks and crevices, and density of the material it is passing through, whether it be air, glass, water, plastic, or whatever. Ambient intensity, on the other hand, simply adds an illumination value to every pixel in the scene, regardless of any physical or environmental parameters. Ambient light, therefore, has the effect of filling in shadows and flattening out shape and form. Because of this, we use ambient light very sparingly in the world of 3D. In rare cases, I have used ambient intensity to lower shadow density for compositing purposes, because sometimes anything is better than completely black shadows.

Figure 7.2: A basic scene with one directional light, area shadows, and no ambient intensity

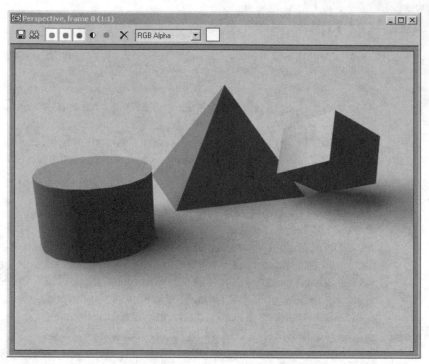

Figure 7.3: A basic scene with one directional light, area shadows, and some ambient intensity. Notice how all the black from the previous image is gone and all the surface values are raised slightly.

Ambient intensity is accessed through the Rendering>Environment menu option.

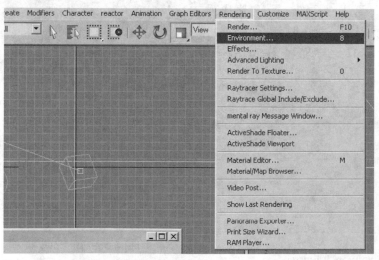

Figure 7.4

Under the Environment and Effects panel, click the Ambient swatch to get the MAX Color Selector.

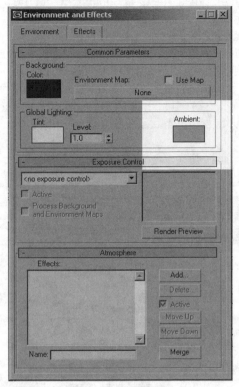

Figure 7.5. Click on the Ambient swatch to access the Color Selector.

Once in the Color Selector you can select any color at any value for your ambient intensity. Bear in mind that it is the grayscale value (black/white value) that determines lighting intensity value, not the color. So a bright blue will add more illumination value to the scene than a dark red.

> **Note:** Here's a trick. A really quick method of creating an ambient light is to add a skylight with Cast Shadows turned off. Simply set the sky color and intensity multiplier, and there you have a quick-and-dirty ambient light source.

Free Lights and Target Lights

Two of MAX's standard light types, the directional light and the spot-light, are available in two flavors. Free lights are just lights that you place in your scene and aim wherever you want by moving and rotating them. Target lights, on the other hand, are directional lights or spotlights that come with an extra feature—a target. The light will automatically aim wherever you place the target.

I use target lights much more than free lights, simply because the target item makes the lights so much easier to aim exactly where you want them to go.

The lights themselves are listed separately from their targets in the Select Objects panel.

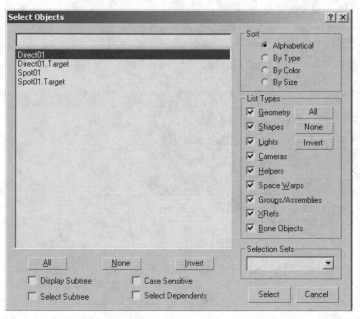

Figure 7.6: The Select Objects panel

Directional Lights

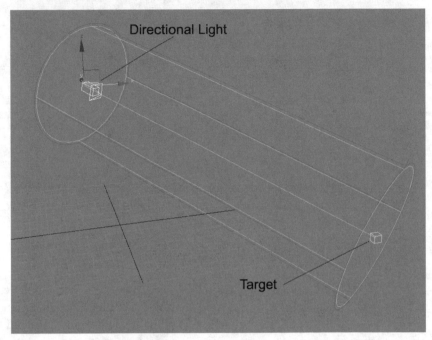

Figure 7.7: Directional light

Directional lights are different from all other lights in that the light rays are parallel. Rather than emanating from a single point as in an omni light or spotlight, or emanating from over an area or a line as with an area or linear light, the directional light's light beams run parallel to each other in a cylindrical shape.

A directional light is intended to behave in some respects like sunlight, because sunlight is often mistaken to be made up of entirely parallel rays of light. Sunlight is not, in fact, made of all parallel rays, as you already know if you've read the first section of this book, but sometimes we can get away with it, if the viewer doesn't look too closely.

Directional Parameters

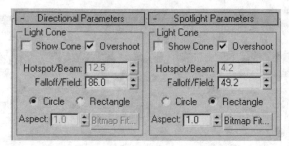

Figure 7.8

The parameters rollout for spotlights and directional lights are identical. The same tools for spotlights and directional lights simply behave slightly differently, as outlined below.

Light Cone

This area describes all of the adjustable parameters of the light "cone," which is in fact not always cone-shaped. A spotlight's illumination shape does look like a cone, but a directional light's light "cone" is cylinder-shaped.

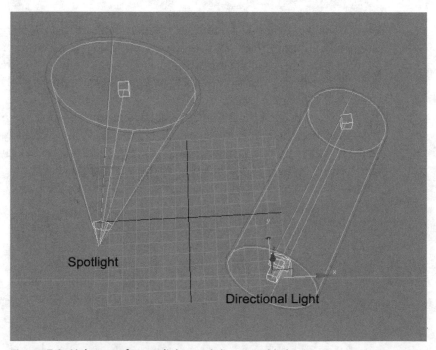

Figure 7.9: Light cone for spotlights and directional lights

Show Cone

Checking the Show Cone check box will allow you to see the light cone even if the light is not selected.

Overshoot

The Overshoot check box allows the directional light or spotlight to illuminate areas outside the light cone. This is helpful in a number of ways. For example, if you have a large outdoor scene, you will have to scale your directional light up to encompass the entire scene. Make a mistake and you'll see the cone edge in your render. But if you select Overshoot, there will be no cone edge and the entire world will be illuminated by the directional light. In this way, a directional light is made to behave a little like the sun. For spotlights, sometimes you have your spotlight in the perfect position, but you just catch the edge of the beam in frame. Instead of having to reposition your light, just check Overshoot.

A secondary advantage to the Overshoot option is that shadow maps are only calculated within the light cone. If you have to move your light far back to encompass a whole scene, then you'll have to use a higher resolution shadow map or you'll see pixelation in the shadow edges. If you use Overshoot, you can keep your cone small and use a lower resolution shadow map but still illuminate all the areas outside of the light cone.

If you check the Overshoot check box, the Hotspot/Beam control becomes inactive.

Hotspot/Beam

Most normal lights have a hotspot somewhere near the center of their light beam. This is usually because directed light, like that from a stage spotlight, is using imperfect optics, and either the reflective mirror behind the lamp or the lenses are causing imperfect light focus to concentrate some light in one area and less in another.

This effect has been replicated in MAX with the Hotspot/Beam control. You can see the Hotspot/Beam cone get larger and smaller as you adjust this setting.

Falloff/Field

Falloff/Field is the area of illumination falling outside of the hotspot and going as far as the edge of illumination.

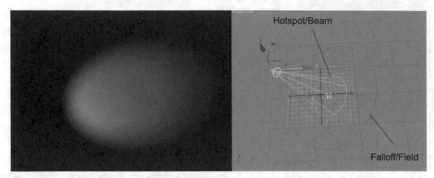

Figure 7.10: Hotspot/Beam and Falloff/Field

Using combinations of Hotspot/Beam and Falloff/Field, you can create very hard-edged theatrical spotlights, very soft-edged light, or anything in between.

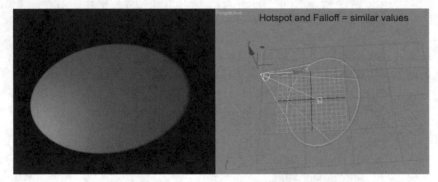

Figure 7.11: Using Hotspot/Beam and Falloff/Field together

Circle/Rectangle

You can easily switch your beam shape from a cone to a rectangle with the Circle and Rectangle buttons.

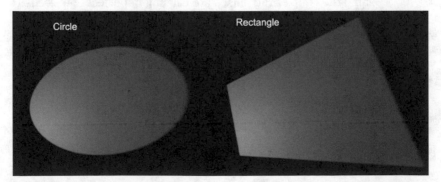

Figure 7.12

Aspect

The Aspect numeric input and spinner control how rectangular a Rectangle beam is. For example, if you enter an aspect of 1.0, the light beam will be perfectly square. If you enter an aspect of 2.0, the beam will be twice as wide as it is high, and so forth.

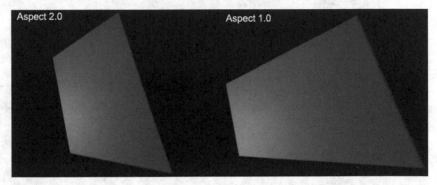

Figure 7.13

Bitmap Fit...

If you choose a rectangular beam, you can automatically set the aspect with the Bitmap Fit... button. Selecting this button brings up a file dialog. When you select a valid image file, the light's aspect will automatically be adjusted to match that of the selected image.

Spotlights

Spotlights are perhaps the most-used lighting instrument in all of CG, regardless of software, gender, creed, religion, or taste in pizza. Spotlights can be used for anything from car headlights and flashlights to skylight sources and sunlight without even breaking a sweat. They're cheap, easy to use and understand, and highly versatile. The fact that they emit light from a point source is a bonus too, since most light sources emit light radially from some sort of special intersection. Spotlights are not perfect though. Since all their light comes from one, nondimensional point, they don't exactly behave like real light sources. There are lots of tools and tricks to help them fake it, though, and those are covered throughout the book.

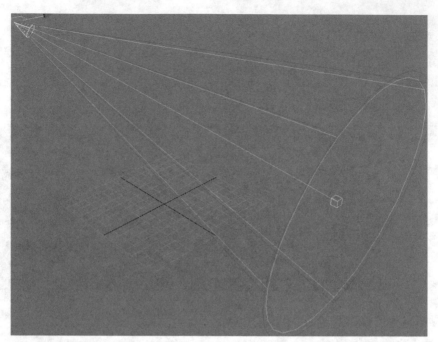

Figure 7.14: Spotlight

The only difference between a spotlight and a directional light is that the directional light is composed of all parallel light beams, while the spotlight's beams all emanate from one point. That's it. All the parameters are exactly the same, so simply refer to the previous discussion on directional lights for ideas on how to fiddle with them.

Omni Lights

Omni lights are so simple that they don't even have a parameters rollout. When I first used an omni light, I hunted around for a rollout. Surely a software package that uses rollouts for every parameter under the sun would have one for its most basic light type. Nope. That's how simple they are.

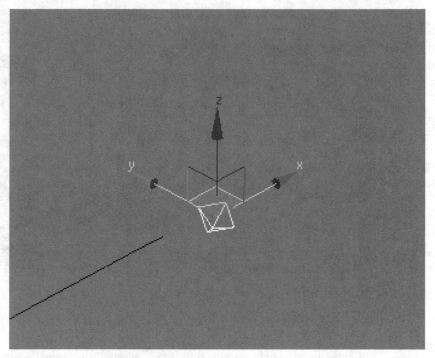

Figure 7.15: Omni light

An omni light is simply a point in space that emits light omnidirectionally. You have the usual shadow, intensity, and color choices in the basic
parameters rollouts.

Omni lights are most appropriately used as candle flames, sparks, or
any other small, luminous material. You could put them inside a lightbulb
or in a rocket flame. If you wanted, they could even make a good fake
sun! You could use them as lens flare elements for small, distant
lightbulbs, stars, or even window light on a distant building. (See Chapter 10 for more information on lens flares.)

There are myriad uses for the omni light. For now, all you need to
know is that you place them in your scene and they emit light in every
direction.

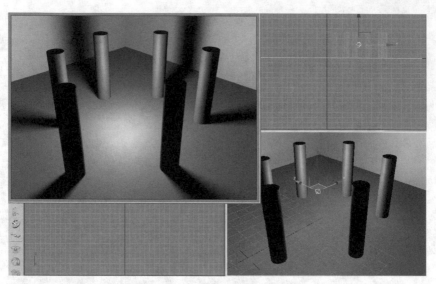

Figure 7.16: Using an omni light

■ ■ ■

By now you should have a good understanding of the basic light types in 3ds max and how to access and manipulate their basic parameters. The following chapters deal with more complex lights, mental ray lights, photometric lights, and other lighting systems available in MAX.

Chapter 8

mental ray Lights

In MAX 6, Discreet added the mental ray Renderer along with two mental ray light types: the mental ray Area Omni light and the mental ray Area Spotlight. These two lights, if used with the Default Scanline Renderer, will behave like regular omni lights. If you want to use these two lights to their full capacity, you must remember to switch to the mental ray Renderer in the Render Scene panel.

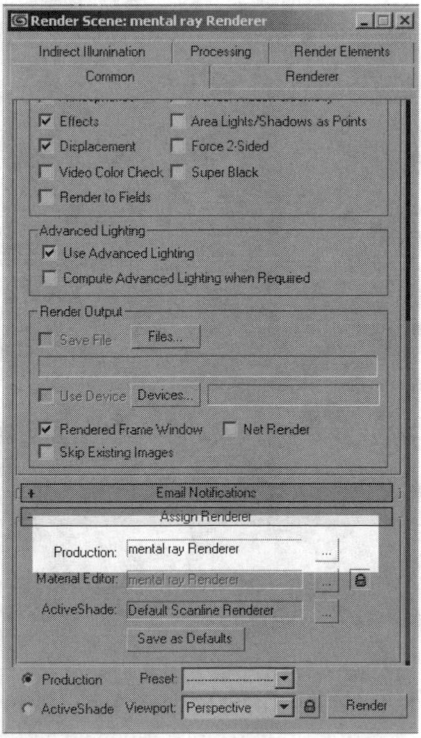

Figure 8.1: The Render Scene panel

mental ray (mr) lights are added just like any
other standard light from the create panel at the
right of the interface.

mr lights can use raytraced shadows, shadow
maps, or mr shadow maps. Considering the
power of mr lights, it seems silly to waste them
on shadow maps. I always use raytraced shadows.
If I want to use shadow maps, I'll switch to a simpler lighting setup. Although there are times you
will need to speed up your render by switching to

Figure 8.2

shadow maps, this will negatively impact your shadow quality.

mr Area Omni Lights

The mr Area Omni is represented on-screen as an octahedron, an
eight-sided shape that looks like two pyramids stuck end-to-end
together.

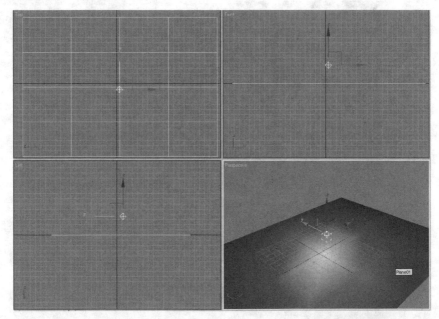

Figure 8.3

The most immediately wonderful thing about the mr Area Omni is that
it behaves very much like a real light source since it has an actual
three-dimensional volume. The mr Area Omni can be defined as either a
sphere or a cylinder, meaning there is a real volume to the light source,
unlike all the other standard light types available in MAX. You don't

always *need* a three-dimensional volume, and often you'll get away with the Area Omni's poor cousin, the mr Area Spotlight. But we'll get to that next.

mr Area Light Parameters Rollout (Area Omni Lights)

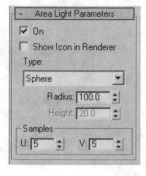

Figure 8.4: The Area Light Parameters rollout for mr Area lights

On

The On check box enables or disables the mr Area light. If you disable the check box, the light will render like a regular omni light source.

Show Icon in Renderer

If you enable the Show Icon in Renderer option, the Area Omni light will render as a flat, white ball if it is within the camera view.

Figure 8.5

97

This feature is quite useful for placing bare, spheroid lightbulbs without using geometry.

Type

An Area Omni light can be defined as a sphere or as a cylinder. The Type drop-down is where you make that choice.

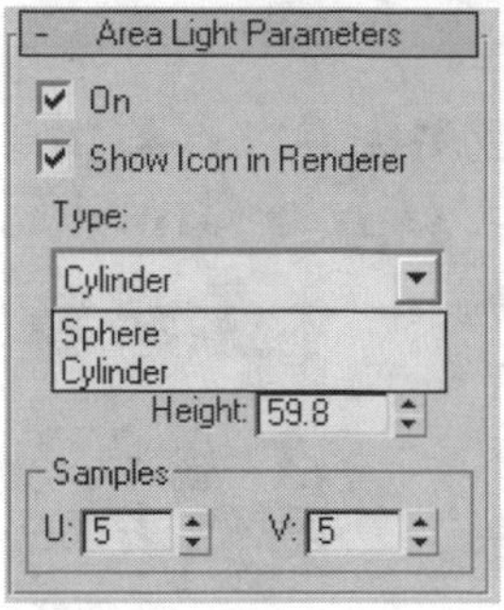

Sphere

If you select Sphere, you will be given the option of changing the sphere radius.

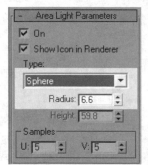

Figure 8.6

When you click on the Radius spinner and alter the value, a radius gizmo will become visible in the viewports.

Figure 8.7

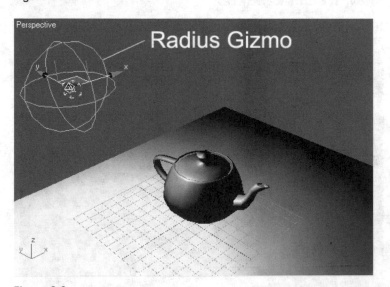

Figure 8.8

A sphere might be used as a nearby lightbulb.

Figure 8.9

Cylinder

If you select Cylinder, you will be given the option of changing the Radius and Height options.

Figure 8.10

When you click on the Radius or Height spinner and alter the value, a gizmo becomes visible in the viewports so you can see the exact size of the light.

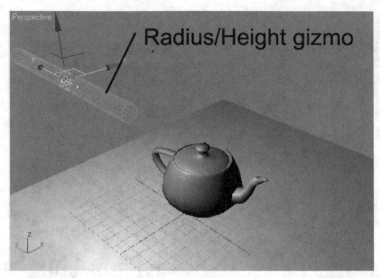

Figure 8.11

A cylinder might typically be used as a fluorescent light fixture.

Figure 8.12

Samples

U and V samples will increase or decrease the shadow quality from the mr Area light. Low values can be used for quick test renders, but higher values will be needed for production renders. As always, higher quality comes at a cost of higher rendering times.

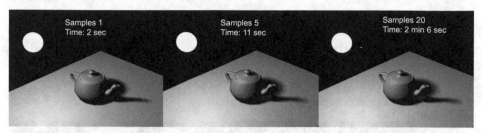

Figure 8.13

mr Area Spotlights

mental ray Area Spotlights are the two-dimensional brother of the mr Area Omni lights. Instead of coming in sphere or cylinder flavors, these come in rectangle and disc flavors. Rectangles are obviously useful as window light sources, while a disc could be used for the sun or any other disc-shaped light source you can think of.

mr Area Light Parameters Rollout (Area Spotlights)

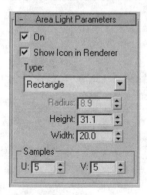

Figure 8.14

On

Just as with mr Area Omni lights, this check box determines whether or not the mr Area Spotlight is active. If disabled, this light behaves like a regular MAX spotlight.

Show Icon in Renderer

The Show Icon in Renderer check box will show the light as either a rectangle or a disc within the render view, depending on which shape you choose. The icon will only be visible if the light is in frame of the current camera or view.

Figure 8.15

Type

The Type drop-down is where you select between Rectangle and Disc as the light source shape.

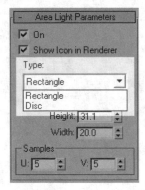

Figure 8.16

Radius, Height, and Width

The Radius, Height, and Width spinners determine the dimensions of the Area Spotlight. If you have selected Disc as the light shape, you will only have the Radius option and the other two will be grayed out. If you select Rectangle, you will have the Height and Width options available, and Radius will be grayed out and unavailable.

In either case, if you click and drag on any of the spinners, a gizmo will appear in the viewport to show you the exact size and shape of your light.

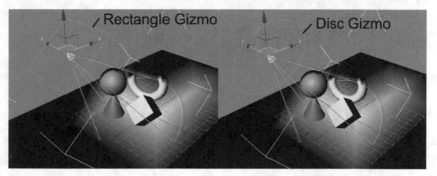

Figure 8.17

Samples

As with Area Omni lights above, higher settings in the Samples area result in higher quality renders, but also higher rendering times. Be sure you don't have this setting higher than you need.

■ ■ ■

That is the basic overview of the two mental ray light types available in MAX. They are fairly straightforward to use and provide good results. For an example showing the use of mental ray lights, see Chapter 25.

Chapter 9

Photometric Lights

The Good...

Photometric lights in MAX are a double-edged sword. On one hand, they are the ultimate tool if you are going for a physically accurate recreation of a real-world lighting environment, especially if you need to use physically correct luminaires in a physically correct environment. Nothing really matches the power and accuracy of these tools, so if you are an architect or a physicist, your prayers have been answered.

The Bad...

On the other hand, if you choose to use photometric lights, you'd better be sure that everything about your geometry is perfect. No light leaks are allowed, and scale must be exactly correct. Structures must be complete in detail; otherwise the lights will not behave correctly. So this means a great deal of extra work—not so good if you're on a TV production deadline.

...and the Ugly

Perhaps the most unfortunate thing about photometric lights is that you are not supposed to use them together with standard lights. According to the documentation, they do not interact correctly and behave very differently. I have had some success mixing light types without too much trouble, but it is not really advisable to do this. You'll have to try out the different combinations for yourself to see if they work for you. I have managed renders using standard, mental ray, and photometric lights together with expected results, so don't forget to try!

If you are an artist more interested in look and effect than in physical correctness, you'll probably want to stick to standard and mental ray lights and leave the photometric lights to the engineers. But I cover photometric lights anyway because there are always some clever artists out there who have learned to make great use of unusual tools for TV and film production, so we certainly should not leave them out here. And of course, you might also be an engineer, architect, or physicist just dying for physically accurate lighting, so this chapter is for you.

Photometric Light Types

Just like standard lights, photometric lights come in free and target flavors. Instead of direct, spot, and omni lights, though, photometric lights come in point, linear, and area light types.

Point Lights

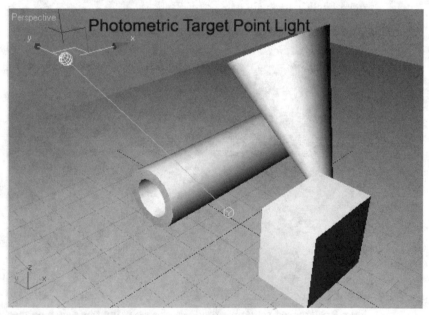

Figure 9.1: A photometric target point light

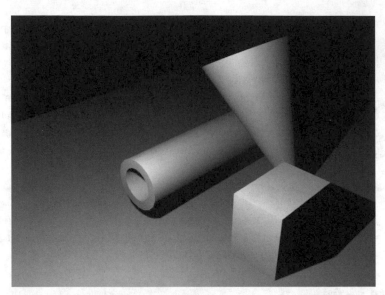

Figure 9.2: Point lights cause hard shadows because all the light emits from a single, nondimensional point in space.

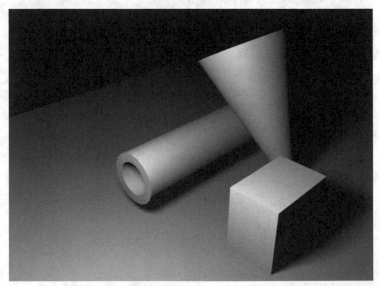

Figure 9.3: You can soften the shadows of a point light by switching the shadow type to Area Shadows.

Point lights behave much like standard omni lights in that they emit light from a single, nondimensional point in space. This is not a physically accurate model since all lights have some size; however, point lights render more quickly than linear or area lights because they are simpler to calculate.

> **Note:** The first time I saw target point lights, I wondered what the point of the target was. But targets can be very useful when you are orbiting or panning the light.

Area Lights

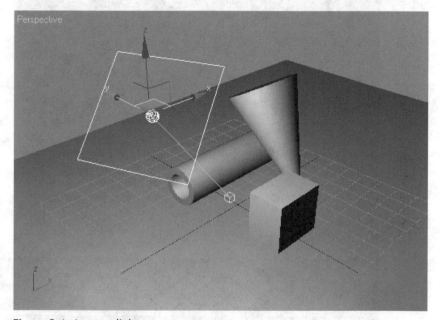

Figure 9.4: An area light

Area lights emit light over a rectangular area. You can set the height and width of the area in the Area Lights Parameters rollout. The area light is the most physically realistic of the three photometric light types, since real lights all have a height and width. In fact, real lights also have depth, making them three-dimensional. Area lights are two-dimensional, but that's close enough for almost all lighting situations. The natural, raytraced shadows from area lights are the most realistic of all the photometric lights.

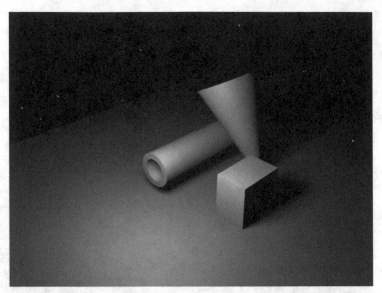

Figure 9.5: This image was rendered with Advanced Raytraced shadows, not with Area Light shadows. The render takes longer than a point light with area shadows, but the shadow quality is much higher.

Linear Lights

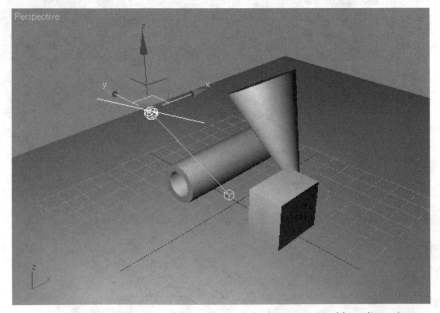

Figure 9.6: Notice in this image that a linear light is represented by a line, since that is the shape of the light source.

Linear lights are intended to reproduce light sources such as fluorescent tubes. The problem is that raytraced shadows from the linear light only soften along the length of the light, not along the width because ... well, because there is no width to a linear light. Linear lights are one-dimensional, and therefore the shadows are only softened over one dimension.

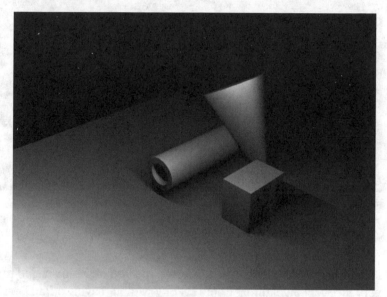

Figure 9.7: Notice how the shadows seem to soften only in one direction, along the length of the linear light.

IES Sky

"IES" refers to the Illuminating Engineering Society. Wherever you see these letters, it means a bunch of physicists have gotten very picky about the light behavior, and while you may not even notice the difference or it might not seem to work the way you'd like, don't worry—at least it's physically accurate.

IES Sky is a photometric version of the skylight that you can use with Light Tracer to create outdoor fill light sources.

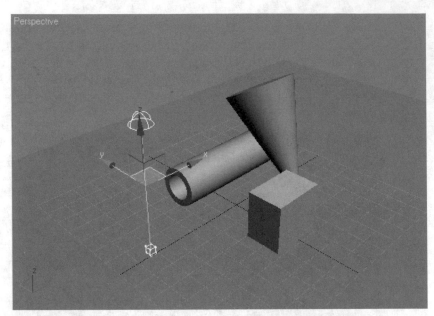

Figure 9.8: An IES skylight looks like a half dome with a target. It looks like a half dome because it represents the dome of skylight outside. The IES skylight, just like the standard skylight, can be placed anywhere in the scene.

Don't worry about the picky physicists, though. I have managed to get very nice-looking lighting from IES Sky without having a Ph.D. or M.Sc. Simply placing the skylight in your scene and dialing in the desired intensity by eye is usually going to be just fine, unless you are writing your doctoral thesis in wave theory or something.

Figure 9.9: Sure, it takes a little longer to render, but the beautiful results are worth it!

IES Sky can also be used with IES Sun in the Daylight System discussed a little later in this chapter.

IES Sun

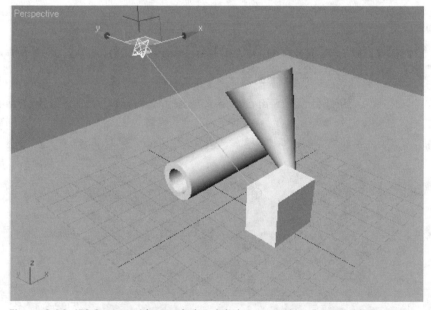

Figure 9.10: IES Sun provides stark, harsh lighting, just like direct sunlight.

IES Sun is another photometrically accurate lighting instrument and is intended to be used with IES Sky for outdoor lighting environments. Once again, being the creative people we are, we certainly aren't obliged to use the tools exactly as directed. I can throw an IES sunlight and an IES skylight together any time I want without using the Daylight System and I will probably never be jailed for it.

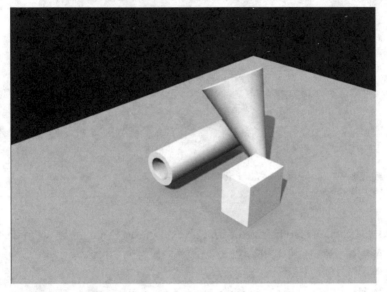

Figure 9.11: An IES sunlight and an IES skylight interact to create an outdoor lighting environment.

Daylight System – Simulated Direct Sunlight Plus a Photometric Skylight

The Daylight System can be accessed through Create>Lights from the main menu.

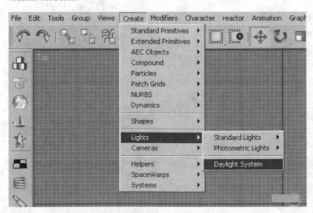

Figure 9.12: Accessing the Daylight System

Once the Daylight System is added to your scene, you will see a parameters rollout that allows you to select the precise location you desire as well as the precise date and time of day. Unfortunately, if you don't live in the United States, your city will not be listed in the Get Location list.

Figure 9.13: Control Parameters rollout for the Daylight System

The Daylight System's purpose is to provide physically accurate daylight models depending on your location on the globe and the time of day. This would likely be very useful if you were creating forensic animations. If you're an artist working in games or visual effects, though, you probably won't have much use for the Daylight System.

For further details on how to set up and use the Daylight System, please see the manual.

Photometric Light Parameters

For details on photometric light parameters, please refer to Chapter 12, "General Light Parameters," where they are covered in detail.

Photometric Light Presets

Here's one particularly cool feature of photometric lights. There are a number of built-in light type presets. Say, for example, you want a 60-watt lightbulb, a halogen lamp, or a streetlight. You can fiddle around and try to find the right settings or, from the Create>Lights>Photometric Lights>Presets menu, you can simply locate your preset, and bing! It's in the scene.

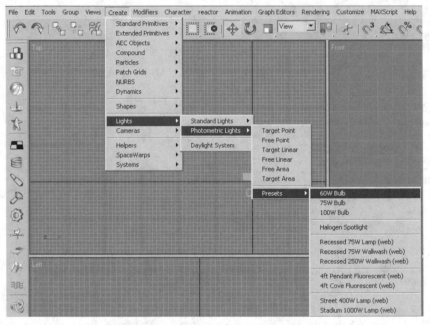

Figure 9.14

Different light types come with different icons. All the settings are changeable in the Modify panel.

Exposure Control (Environment Control)

Exposure control can be accessed through the Environment and Effects panel.

This tool allows you to process the exposure of your image, just as though you were opening or closing the aperture on a camera. When using standard lights, you will probably not use this tool very often; however, when using photometric lights, the light energy calculations can be a little unpredictable and you may find the exposure control settings to be quite useful.

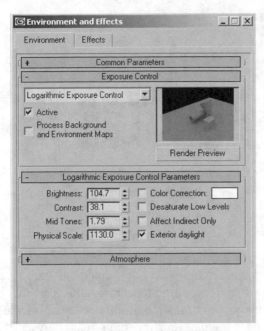

Figure 9.15: The Environment and Effects panel

There are a lot of details in the MAX documentation about how to use this tool, but it's really quite easy to pick up if you just fiddle with it for a minute.

Keep in mind, though, that exposure control doesn't have any effect over radiosity, so be sure you set your exposure before enabling radiosity in your scene.

■ ■ ■

By now, you should have a basic understanding of the photometric lighting tools available in MAX. In Part III of the book, we'll be putting most of these tools through their paces to see what can be done with them.

Chapter 10

Other Lighting in MAX

In addition to standard lights, mental ray lights, and photometric lights, 3ds max is equipped with other lighting tools that help us create physical lighting effects like radiosity and caustics, atmospheric effects like volumetrics, lens flares, and even materials that emit light energy.

Light Tracer and Radiosity (Default Scanline Renderer)

Radiosity, also known as Global Illumination in MAX, can be handled in a couple of different ways. Both Light Tracer and Radiosity can be found in the Advanced Lighting tab of the Default Scanline Renderer panel.

Figure 10.1: The Default Scanline Renderer panel Advanced Lighting tab

The first solution is called Light Tracer.

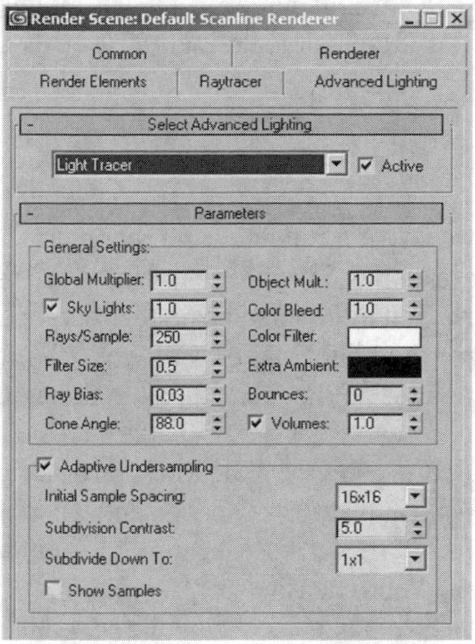

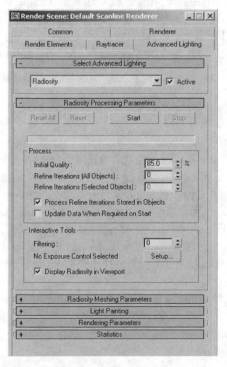

Figure 10.2:
Light Tracer
options

Light Tracer is not a physically accurate radiosity model, but it does provide light bounces and color bleed that simulates radiosity and will often be sufficient.

Figure 10.3:
Radiosity options

Radiosity, on the other hand, provides a physically accurate model and includes some special tools and settings not available with Light Tracer. For a detailed discussion of both Radiosity and Light Tracer, please refer to Chapter 14.

Caustics

Caustics in MAX come in two flavors: reflected and refracted.

When we use the word "caustics," we are referring to the redirection of light into a more dense and intensified beam, usually focused on a nearby surface. For example, when light shines through a glass of wine, you see an intensified area of light on the table opposite the light. This is because the glass and its liquid contents are acting like a lens and are refracting and focusing the light. A shiny ball bearing can also result in a caustic lighting effect. While a ball bearing is opaque and will not let light pass through, it is very shiny and reflective; therefore the light will reflect off the shiny surface and onto nearby surfaces. Because the ball bearing is spherical, its surface acts like a focusing mirror, causing the reflected light to intensify on nearby surfaces. A gold ring will also act like this. The interior face of the ring acts like a focusing mirror, also making a caustic reflection appear on nearby surfaces.

MAX is capable of both types of caustic effects when using the mental ray rendering engine. But the fact is that caustics are rarely, if ever, used in actual production. I'm not going to dedicate space to this lighting effect, but complete tutorials and tool descriptions are available in the MAX documentation.

Volume Lights

Volume lights simulate particles in the atmosphere. Take a smoky bar, for example. If you are in a smoky bar and the bright stage spotlights come on, you will "see" the smoke in the light beams. In fact, the smoke is everywhere in the room, not just in the light beams. However, to save on rendering time, it is more efficient to only render the smoke where the light beam is located. This is what is meant by a "volume light." It is a light that includes particulate density or volume within the light beam, without calculating that particulate density in the rest of the environment. Quite clever, if you think about it.

Volume lights work with all light types in MAX, including mental ray lights. They are extremely easy to add to your scene.

To demonstrate, simply add a light, such as a spotlight. I'm going to add a spotlight, a direct light, and an omni light to show the different volumetric effects. In Figure 10.4, you can see the spotlight cone and volumetric shape. This shows where the volumetric effect will render.

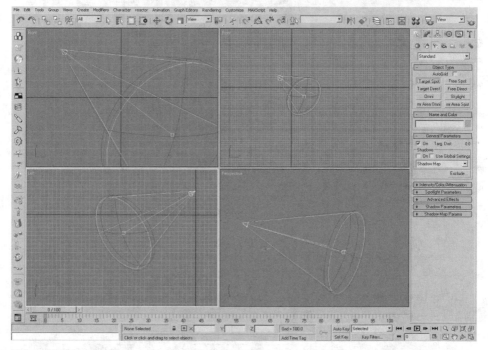

Figure 10.4

> **Note:** Different light types will provide differently shaped volumetrics. For example, the spotlight will create a cone-shaped volumetric, the omni light will create a sphere-shaped volumetric, and a distant light will create a cylinder-shaped volumetric.

Open the Atmospheres & Effects rollout on the Light Modify panel.

Figure 10.5

119

Click the Add button.

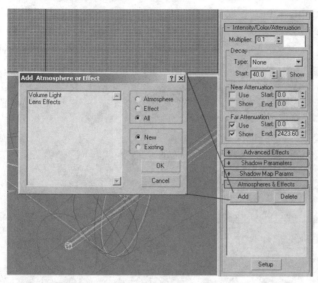

Figure 10.6

Click on Volume Light and click OK.

Now set the near and far attenuation options for each of the lights and render a frame to have a look.

Figure 10.7

The volumetric will adhere to the shape of the light volume, even if it is occluded by geometry, taking on the shape of the shadows.

Figure 10.8

Volume lights can be extremely helpful for creating car headlights, jet blasts, flashlight beams, lasers, and, you guessed it, spotlights in smoky bars.

Objects as Lights

One of the greatest single uses for radiosity is the ability to use the Advanced Lighting Override material to make self-illuminated objects emit light into the scene. This allows us to build custom lights of any size and shape. If, for example, you need a frosted lightbulb or a neon sign, this is a perfect solution for correctly and beautifully illuminating your scene.

Making a self-illuminating object is incredible simple. First, click on the Standard button next to the material name in the Material Editor.

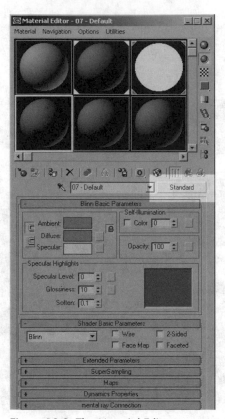

Figure 10.9: The Material Editor

This will open up the Material/Map Browser.

Figure 10.10: The Material/Map Browser

Click on Advanced Lighting Override and click OK.

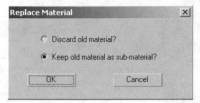

Figure 10.11

You will get a dialog asking whether you want to discard the existing material or keep it as a sub-material. If you want to build a new material, click the discard option. If you already have a material that you like but you just want to make it luminous, keep the old material and click OK.

Now, you will see the Advanced Lighting Override Material rollout in the Material Editor.

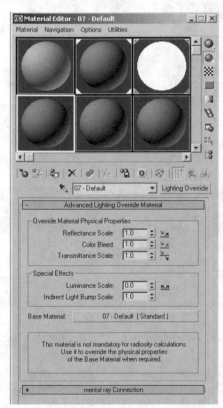

Figure 10.12: The Advanced Lighting Override Material rollout

In the Special Effects section, turn the Luminance Scale up to 1000.

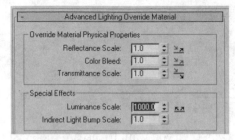

Figure 10.13

Now, in the Render Scene panel, make sure you have the Default Scanline Renderer selected, and add the Radiosity plug-in in the Advanced Lighting tab under the Select Advanced Lighting rollout.

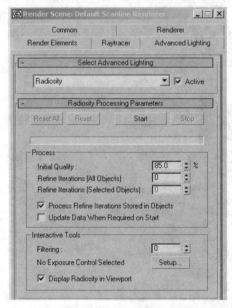

Figure 10.14: The Render Scene panel

With Radiosity active, click the Start button on the Radiosity Processing Parameters rollout. This will let MAX calculate the lighting solution for the luminous material. Once the calculation is finished, render a frame and enjoy your luminous object!

Figure 10.15: A self-illuminated object that emits light

Lens Flares

Lens flares, also known as "lens effects" in MAX, are another real-world lighting effect. Strangely, this tool is less often used to simulate its real-world counterpart than it is to create other, completely different effects.

Lens Flares Defined

A camera lens is really a tube filled with a number of different lenses. Each of these lenses has a highly polished optical glass surface. Because the glass is highly polished, it is also highly specular and, therefore, highly reflective. Camera and lens manufacturers go to great lengths to prevent reflection from occurring within the lens housing. They paint the inside of the tube black and apply antireflective coatings to the lens, but these measures are of little help when a very bright light source like the sun or a car headlamp shines directly into the front of the lens. When this happens, bright light will reflect back and forth between the lens surfaces, creating a visible reflection called a *lens flare*. You have probably seen many lens flares on television and in movies whenever the camera pans past the sun or when a car drives by at night with head-lights on.

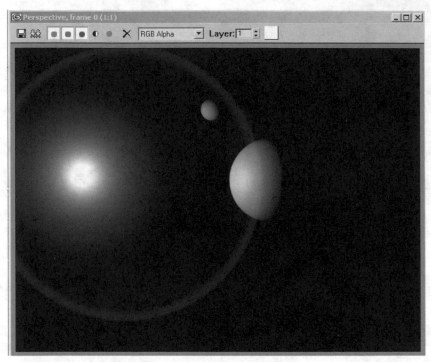

Figure 10.16: A lens flare occurs when a very bright light shines directly into a camera lens.

Figure 10.16 was created using the lens effects tools available in the Atmospheres & Effects rollout of an omni light. This phenomenon is common in outdoor shots where the sun is in-frame.

Why Not to Use Them

When lens flare tools were first added to 3D animation software it was thought that this effect added a new, unparalleled realism to CG renders. Since the main problem with CG renders is a lack of errors, it was thought that these lens flares would add a natural error into the shot, making it seem to be real photography. At first this was true. There was a very high "cool" factor attached to the use of lens flares. The problem was that this tool became seriously overused, both in intensity and in frequency.

Lens flares soon became cliché. They clearly identified shots as computer generated, creating the exact opposite effect that the artist desired. Less-experienced artists began to use lens flares all over the place, at intensities much too high to be real. A dead giveaway of an inexperienced artist is overuse, or even any use, of lens flares on the demo reel.

Good Uses for Lens Flares

Just because a lot of artists over the years have made lens flares cheesy and obvious doesn't mean you can't use them in other great, less obvious ways. Of course, sometimes you will actually have to use a lens flare for a real lens flare effect.

Lens flares should be used judiciously. First of all, there absolutely must be a valid and pressing reason to use a lens flare, such as our example of the sun crossing the field of view. If this happens, lens flares should be subtle. Don't overdo it.

Figure 10.17: Lens flares (See color image.)

Any light type can have a lens flare. Simply open the light's Modify panel, open the Atmospheres & Effects rollout, and click the Add button.

Figure 10.18

When you click the Add button, you will get the Add Atmosphere or Effect panel. Click on Lens Effects and then click OK.

Once you've done this, you will see "Lens Effect" listed in the Atmospheres & Effects rollout.

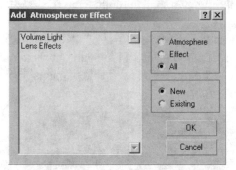

Figure 10.19

Figure 10.20

Enabling Lens Effect features is a multi-step process. To begin, simply select Lens Effects from the Atmospheres & Effects rollout and click the Setup button. When you do this, you will be presented with the Environment and Effects panel, open on the Effects tab.

When you click on the Lens Effects entry in the Effects list, all the appropriate rollouts will appear below.

Figure 10.21: The Environment and Effects panel

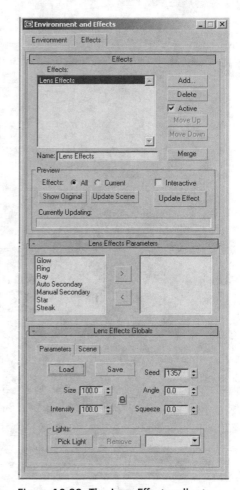

Figure 10.22: The Lens Effects rollouts

You can start adding lens effects in the Lens Effects Parameters rollout. If you decide to add all of them, just multi-select the whole list and click the little arrow pointing to the right. This takes all the available effects and makes them active.

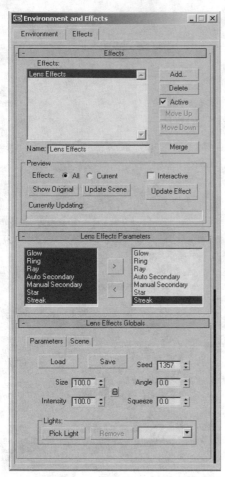

Figure 10.23: Multi-selecting lens effects
parameters

Figure 10.24 shows a render with an omni light that has all the lens
effects active.

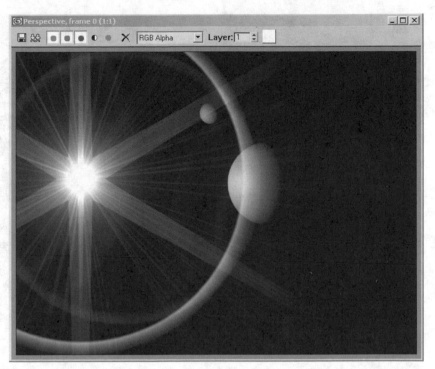

Figure 10.24: An omni light with every lens effect

That's a lot of effects, and is definitely over the top, but fun to try out. Each of the lens effects has parameters that can be altered to your taste. Since lens effects are so seldom used, I won't put much effort into describing all the different settings here. You can find them in the manuals and other resources, and besides, if you just start fiddling with the controls, it quickly becomes obvious what each does.

In truth, I have only once had the need in production to use this tool for creating lens flares. It was for a shot in *I, Robot* where a very large, nasty robot comes to life and as it does so, its bright spotlights shine directly into the camera view. That is not to say that I don't often use lens effects in production; it's just that I almost never use them for lens flares.

I have found lens flares to be an extremely useful tool, not as lens flares, but instead as small, distant light sources such as those warning lights you might see at the top of an antenna so that aircraft don't come too close. You see, lens effect "glow" creates a small area of intense brightness right near the light source. So you may, for example, take an omni light, stick it to the top of your antenna, and turn on Lens Effects. Add Glow only and you will find that your omni light is now a visible light source.

Figure 10.25: Omni lights with a Glow lens effect

When using this technique, you will usually want the lens flare to take on the color of the light. In this case I used omni lights with a color of 255, 0, 0. It is a very versatile little technique that can be used in innumerable ways. Picture street lamps as viewed from a helicopter. Or imagine how useful this effect might have been in the days of *Blade Runner* when a nighttime cityscape was composed mainly of bright point source lights just like this.

This technique is by far the best use I have found for lens flares in MAX. But you may very well find a place where you need a real lens-reflection type lens flare. Go ahead and use it. But remember, as with all effects and techniques, subtlety is usually the key to success.

I once set up a scene with 15 lens flares interacting with five render passes of particles to create a magical effect. The lens flares were nothing more than drifting light sources floating around in space. One of the double-edged swords in MAX is that the light sources themselves are not visible. This is good because it means you can place a light anywhere on the set, including directly in front of the camera, and not worry about seeing it. On the other hand, when you want to see the light source, you're out of luck. This is where lens effects come in handy. If you only use the Glow effect, you are left with a single intense point where the light's pivot point is. This is a great visible light source that is useful for all sorts of effects and situations.

My last bit of advice about lens flares is to use them sparingly and wisely. Overuse of this effect is a dead giveaway that the work is CG.

■ ■ ■

You should now have a basic understanding of the use and purpose of lens effects, volume lights, objects as lights, and basic radiosity in MAX. Remember, it is usually the creative and uncommon uses of these tools that get you noticed as an artist.

Manipulating Lights

This chapter will help springboard new artists and artists inexperienced with MAX into a complete understanding of how to add and manipulate lighting instruments. By the time you have finished this chapter, you should know how to create all MAX light types and position them so they will illuminate your scene just the way you'd like. This chapter deals mainly with creating and moving lights. For instruction on how to change light settings and properties, please see Chapter 12, "General Light Parameters."

Creating Lights

All lights in 3ds max are created from the Command Panel's Create tab.

Figure 11.1: The Create tab

You simply click the Light icon, choose between Standard and Photometric lights in the drop-down, click on the light type you wish to create, and then click in one of the viewports to place the light.

For target lights, you click and drag. Wherever you click is where the light is placed. Wherever you drag and let go of the mouse button is where your target is placed.

Skylights can be placed anywhere in the scene because their position is not important. They will create a skylight source regardless of where you place them.

Once you have placed your light in the scene, you can name it, change its color, type, and parameters, move it around, and perform any other type of manipulation you choose.

Selecting and Transforming Lights

To "transform" a light means to move it in space, rotate it, or change its size or scale. Before you can transform a light, though, you must select it. There are a number of ways to select items in MAX, but with complex scenes and overlapping items, perhaps the easiest and quickest way to select items is via the Selection Floater.

Selecting an Item

There are a few ways of bringing up the Selection Floater:

1. You can open the Selection Floater from the Tools menu at the upper left of the MAX interface.

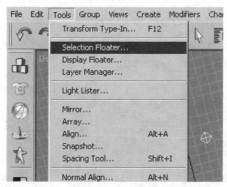

Figure 11.2: Opening the Selection Floater from the Tools menu.

2. You can click the Select by Name icon on the main toolbar.

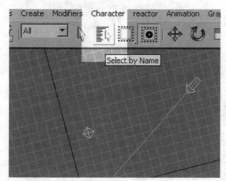

Figure 11.3: Opening the Selection Floater from the main toolbar.

135

Once you have the floater open, you can select from the list.

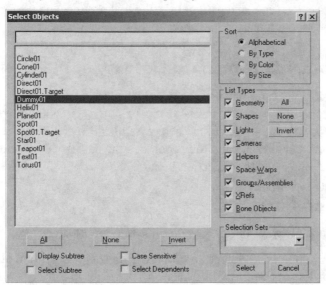

Figure 11.4

If you have too many items in the scene and only wish to list the lights, simply filter out all the other items by clicking their check boxes at the right of the list.

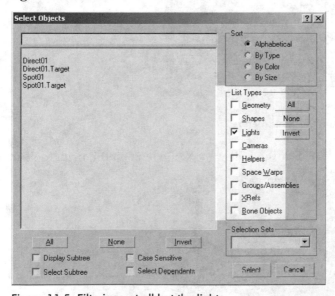

Figure 11.5: Filtering out all but the lights.

Once you have selected either a light or its target, you can move things around. If you are using a target light, you must select the light to change the origin of the light source, and you must select the target to change the direction the light is facing, unless you are using one of the light navigation controls discussed later in this chapter.

Moving an Item

To move a light, simply select it and click on the Select and Move icon in the main toolbar, or click the Select and Move icon and then click within a viewport to select the light. The only disadvantage to this method is that you can accidentally select the wrong item if your scene is moderately complex.

Figure 11.6: The Select and Move icon

When you have clicked on the Select and Move icon, you will see the move gizmo attached to the light. You can constrain which direction the light moves by only selecting one leg of the gizmo. You will see the leg turn yellow when it is selected and the light will move only in that axis.

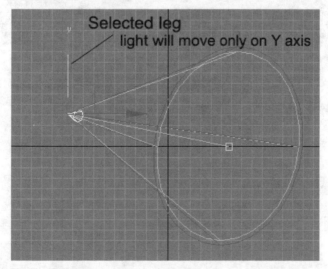

Figure 11.7

137

If you select the square in the middle of the transform gizmo, the light will move on two axes at once, or a plane. The square represents the plane of motion. Which plane depends on which viewport you are currently looking through. If you are looking through a perspective, light, or camera viewport, you will have access to all planes and will not have to switch viewports to select a different plane.

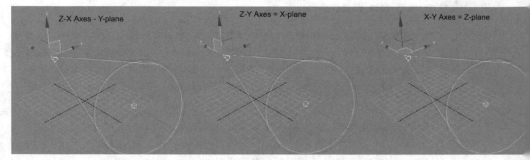

Figure 11.8

Now that you know how to transform a light, you can move the light and its target around as much as you like. Incidentally, this is how you move around anything else in MAX too.

Rotating an Item

Rotating items is very much like moving them in terms of how the controls work. The main difference is that instead of clicking the Select and Move icon, you click the Select and Rotate icon.

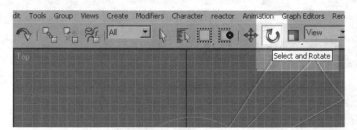

Figure 11.9: The Select and Rotate icon

You also get a rotate gizmo in the viewports instead of a move gizmo. The rotate gizmo works similarly to the move gizmo. When you have a single axis of rotation selected, that axis will turn yellow.

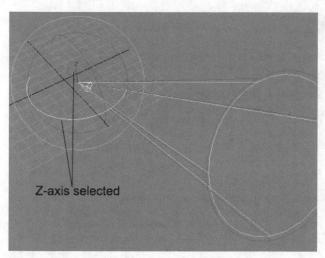

Figure 11.10

In a perspective viewport, you are able to select all axes at once and freely rotate the light. The axis ball turns dark gray when you have all axes selected.

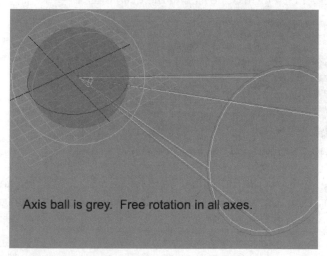

Figure 11.11

What is really cool about the rotation gizmo is that when you are rotating your item, MAX displays the angle of rotation numerically, gives you a direction arrow on the rotation gizmo to show you the direction of rotation, and also shades the angle of rotation so you can tell exactly how far you have rotated the light. This is all valuable information presented in an intuitive manner.

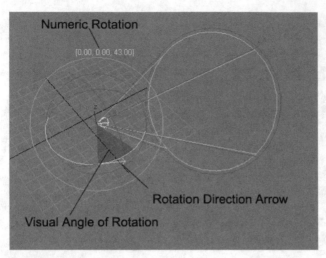

Figure 11.12

Scaling an Item

Similar to rotation and moving, scaling an item requires that you click on the Select and Uniform Scale icon in the main toolbar.

Figure 11.13: The Select and Uniform Scale icon

The scale gizmo works much like the move gizmo, except instead of moving an item, this gizmo will stretch it. If you select the middle triangle on the scale gizmo, the item will be scaled on all axes at once, making the entire item larger or smaller.

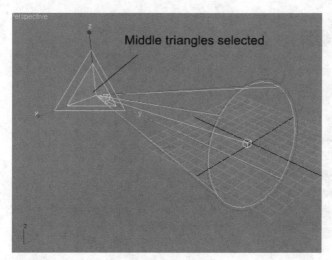

Figure 11.14

If, on the other hand, you select one of the outer rectangular shapes on the gizmo, the item will stretch along that plane and stay unchanged in the other planes.

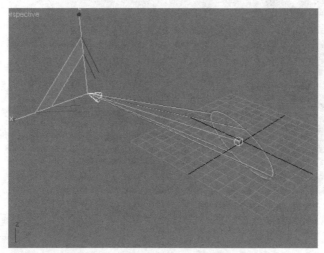

Figure 11.15: Selecting and dragging the X-Z scale plane squashes the light cone.

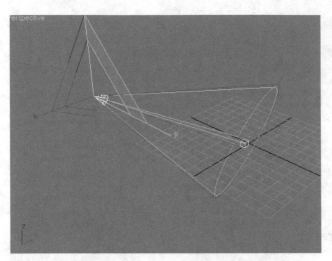

Figure 11.16: Selecting and dragging the Y-Z scale plane squashes the light cone in the other direction.

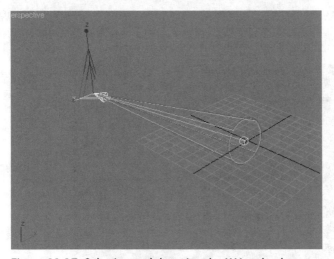

Figure 11.17: Selecting and dragging the X-Y scale plane makes the light cone wider or narrower.

By simply fiddling with these controls for a few minutes, you should be able to achieve a solid grasp on exactly how and why they work. Discreet has obviously put a great deal of effort into ease of use, and these controls are logical, sensible, and straightforward.

Transforming Target Lights

You have three options when transforming target lights. First, you can select the light and move, rotate, or scale it. Second, you can select the target and move, rotate, or scale it. Third, you can select both the light *and* its target by clicking on the line that connects the two. This will allow you to move, scale, and rotate the light and its target together.

Scaling both the light and its target will change the cylinder or cone size and affect the distance between the target and the light.

The Light Viewport

You can switch any of your viewports to light viewports by right-clicking on the viewport name, scrolling down to Views to open the view list, and then selecting the light you desire.

Figure 11.18

This viewport will now display the scene from the point of view of the selected light.

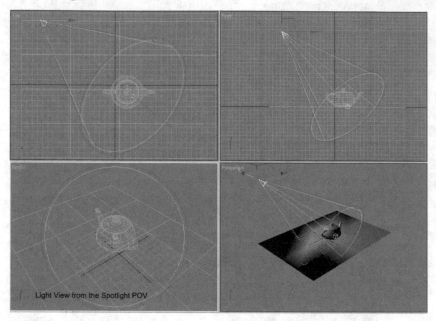

Figure 11.19

When you have a light viewport selected, you are presented with a number of new viewport navigation controls in the bottom right of the MAX interface. These are discussed in the following section.

Light Navigation Controls

Dolly, Target, Both

You'll notice the Dolly control has a small triangle at the bottom right. This means there are additional controls available. In this case, you can select among Dolly Light, Dolly Target, or Dolly Both.

Figure 11.20: Light navigation controls

Figure 11.21: Dolly control

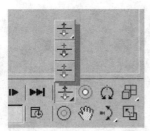

Figure 11.22: Dolly control
options

To "dolly" an item means to move it forward and backward along its axis
or the direction it is facing.

> **Note:** If you are using a free light (a light with no target), the additional Dolly tools will not be available.

When you select the Dolly Light tool, the light will move back and forth
toward or away from the target. When you select the Dolly Target tool,
the target will move back and forth toward or away from the light. When
you select the Dolly Both tool, the light and target will move together
back and forth along the axis created by the line that joins the light to
the target.

Light Hotspot

Figure 11.23: Light Hotspot
control

The Light Hotspot control allows you to focus most of the light into the
center of the light cone or cylinder. Most directed lights in the real world
such as ellipsoidal reflector spotlights, Fresnels, PARs, floodlights, etc.,
have a hotspot. Although light designers go to a great deal of trouble to
remove hotspots from lighting instruments, they still exist and can
serve to add a sense of realism to a light source.

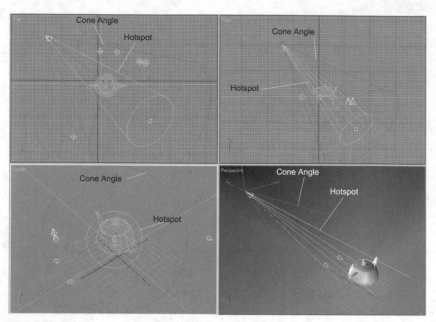

Figure 11.24

When you adjust the hotspot, you will see a separate light cone or cylinder within the cone angle. This defines the distance from the center at which light falloff to the cone angle begins.

Figure 11.25: No hotspot adjustment

Figure 11.26: Spotlight with hotspot adjustment

Roll Light

Figure 11.27: Roll Light
control

The Roll Light tool simply allows you to spin your light along its own
axis. That is, whichever way the light is pointing is the roll axis and the
light spins about this axis. Try it. It's so simple it's not worth any further
text or images.

Light Falloff

Figure 11.28: Light Falloff
control

This is a very important tool, since, like the Hotspot tool, it softens the
light cone edge. Where the Hotspot tool moves the cone edge inward to
calculate falloff and create a hotspot, the Light Falloff tool moves the

outer cone edge outward to maintain the area of illumination within the original cone, while softening the edge outward. Just like the Hotspot tool, the cone angle gizmo can be seen in the viewports.

Figure 11.29: Spotlight with no falloff

Figure 11.30: Spotlight with falloff

> **Note:** Note that while the Hotspot and Light Falloff tools affect the softness of the cone angle edge, they do not affect the softness of the shadows cast by objects within the cone. For shadow control options, see Chapter 12, "General Light Parameters."

Truck Light

Figure 11.31: Truck control

To "truck" a light means to move it up and down, left and right, along its own axes. Go ahead and try it; you'll figure it out quickly.

Orbit, Pan Light

Figure 11.32: Orbit and Pan control

Just like the Dolly tool, this tool has additional modes to choose from: Pan and Orbit. You can choose between them by clicking and dragging off the button.

Figure 11.33: Orbit and Pan control options

The Orbit tool will make the light rotate around the target, while the Pan tool will make the target rotate around the light.

> **Note:** The Pan tool makes a target light behave like a free light.

The Light Lister

Although the Light Lister does not allow you to physically move your lighting instruments, I have included it here especially for inexperienced artists who want to get up and running quickly.

You can bring up the Light Lister through the Tools drop-down.

Figure 11.34: Selecting the Light Lister.

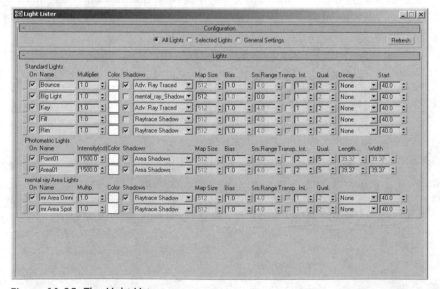

Figure 11.35: The Light Lister

There is a great deal of information in the Light Lister, all of which can be altered elsewhere, but the most common parameters for each light are listed here, like a spreadsheet. The Light Lister is probably the most valuable single tool in the lighting arsenal, as it gives you a quick overview of all your lighting parameters and allows you to change them quickly and easily.

Here, you can turn shadows on and off, change the light's name, intensity, color, and shadow type, and adjust many other parameters. For a full overview of the scope and function of all these parameters, please see Chapter 12. In the meantime, however, I suggest you throw a couple of objects in the scene, turn on a light or two, and start playing with the Light Lister. I think you will find it to be a fast and intuitive way to change your light's parameters without having to go through the long list of parameter rollouts.

■ ■ ■

This chapter has covered basic manipulation tools for the lights in 3ds max. By now you should have a good idea of how to get lights into your viewports and how to move them around to your desired position and orientation. The next chapter will deal with individual light parameters in detail.

Chapter 12

General Light Parameters

The Command Panel is found at the right of the default MAX layout. At the top of the Command Panel there are six icons representing the Create, Modify, Hierarchy, Motion, Display, and Utilities tabs.

In this chapter, we're most interested in the Modify tab.

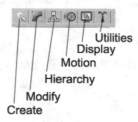

Utilities
Display
Motion
Hierarchy
Modify
Create

Figure 12.1: The Command Panel tabs

Figure 12.2: The Modify tab icon

The lights you use in MAX have specific parameters; in other words, they have controls to adjust all the different settings of the currently selected light. There are some different settings for different light types and the rollouts are context sensitive; that is, they change depending on what current light type you have selected. This chapter should cover most of the controls for the various light types in enough detail to give you a solid understanding of all the basic parameters. For complete details, consult the manuals.

The top of the Modify tab shows the currently selected item, in this case a directional light. This box contains the name of the light, which you can change by simply clicking within the box and typing any name you choose. To the right of the item

Figure 12.3: The Modify tab

name is a color swatch. This color does not affect the color emitted by the light, but instead shows the color of the light in the viewport workspaces.

Below the light name is the modifier list drop-down and the modifier stack, which won't be dealt with here. Chapter 11 deals with a number of settings that are not covered here, most of which deal with light shape, size, and position.

General Parameters Rollout

Beneath the modifier stack is the General Parameters rollout.

Figure 12.4: General Parameters rollout

This rollout contains the most basic properties of your light.

Light Type

Within the Light Type area, you have a few simple options.

On

You can turn the light on or off by using the On check box. Turning the light off makes it inactive within your scene.

Figure 12.5: The On check box

153

Type

The Type drop-down lets you change the type of light. The choices for standard lights are Spot, Directional, and Omni, while the choices for photometric lights are Point, Linear, and Area.

Figure 12.6: The Type drop-down

Targeted

You can use the Targeted check box to change your spot or directional light from targeted to free or vice versa. The number to the right of the Targeted check box is the target distance. If you are using a targeted light, the number will show the distance to the target. To change the target distance you must select and move the light's target. If you have a free light, however, there will be a spinner visible next to the number. Use this spinner to change the target distance for free lights.

Figure 12.7: The Targeted check box

Shadows

In the Shadows area, you will find basic shadow settings.

On

The On check box is used simply to turn shadows on or off for the currently selected light.

Figure 12.8: The On check box

Use Global Settings

If the Use Global Settings check box is on, the shadows for the currently selected light will be determined by the global parameters. All lights in the scene with this box checked will use the global parameters to determine shadow settings. If this box is not checked, the local parameters will determine the shadow settings for the currently selected light only.

Figure 12.9: The Use Global Settings check box

155

Shadow Type

This drop-down allows you to select from among the available shadow types. The choices available include Advanced Ray Traced, mental ray Shadow Map, Area Shadows, Shadow Map, and Ray Traced Shadows. The purpose and use of the various shadow types is discussed in detail in Chapter 13.

Figure 12.10: The
Shadow Type drop-down

Exclude

At the bottom of the General Parameters rollout is the Exclude button.

Figure 12.11: The Exclude
button

Clicking this button brings up the Exclude/Include panel.

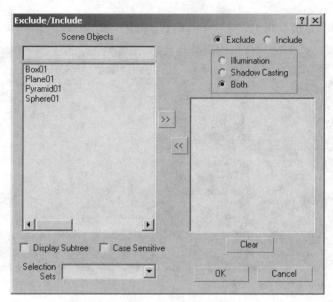

Figure 12.12: The Exclude/Include panel

The Exclude/Include panel allows you to selectively include or exclude illumination, shadowing, or both on an object-by-object basis.

For example, you could exclude an object from illumination and shadowing.

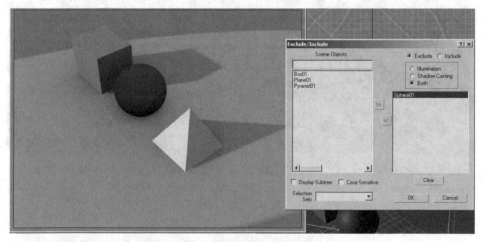

Figure 12.13: The sphere has no illumination or shadowing.

Or you could exclude an object from illumination but not shadowing.

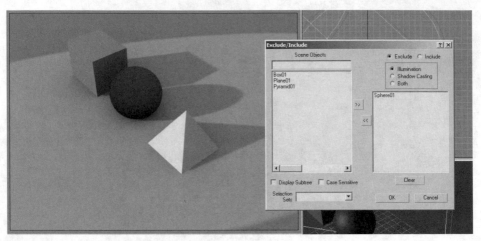

Figure 12.14: The sphere has no illumination.

Or you could exclude an object from shadowing but not illumination.

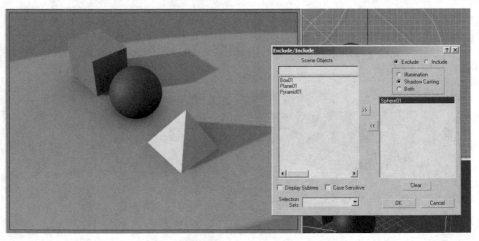

Figure 12.15: The sphere has no shadowing.

Intensity/Color/Attenuation Rollout (Standard Lights)

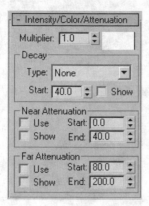

Figure 12.16: Intensity/ Color/Attenuation rollout

If you are using a standard spot, directional, or omni light, attenuation controls are available for standard light types. The rollout is different for photometric lights; see the "Intensity/Color/Distribution Rollout" section below.

Multiplier

The first item in this rollout is the intensity multiplier. This setting determines the intensity level of your currently selected light.

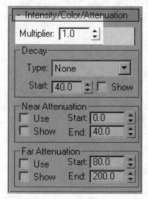

Figure 12.17: The intensity multiplier

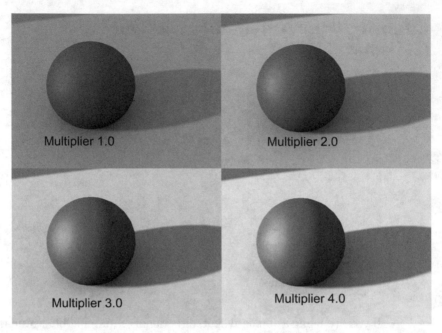

Figure 12.18: Several renders with different intensity multiplier levels

Using an intensity multiplier rather than a percentage level makes a lot of sense. It's not like turning on a lightbulb in your house where full power is 100%. In the virtual world there are no practical limits to light intensity and no specific intensities that can be identified in terms of "full power." Lights can be set to any power, either positive or negative; it's only numbers! Therefore, a simple intensity multiplier prevents the artist from getting "brain locked" into the idea that 100% is top power.

Color Swatch

Next to the intensity multiplier is the color swatch. By clicking the swatch, the MAX Color Selector becomes available, allowing you to select the color of illumination emitted by the currently selected light.

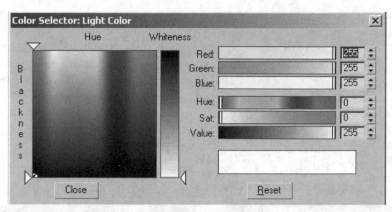

Figure 12.19: The Color Selector

Decay

Every light in the real world has a decay or fall-off. In other words, the farther away you get from a light, the dimmer the illumination from the light becomes. This is because the light waves (or particles) are spreading out and becoming less dense over distance.

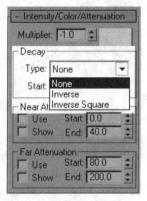

Figure 12.20: The Decay options

Type

In MAX, you have several types of decay to choose from: None, Inverse, and Inverse Square.

None

Your first option is None. This means that there will be no illumination decay over distance. No matter how far away you get, the illumination from the light source will remain just as powerful.

Inverse

Inverse is a fancy way of describing a linear decay. If the light has an intensity of 1.0 at the source and in intensity of 0 at a distance of one meter, then we know that at 0.5 meters, the intensity will be 0.5.

Inverse Square

This is how light behaves in the real world. Because light is spreading out both horizontally and vertically as it is transmitted away from the light source, its intensity, and therefore the density of photons, must be spread out both horizontally and vertically. This means that the intensity will be measured by the inverse square of the distance from the light source. Light using the Inverse Square Decay setting will tend to be much brighter at the source and will decay in brightness much more quickly. This is how it works in the real world, but most people don't notice because they don't spend much time staring at light sources.

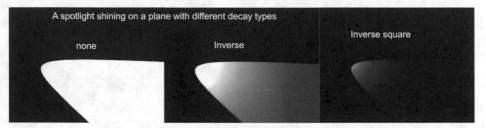

Figure 12.21

Start

The Decay Start spinner determines at what distance from the light source the decay will start. If you set this to 1 meter, the light intensity will remain at your maximum setting within one meter of the light source. After one meter, the light will begin to decay at the rate specified.

Show

If you have the Show check box checked, MAX will display the decay distance even if you don't have any decay selected.

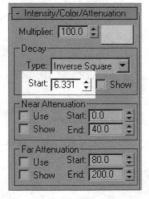

Figure 12.22: The Start option

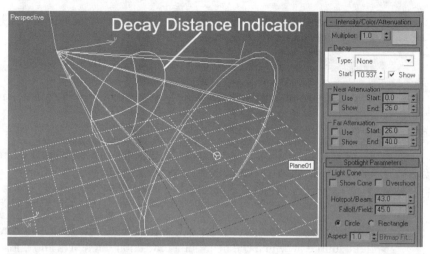

Figure 12.23

Near and Far Attenuation

Near attenuation is sort of like reverse decay. The Near Attenuation setting determines at what distance from the light source the intensity begins. Using near attenuation, you can create a light source that has no illumination in the center or less illumination in the center, unlike real lights. You can specify the start and end distances of near attenuation.

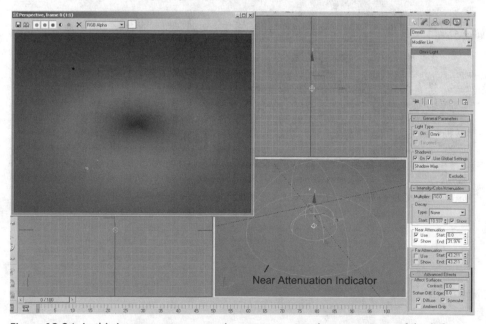

Figure 12.24: In this image, near attenuation starts at zero, the exact center of the light source.

Far attenuation is like normal decay, but you can specify the exact start and end distances of that decay.

Use

The Use setting enables or disables the near and far attenuation tools.

Show

If the Use check box is not selected, you can still see where the near and far attenuation are located by turning on the Show check box.

Start/End

The Start and End numeric input boxes indicate the distance from the light source at which the near and far attenuation starts and ends. For example, you can set where the near attenuation starts and ends, and where the far attenuation starts and ends.

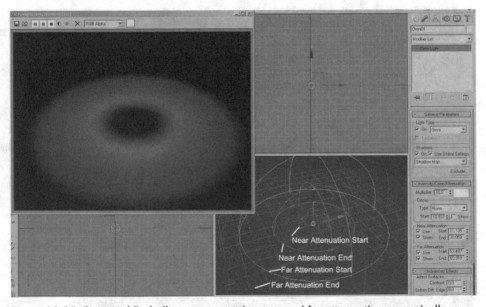

Figure 12.25: Start and End allow you to set the near and far attenuation numerically.

Intensity/Color/Distribution Rollout (Photometric Lights)

For photometric lights, you see the Intensity/Color/Distribution rollout instead of the Intensity/Color/Attenuation rollout.

Distribution

Lights in the real world do not distribute illumination perfectly evenly. Because photometric lights are designed to replicate real-world light sources, they have been equipped with a number of different light distribution parameters that reflect real-world distribution. If you are using a point light, your distribution options are Isotropic, Spotlight, and Web. If you are using a linear or area light, your distribution options are Diffuse and Web.

Figure 12.26: Intensity/Color/Distribution rollout

Isotropic

Isotropic distribution emits light equally in all directions, somewhat like an omni light.

Spotlight

Selecting the Spotlight distribution mode enables the Spotlight Parameters rollout. The light will behave very much like a spotlight.

Diffuse

Diffuse distribution makes linear and area lights behave much like standard lights, illuminating the diffuse surfaces of materials.

Web

For those who are nitpicky about perfect light distribution (such as engineers and architects) the Web distribution option lets you load an .ies file onto the light. IES stands for Illuminating Engineering Society. This society has established a standard file type for describing the distribution properties of specific light types. The .ies files will usually be available from manufacturers of the specific luminaire, if necessary.

Color

A number of standard light colors have been listed for your convenience. All these settings are based on the actual real-world color temperature of the light source. You have a wide variety of standard settings such as quartz, high-pressure sodium, mercury, fluorescent, and cool white, to name just a few.

Kelvin

If you don't wish to use one of the color presets, you can set a custom color by using the Kelvin option. The Kelvin scale says that light of longer wavelengths is cooler than light of shorter wavelengths. Since red is at the long end of the spectrum, it is considered to be cooler than blue, which is at the short end of the visible light spec-

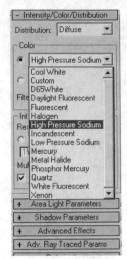

Figure 12.27: Color options

trum. This is sort of backward to how we think of warm and cool. A fire, for example, is warm—red, orange, and yellow—while ice and water are cool—blue and green. But that is just our perception. In reality, if we heat up a piece of metal, it starts by glowing dull red, then orange, yellow, white, and, if it hasn't melted yet, will eventually begin to emit blue light. That is why blue is actually much hotter than red.

In the world of visible light, the Kelvin scale is limited to a range between 1,000 and 20,000 degrees.

What's so great about Kelvin? Well, if you have any experience on set, you'll know that the most often used lighting gels all have a color temperature that corresponds to their color filtering properties. So for matching a plate, if you knew the color temperature of the gels, you would know exactly what color to make your lights. Furthermore, most natural lighting colors are within this range. Here is a short list of some of the most common natural light sources and their color temperatures:

Color Temperatures of Various Sources

Lighting Source	Kelvin Degrees
Candle	1900
Lightbulb	2000-2500
Tungsten/halogen bulb	3200
Afternoon sunlight	4500
Summer sunlight	5500-5700

Lighting Source	Kelvin Degrees
Sunlight with blue/white sky	6500
Summer shade	7000
Overcast sky	7000
Skylight	10,000-20,000

From *Set Lighting Technician's Handbook: Film Lighting Equipment, Practice, and Electrical Distribution* by Harry C. Box (Focal Press, 1993).

Figure 12.28: Kelvin options

The Kelvin spinner is used to set the Kelvin color temperature.

Color Swatch

The color swatch represents the color selected by the spinner to its left. You cannot select the Kelvin color temperature directly by clicking on this swatch, as you can by clicking on the color swatch for standard lights. This is only a display of the color temperature.

Filter Color

On set, colored filters called "gels" are often placed in front of lights. Using the Filter Color tool, you can select the color of the gel, thereby altering the final, emitted color of light. Clicking the Filter Color swatch will open the Color Selector.

Intensity

All lights in MAX have intensity control. For photometric lights, however, the intensity control is a little different. For example, all photometric lights use an inverse square intensity decay, because that is how real lights behave, and photometric lights are designed to behave like real lights. Standard lights are not designed this way because most of the time you can't tell the difference, and simpler lighting models are quicker to calculate and therefore quicker to render. So keep this in mind when you're under a tight deadline.

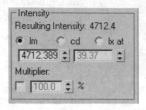

Figure 12.29: Intensity options

Resulting Intensity

The Resulting Intensity number reflects the final, actual light intensity you've assigned to the light. You can select from a variety of units: lm (luminous flux), cd (luminous intensity), or lx at (illuminance at a distance).

- lm — The documentation says the lm setting determines the "overall output of a light fixture in lumens."

- cd —This, according to the documentation, "measures the maximum light intensity of a fixture in candela." (1 candela is equal to the light output of one candle, so 10 candela is equal to the light output of ten candles.)

- lx at — This measures the intensity of light at a set distance, measured in lux. (1 lux equals 1 lumen per meter squared.)

- fc at — This is the same as lx at, except that the units are measured in foot-candles, where 1 foot-candle equals 1 lumen per foot squared. Foot candles are only available if light units are set to American.

The number below lm shows the value you have selected for your current units. For example, if you wish to set a light intensity of 1500 candela, simply click the cd button, enter 1500 in the numeric box, and set Multiplier to 100% or leave the Multiplier check box unchecked.

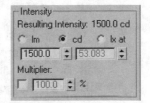

Figure 12.30

If you select "lx at" or "fc at" as your current unit, the numeric box to the right becomes available. This box sets the distance at which your intensity value is measured. For example, if you set your intensity to 1500 lx and you set the distance to 10 meters, then the measured light value 10 meters from your light source will be 1500 lux. The light intensity is 1500 lux *at* 10 meters.

Multiplier

You can change your final intensity value by simply checking the Multiplier check box and entering a numeric value from 0% to 100%, or you can use the spinner. For example, if you have an illumination value of 1500 candela and you set your multiplier to 50%, the resulting intensity will be half of 1500 cd, or 750 cd.

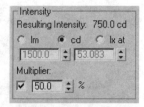

Figure 12.31: The Multiplier option

Linear Light Parameters Rollout

If you are using a photometric linear light, there is only one parameter in the parameters rollout: Length. A linear light is roughly analogous to something like a fluorescent tube, so it has a length. This is where you enter that length. Very straightforward.

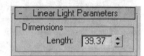

Figure 12.32: The Linear Light Parameters rollout

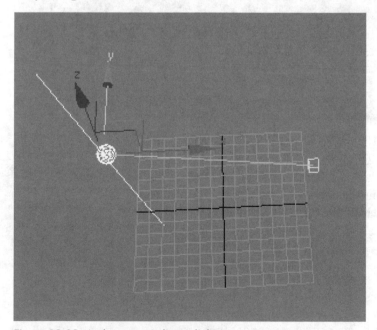

Figure 12.33: A photometric linear light

Area Light Parameters Rollout

Similar to linear lights, the Area Light Parameters rollout contains simple dimension controls for length and width.

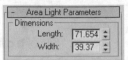

Figure 12.34. The Area Light Parameters rollout

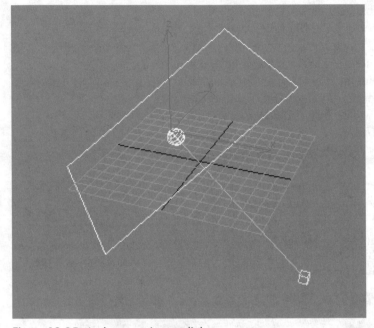

Figure 12.35: A photometric area light

Shadow Parameters Rollout

All light types have their own shadow settings. Bear in mind that lights themselves do not cast shadows, but these parameters affect the look of the shadow that is cast by an object placed within the illumination zone of the light.

Object Shadows

Pay attention now. Here are some extremely valuable tools that, when used subtly, can fake some of the most important lighting effects without adding any render time.

Figure 12.36: The Shadow Parameters rollout

Color

Why would we want to color a shadow? Shadows are just the absence of light, aren't they? So they should just be gray, shouldn't they?

Well, no, not really. Shadows are certainly the absence of light from one or more light sources, but almost never are they total absence of all light from all light sources. This implies that there is some other light source of lower intensity filling in the shaded area. This secondary "fill" light almost certainly has some sort of color, and you can, if you wish, add a second light with a different color to fill in the shaded area. Or, if you are very pressed for render time, you can simply change the shadow color.

For example, on a clear, sunny day outdoors, the areas that are shaded from direct sunlight are filled in by skylight. As we all know, the sky is blue and therefore the shadow is tinted with blue light. Simply click on the shadow color swatch to open the Color Selector, select a nice sky-blue color, and then render. You'll be able to see details within the shaded area.

Shadow color is also related to shadow density. One way to decrease shadow density is to simply make the color value higher. A very light blue shadow is less dense than a very dark blue shadow. Try it, you'll see.

Density

Shadow density is one of the tools I use most often these days. In photo-real work, it is often impossible to take the render time necessary to use radiosity; therefore you end up with pockets of darkness through-out your geometry that just look too dark. Since radiosity is out, we need another solution. Simply reducing the shadow density helps lighten up those dark areas without affecting the brightness of the light or the values of the fully illuminated materials.

A shadow density value of 1.0 means the shadow is 100% dense. In other words, the shadow alone should be the exact shadow color you selected in the shadow color swatch. If you choose a shadow density value of 0%, there will be no shadow. 50% means the shadow will be lighter than the shadow color by half. You can also set values higher than 1.0 if you want your shadow to become even denser.

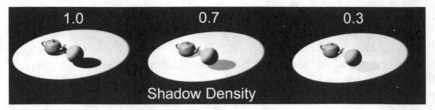

Figure 12.37: Shadow density examples

Map

Figure 12.36 shows the Map check box and button. If you click the None button, you will get a file dialog, allowing you to select an image map. Clicking on the check box will enable that map in the light's shadow. This image map, when applied, will be projected within the shadowed areas of the light. You can imagine how many different effects you could create within shadows using this feature!

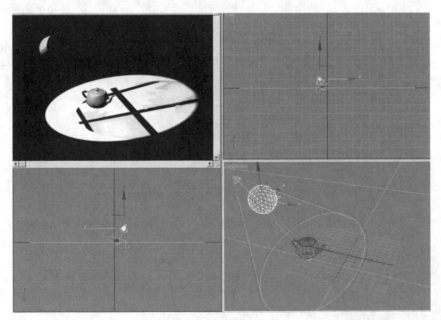

Figure 12.38: A "broken window" bitmap is used to create the look of light shining through a broken window within the area of shadow.

Figure 12.39: The "broken window" image. This is available on the companion CD.

Light Affects Shadow Color

Checking the Light Affects Shadow Color box multiplies the light color by the shadow color and density, allowing you to roughly fake color bleeding or a secondary light source that is tinted similarly to your key light.

Atmosphere Shadows

Atmosphere Shadows is a rather unusual tool. The documentation states that this tool is used to ensure that certain atmospheric effects such as fire and explosions cast shadows. I suppose if you had a big, dark smoke cloud or heavy rain clouds, this might be handy, but in my experience explosions or fires are usually the brightest light sources in the vicinity and don't usually cast shadows themselves.

Nonetheless, no doubt some find it very handy for their specific purposes.

The controls are fairly simple.

On

The On check box enables and disables the atmosphere shadows effect.

Opacity

The Opacity setting works like the shadow density tool. Higher opacity makes the atmospheric effect cast deeper shadows.

Color Amount

The Color Amount setting determines how much of the atmospheric effect's color is transmitted into the shaded area.

Atmospheres & Effects Rollout

The Atmospheres & Effects rollout allows you to add lens effects, volume light, or both to your light. The Add button opens a dialog that allows you to select these options.

Figure 12.40: The Atmospheres & Effects rollout

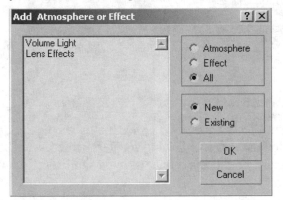

Figure 12.41: The Add Atmosphere or Effect dialog

The Delete button will remove a currently selected effect.

The Setup button will open the Environment and Effects panel where you set the parameters of the selected effect.

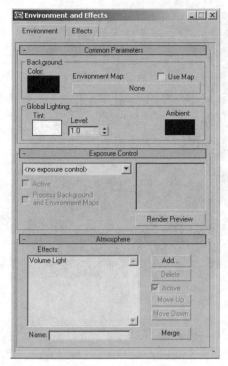

Figure 12.42: The Environment and
Effects panel

Lens flares and volume lights are covered in more detail in Chapter 10.

Advanced Effects Rollout

Affect Surfaces

Under this rollout, there are a number of controls that affect how the light appears on materials.

Figure 12.43: The
Advanced Effects rollout

Contrast

By default, the contrast is set to 0.0. A ball under a spotlight looks like Figure 12.44 under default settings.

Figure 12.44: Contrast at 0.0

The range is 0.0 to 100. The higher the contrast, the sharper the shadow terminator line becomes. Below is an image with a contrast of 100.

Figure 12.45: Contrast at 100

Soften Diff. Edge

This tool has the opposite effect of Contrast. The range is from 0.0 to 100. A higher value makes the shadow terminator become softer. Figure 12.46 shows an image with Soften Diffuse Edge at 100.

Figure 12.46: Soften Diff(use) Edge set at 100

Diffuse/Specular

The Diffuse and Specular check boxes turn diffuse lighting and specular lighting on and off. If diffuse lighting is off, there will be no light cast onto diffuse materials. If specular lighting is off, there will be no specular highlights, even on materials with high specular settings. The advantage of turning off diffuse light is that sometimes you only want to see reflection or specularity without changing the material. The advantage of turning off specularity is that sometimes you only want to see the material without specular highlights. Also, turning off the specular highlight can decrease the directional appearance of a light, making it appear more like an area light source.

> **Note:** The larger the light source, the wider the specular highlight. As a matter of fact, some light sources are so large that the specular highlights are too wide to notice. This is why area lights and skylights don't show much specularity. Turning off specularity can fool the viewer into believing you are using a larger (and more render-intensive) light source.

Figure 12.47: Diffuse lighting off and specular lighting on

Figure 12.48: Specular lighting off and diffuse lighting on

Ambient Only

The Ambient Only check box disables all the other controls in the Affect Surfaces area. If this box is checked, the light provides flat lighting with no shadows.

Figure 12.49: Ambient Only on

Projector Map

If you select the Map box in the Projector Map area, you can select an image map or material from the adjacent button and have that material or image projected through the light. When you click the button, you are presented with the Material/Map browser. You may choose any material or map.

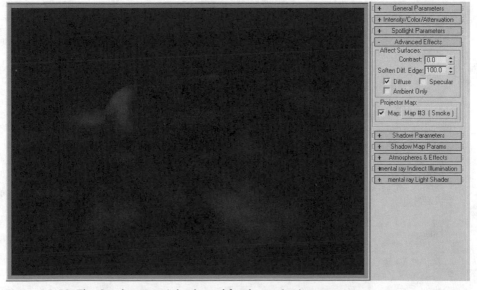

Figure 12.50: The Smoke material selected for the projection map

179

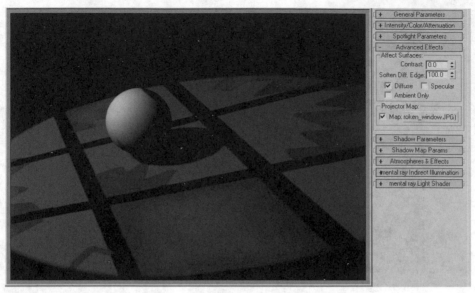

Figure 12.51: The "broken window" image selected for the projection map

Chapter 13

Shadow Types and their Typical Uses

Shadow Maps

Shadow maps are the fastest form of shadows in MAX. This is because they are calculated by mapping the shapes of objects as seen from the light's point of view. These are rough, two-dimensional cutout shapes, which makes them very quick. Also, the cutout shape has a resolution that you set in the shadow map Size parameter. The smaller the shadow map size, the quicker the render. Shadow maps can be used to great effect to fake all sorts of lighting situations and environments. They do have their shortfalls, however. Shadow maps can be made sharp or fuzzy, but they are the same sharpness or fuzziness all the way around the shadow edges. This doesn't reflect the shadow properties of real shadows, but often times it is enough to get by.

Shadow Map Parameters Rollout

Bias

The Bias setting determines whether or not the shadow starts at the object casting it. The higher the bias, the farther away from the object the shadow will begin. Too high a Bias setting can make an object appear to be "floating" above the ground because the shadow does not touch the object casting it as it would in the real world.

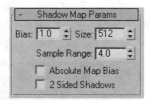

Figure 13.1: Shadow Map Parameters rollout

Figure 13.2: Bias settings

Size

Shadow map size determines how fine the edges of shadow-mapped shadows appear. A very low-resolution shadow map will look blocky because it is only a few pixels square. A higher resolution map may be required for very subtle curves. Note that higher resolution shadow maps require longer rendering times, so try to keep this value as low as possible.

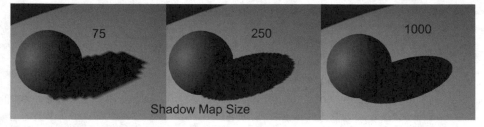

Figure 13.3: Shadow map size settings

Sample Range

Sample Range is a really, really important tool. We'll be referring to it a lot later on.

The Sample Range setting will give fuzziness to the shadow map edges. This is a good way to keep your shadow map size down. You can always blur the edges to hide the "pixelly" look.

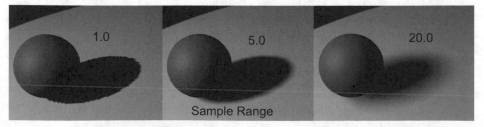

Figure 13.4: Sample Range settings

This is an especially important tool because it allows us to soften shadows without having to use area lights or calculate area shadows. Much faster, nice softness, maximum bang for the buck!

Absolute Map Bias

The documentation says that the shadow map bias is computed by looking at the whole scene's size, and that if you change the size of the scene quickly, flickering can occur in the shadows. To solve this problem, turn on Absolute Map Bias.

2 Sided Shadows

Most faces and polygons are single-sided unless you explicitly tell them to be two-sided. Because of this, a light will not "see" a polygon that has its normal facing away. This light is looking at the "backface" of the polygon, and no shadows are cast by the object because the backface is effectively transparent.

In order to make transparent backfaces cast shadows, even if the polygon does not have 2 Sided enabled, turn on this 2 Sided Shadows button. The light will see all the faces regardless of which side is facing the light.

mr Shadow Maps

You can use mental ray shadow maps with standard lights, provided you switch the renderer to the mental ray Renderer. If you don't use the mental ray Renderer, the mental ray lights will behave just like standard MAX lights but render a little slower. You'll get the best quality from mr shadow maps by using mental ray lights. Standard lights will render more quickly with mental ray shadow maps, but at a cost of quality.

In general, mr shadow maps produce a better quality shadow than standard MAX shadow maps.

mental ray Shadow Map Parameters Rollout

The mr Shadow Map Parameters rollout has three settings, which are discussed below.

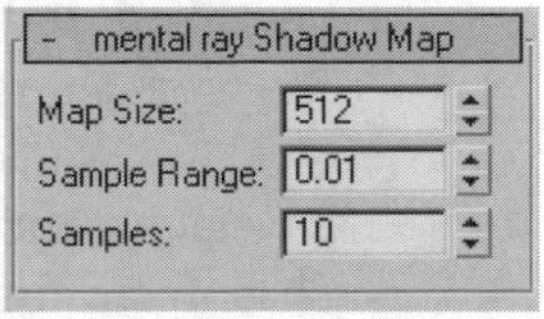

Map Size

Map Size refers to how many pixels high and how many pixels wide the map will be when calculated. Larger map sizes result in more

Figure 13.5: mental ray Shadow Map Parameters rollout

accurate maps and smoother shadow edges. Higher settings are especially important when you are using a hard-edged shadow. If you are using a very soft shadow edge, you can usually get away with much lower map sizes. See Figure 13.3.

Sample Range

As discussed earlier, Sample Range is one of the most important lighting settings, at least for shadow maps. This setting determines how hard or soft edged your shadow is. Lower settings make harder shadows, while higher settings make softer shadows. See Figure 13.4.

Samples

The Samples setting determines the quality of the shadow map. Harder-edged shadows can get away with a lower Samples setting, while softer shadows with wider sample ranges will require a higher Samples setting.

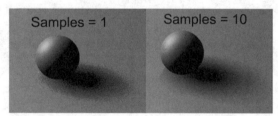

Figure 13.6:Samples settings

Ray-traced Shadows

Ray-traced shadows are second in speed only to shadow maps. They render by tracing lines from the light source, along the edges of objects, and continuing until they hit geometry. This works much like real light "rays." The only problem with this shadow type is that the shadows are always hard-edged. You can get away with this in some situations, such as direct sunlight, because shadows in direct sunlight often appear to be very hard all the way around (even though they are not). Considering the great alternatives available, though, this is the least likely type of shadow I would use in any case. One good thing about ray-traced shadows is that they will trace through transparent materials, where shadow-mapped lights will not.

Ray Traced Shadow Parameters Rollout

Ray Bias

A Ray Bias of 0.0 will trace shadows right to the edge of the geometry. A higher setting will tend to "push" the shadows inward. A very high Ray Bias setting tends to decrease the quality of the shadow edge.

Figure 13.7: Ray Traced Shadow Parameters rollout

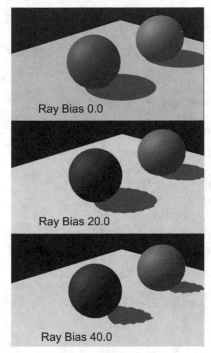

Ray Bias 0.0

Ray Bias 20.0

Ray Bias 40.0

Figure 13.8: Using Ray Bias

2 Sided Shadows

Most faces and polygons are single-sided unless you explicitly tell them to be two-sided. Because of this, a light will not "see" a polygon that has its normal facing away. This light is looking at the "backface" of the polygon and no shadows are cast by the object because the backface is effectively transparent.

In order to make transparent backfaces cast shadows, even if the polygon does not have 2 Sided enabled, turn on the 2 Sided Shadows button. The light will see all the faces regardless of which side is facing the light.

185

Max Quadtree Depth

Max Quadtree Depth determines the size of the data structure used to calculate the shadow. A lower setting will take up less RAM but will also take longer to render. Values available range from 1 to 10. Naturally, if you have enough RAM, the higher the setting the better.

Advanced Ray-traced Shadows

Advanced ray-traced shadows are an updated and refined version of ray-traced shadows. The main difference is that you can set soft edges and quality for advanced ray-traced shadows. Naturally, higher quality means higher rendering times, so experiment to find the lowest possible settings before setting a final render.

Advanced Ray Traced Parameters Rollout

Your first option is to select Simple, 1-Pass Antialias, or 2-Pass Antialias.

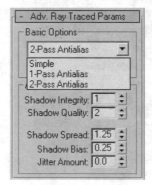

Figure 13.9: Advanced Ray Traced Parameters rollout

Figure 13.10

The Simple option will disable most of the quality settings in the rest of the rollout and make the shadows behave like regular ray-traced shadows. 1-Pass will antialias the shadow edges, and 2-Pass will antialias the shadow edges twice, improving the quality. Be sure to use the lowest quality you need, as higher settings really increase render times. With 2-Pass, you will also have the option to determine the shadow quality.

2 Sided Shadows

See the discussion about the 2 Sided Shadows option earlier in this chapter.

Shadow Integrity

Advanced ray-traced shadows are softened by overlaying several copies of the shadow, which are slightly offset from each other and then blurred. The Shadow Integrity setting determines how much the shadow copies or layers are blurred together

Figure 13.11: Shadow Integrity settings

Shadow Quality

Higher Shadow Quality settings will provide better shadow edges. A higher setting means more rays are traced to determine the shadow edges. Once again, higher settings equal longer rendering times.

Shadow Spread

Shadow Spread determines how far apart the "layers" or "copies" of the shadow are spread out. The higher this setting, the farther the shadow layers are spread out and the more obvious the layers become. As you move this setting higher, you will need to improve shadow integrity and quality to hide the layer stepping. Conversely, the lower you keep the Shadow Spread value, the lower the quality and integrity settings you can use, and therefore the quicker renders you can achieve.

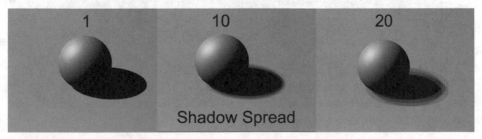

Figure 13.12: Shadow Spread settings

The main disadvantage to this setting is that it is measured in pixels. This means that if you back the camera away, the spread will change relative to the scene.

Figure 13.13: Shadow Spread settings

This can be a real problem if you have a camera fly-through and soft shadows due to a high shadow spread.

Shadow Bias

Just as with the other shadow types, Shadow Bias determines how close to the object the shadow begins. Higher values bring the shadow closer to the object casting it.

Jitter Amount

Jitter Amount breaks up the rays traced into the shadow edges, creating a random effect and softening the shadow edge. Higher Jitter Amount values require higher Shadow Quality settings; otherwise they look too grainy.

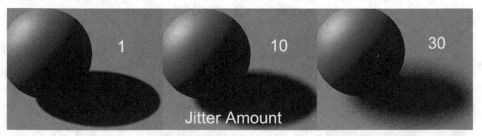

Figure 13.14: Jitter Amount settings

Area Shadows

All real light sources have size. This is the main difference between real lights and basic CG lights like spotlights, directional lights, and omni lights, which all have no size, being defined only by a single, nondimensional point in space. Lights with size cause shadows with a penumbra that is sharpest near the object casting the shadow and softer proportionally to the distance from the object. Since basic CG lights do not have size, they generally do not create natural-looking shadows —except for the fact that they can use area shadows. As a matter of fact, all MAX light types can use area shadows.

For basic light types like omni, directional, and spot, area shadows are fantastically useful. The greatest thing about them is that they behave much like real shadows. Area shadows aren't the answer to every problem, but they are definitely one of my favorite lighting tools in MAX.

Area Shadows Parameters Rollout

Basic Options

The drop-down in the Basic Options portion of the rollout allows you to determine the initial shape of the light. Now bear in mind that none of the settings in this rollout affect how the light *illuminates* the subject, only how the shadows are formed.

Figure 13.15: Area
Shadows rollout

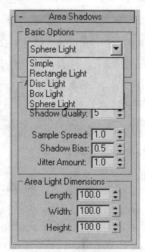

Figure 13.16: Basic
Options choices

The Simple setting effectively turns off area shadows and makes the shadows behave like basic ray-traced shadows. This is sort of an enable/disable feature in case you want to do quick test renders.

The Rectangle and Disc choices allow you to simulate shadows from a window or a television, which are both rectangular, or perhaps from the sun, which, as far as we are concerned, is just a disc in the sky.

The Box and Sphere choices add an additional dimension to the light. These are actually the most realistic, since all lights have volume, but they are also the most expensive to render and usually make very little difference to the final look.

Most of the time, you'll find yourself using a rectangle, I'll bet, unless you have a very specific purpose in mind. Rectangle is my setting of choice.

Antialiasing Options

All the Antialiasing controls in the Area Shadows parameters rollout work just like those in the Advanced Ray Traced Shadows rollout, so take a look at that section of this chapter for information on how to use them. No use wasting space when there's so much other goodness to fill the pages.

Area Light Dimensions

Obviously, these settings control the length, width, and height of the area light. Straightforward. Larger lights result in softer shadows.

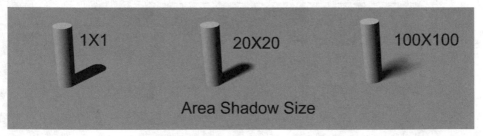

Figure 13.17: Area Light Dimensions settings

■ ■ ■

By now you should have a fairly good understanding of the different shadow types available in MAX and perhaps a little idea as to how and where best to use each type. As with everything in CG, the highest quality and best results usually come at a cost of high render times, with few exceptions.

Chapter 14

Radiosity

Radiosity Defined

What is radiosity?

Radiosity happens every day, everywhere in the universe. Radiosity occurs when photons strike a material and bounce off it in another direction. In the real world, radiosity light reflections happen hundreds or thousands or millions of times until all the energy is absorbed. A good example of radiosity is the indirect illumination you see on the underside of people's chins when they are outside sitting at a table with a white tablecloth that is lit by direct sunlight. Actually, if you take a moment to look around you, you'll see that there is light almost everywhere you look, even though much of your environment is not directly illuminated. Where does the light come from? Some people call it "ambient" light. Sure, you can call it ambient light if you like, as long as you don't confuse it with the ambient lighting within 3D software. This real-world "ambient" light is simply light that has reflected from one surface to the next over and over again until the room is generally lit.

So why do we need radiosity in MAX?

Well, we can always get away with tricks and cheats. Visual effects artists have been faking radiosity for years simply by understanding the properties of light reflection and cleverly faking these properties using other light sources. But the fact remains that nothing looks quite as good, as real, or as subtle as real, calculated radiosity reflections.

Global Illumination Defined

In 3ds max, there are primarily two types of lighting. One is *local illumination*, that illumination in which scenes and objects are directly lit by lights such as spotlights, omni lights, and direct lights. The other kind of lighting in MAX involves indirect lighting such as radiosity reflections and image-based lighting. This kind of lighting is known as *global illumination*.

191

The Tools

MAX is equipped with a number of tools to help you create beautiful global illumination in your scenes. Light Tracer, Radiosity, and mental ray's Indirect Illumination are just a few of the many rendering solutions available for MAX to create beautiful radiosity renders.

Following are brief discussions of the radiosity tools available in MAX, along with tutorials that will help you get up and running with the radiosity tools quickly. For a complete, detailed discussion of all the radiosity tools and settings, please consult the MAX documentation.

Radiosity

When using the Default Scanline Renderer in MAX, you can enable radiosity by opening the render panel and choosing the Radiosity plug-in in the Advanced Lighting tab.

Figure 14.1: Selecting the Radiosity plug-in

Radiosity settings are found in the Advanced Lighting tab and are fairly self-explanatory. The rollouts here deal mainly with quality settings.

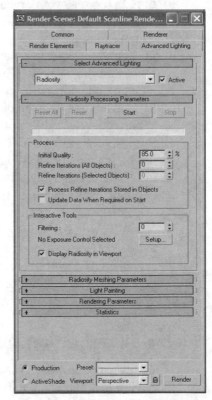

Figure 14.2: The Advanced Lighting tab

Using the Radiosity plug-in is relatively simple. In order to get a good-looking solution, however, you'll probably find yourself fiddling with the Exposure Control settings in the Environment and Effects panel.

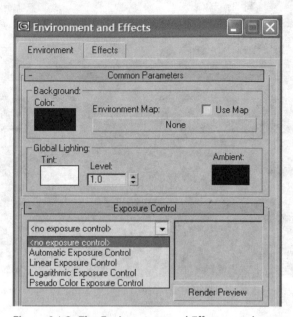

Figure 14.3: The Environment and Effects panel

Radiosity Tutorial

Here's a very simple radiosity tutorial to get you up and running.

First, load up the radiosity.max scene from the companion CD. This scene is just a bunch of primitive geometry and a single omni light. Nothing special. No special materials required. Figure 14.4 shows what a basic render should look like.

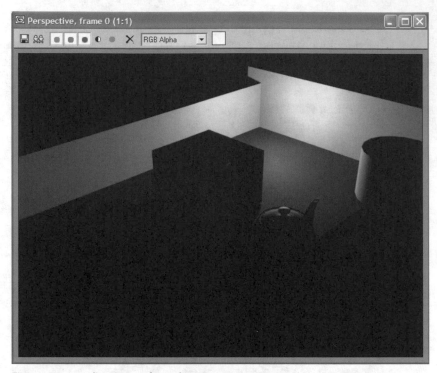

Figure 14.4: radiosity.max from the companion CD

Now choose the Radiosity plug-in in the Advanced Lighting tab of the render panel and click the Start button to calculate the radiosity solution.

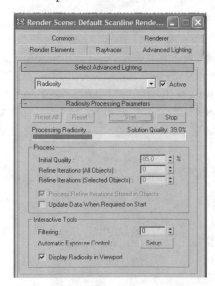

Figure 14.5

A new render will look pretty much like the original one calculated without radiosity.

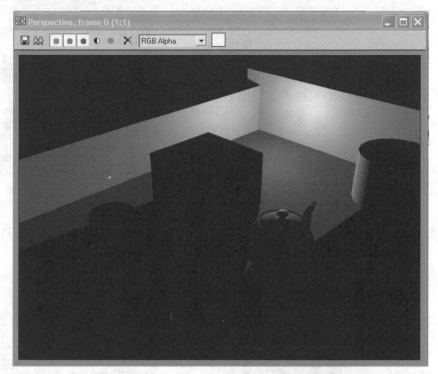

Figure 14.6: Scene with Radiosity on

In the Environment and Effects panel, select one of the Exposure Control methods.

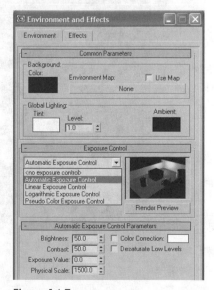

Figure 14.7

I like to start with Automatic Exposure Control as it's easiest.

When you become more familiar with the other controls and parameters, you can start using them.

Make sure Automatic Exposure Control is active and render a new frame. It should look like Figure 14.9.

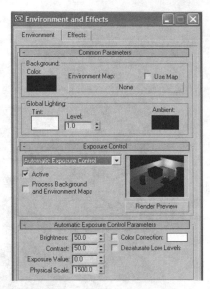

Figure 14.8

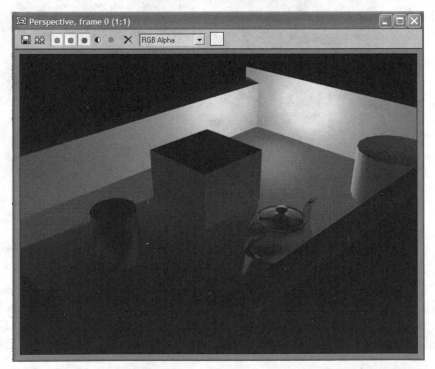

Figure 14.9: Scene with Radiosity on and Automatic Exposure Control option

You can see that radiosity bounces are providing indirect lighting in areas where the omni light does not directly reach. Try fiddling with the Exposure Control settings to get a better illumination solution. Remember, if you move the light or any items in the scene or if you change any radiosity parameters, you will need to reset the radiosity solution and calculate it again by pressing the Start button on the radiosity panel.

Figure 14.10

Light Tracer

Light Tracer is by far the simplest of the global illumination solutions in MAX. It is also the least physically accurate, but the truth is, you will probably get more use out of Light Tracer than you will out of Radiosity or mental ray Indirect Illumination simply because it is simple, easy to use, and provides nice-looking and predictable results. No preprocessing is required as it is with Radiosity, which makes it faster to work with as well.

You activate Light Tracer just as you do Radiosity by selecting the Light Tracer plug-in in the Advanced Lighting tab of the render panel.

Aside from being self-explanatory, the few controls in the Parameters rollout are well documented. The most important control is the Bounces control. This determines how many light bounces are calculated at render time. This setting goes up to a maximum of 10.

Following is a short tutorial that will quickly get you up and running with Light Tracer.

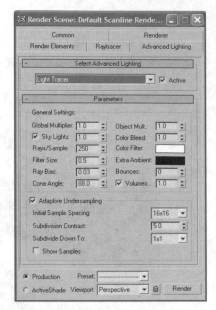

Figure 14.11: Selecting the Light Tracer plug-in

A Short Light Tracer Tutorial

First, load up the scene from the companion CD titled light_tracer.max. This is similar to the radiosity scene file. A basic render should look like the following.

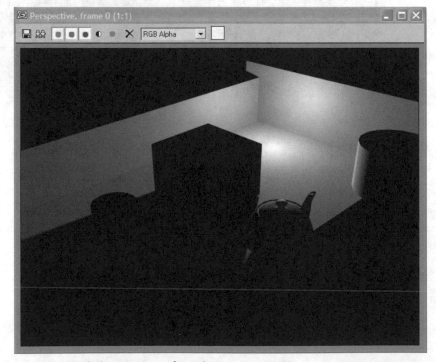

Figure 14.12: light_tracer.max from the companion CD

Now, in the render panel, choose the Light Tracer plug-in.

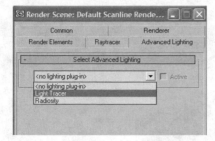

Figure 14.13

You'll now see the Light Tracer Parameters rollout.

Leaving all the other settings at their default levels, change Bounces to 3.

Figure 14.14: Default settings

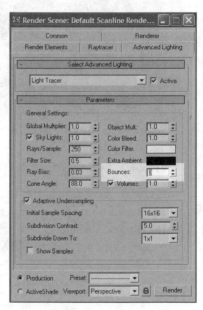

Figure 14.15: Choose 3 for Bounces.

Now hit the Render button and check out the difference!

Figure 14.16: Scene with Light Tracer on and three bounces (See color image.)

Another Short Light Tracer Tutorial

Here's a great way to use Light Tracer for outdoor scenes. One of the most difficult aspects of exterior lighting is achieving the wide illumination and soft shadows created by the biggest light source on the planet — the sky. Fortunately, MAX gives us skylights and Light Tracer.

Load up a plane and any geometry you'd like to start with. Your perspective viewport should look something like Figure 14.17.

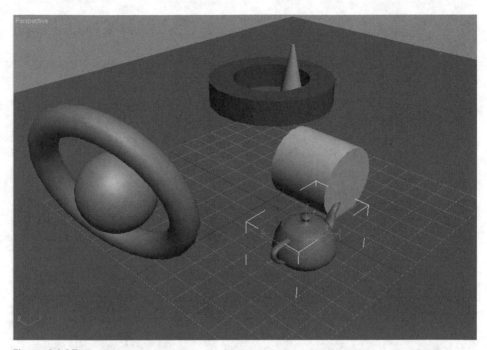

Figure 14.17

A simple render with default lighting looks pretty basic and boring.

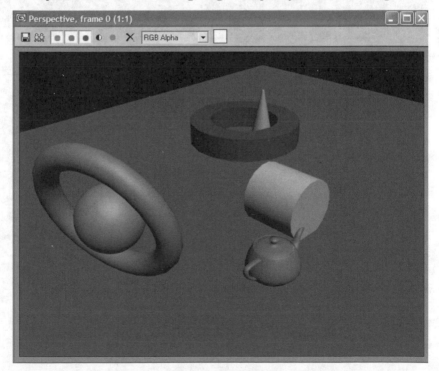

Figure 14.18

Now add a skylight. It doesn't matter where in the scene you place the skylight, but the orientation of the light *does* matter. Make sure the half-dome is oriented as though it were a sky dome, with the flat side down.

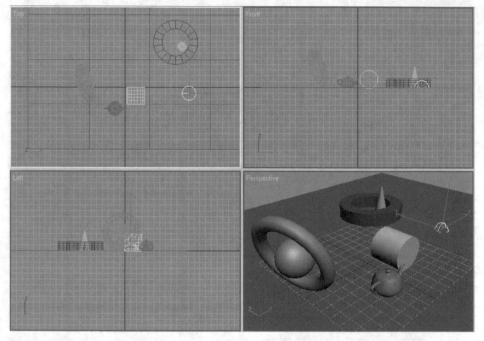

Figure 14.19

Now, in the Advanced Lighting tab of the render panel, choose the Light Tracer plug-in.

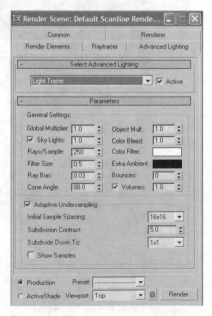

Figure 14.20

If the sun's rays were all parallel, the shadow behind earth would look like this

Figure 3.4

Figure 6.4

Figure 1.3: This photo has three main light sources. The sun is the key light, and there are two fill lights: the skylight and reflected light.

Here is a good example of a highlight in nature. In this example one could argue that the key light is the highlight or rim light. Others may say there is no key, just a fill and a rim.

Figure 6.10: In this image, the "bounce" light behaves like radiosity reflected from the floor or road in front of the man, also filling in where lesser experienced lighting artists might be tempted to use ambient intensity — a big no-no in most cases.

Figure 6.6: McCandless lighting.

Figure 6.8: Three-point lighting.

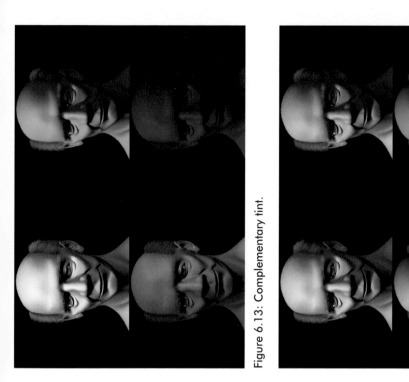

Figure 6.13: Complementary tint.

Figure 6.14: Related tint.

Figure 6.11: Sidelight.

Figure 6.12: Footlight.

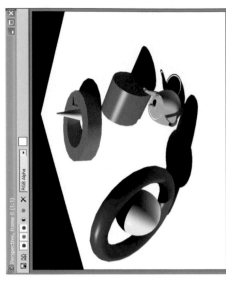

Figure 14.27: Using Global Illumination.

Figure 14.28: Using Final Gather.

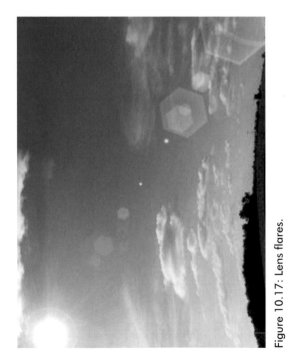

Figure 10.17: Lens flares.

Figure 14.16: Using the Light Tracer plug-in.

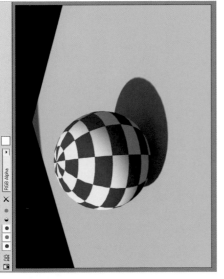

Figure 15.7: Render with Light Tracer.

Figure 15.8: Increasing light bounces.

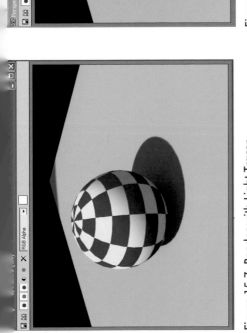

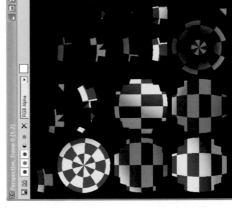

Figure 15.14

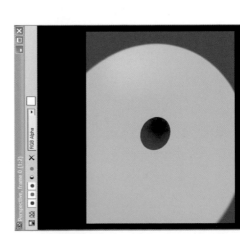

Figure 15.13: Rendering to texture.

Figure 15.23

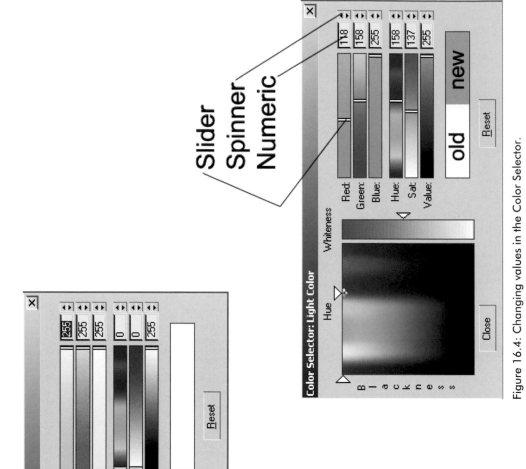

Figure 16.1: The Color Selector.

Figure 16.2: Selecting the color swatch.

Figure 16.4: Changing values in the Color Selector.

Figure 17.1: Render on left with HDR image on right.

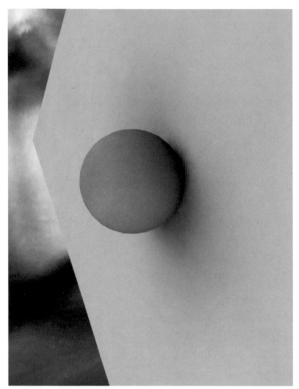

Figure 17.16: Using an HDR image.

Figure 17.2: LightGen render.

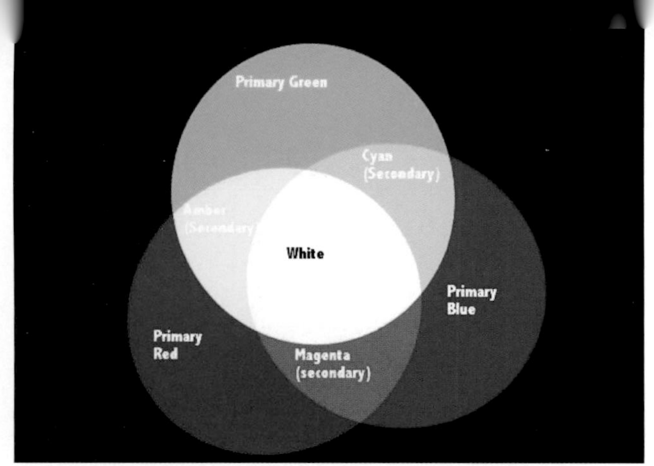

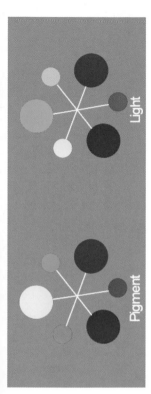

Figure 20.3: Primaries and secondaries.

Figure 20.4: Hue.

High Saturation   Low Saturation

Figure 20.5

High Value   Low Value

Figure 20.6

Figure 20.1: Primary and secondary colors of lighting.

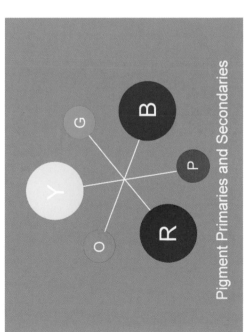

Pigment Primaries and Secondaries

Figure 20.2

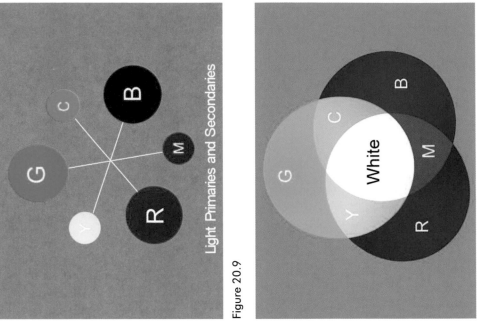

Figure 20.9

Figure 20.7: Color model showing the interaction of hue, saturation, and value.

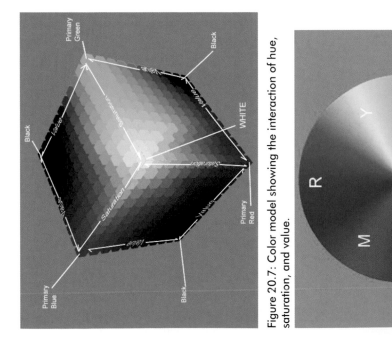

Figure 20.8: Example of color wheel.

Figure 20.10: Example of color wheel.

A graphic
representation
of all three light
colors.

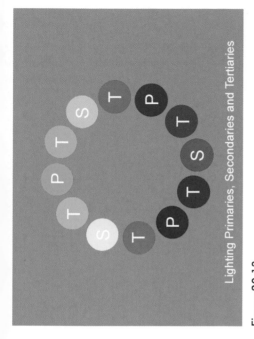

Lighting Primaries, Secondaries and Tertiaries

Figure 20.13

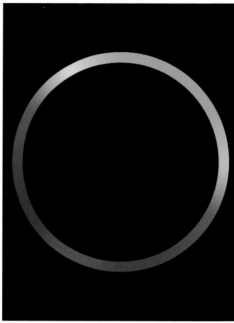

Figure 20.14: Color wheel showing intermediate colors.

A typical
wavelength
transmission
graph for a
lighting filter.

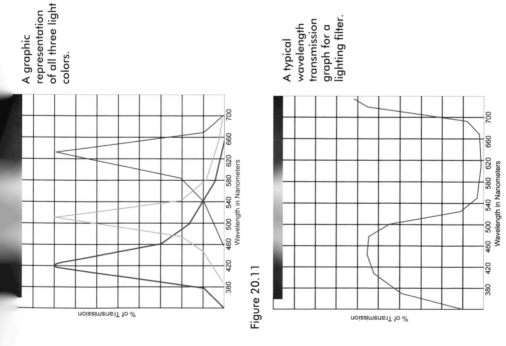

Figure 20.11

Figure 20.12

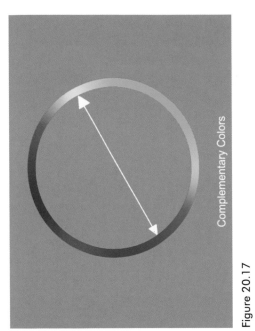

Monochromatic Color Harmony

Figure 20.15

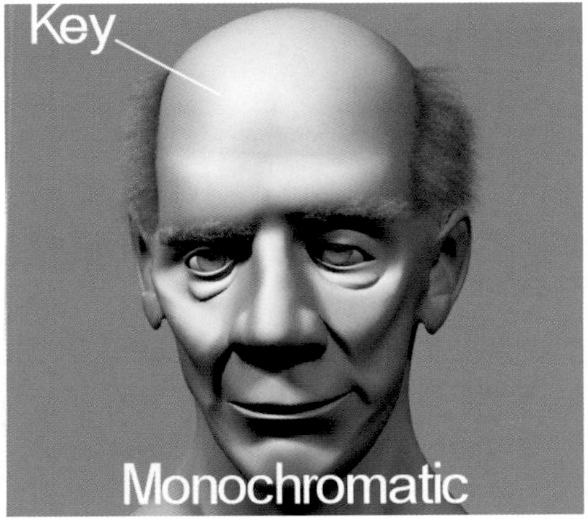

Complementary Colors

Figure 20.17

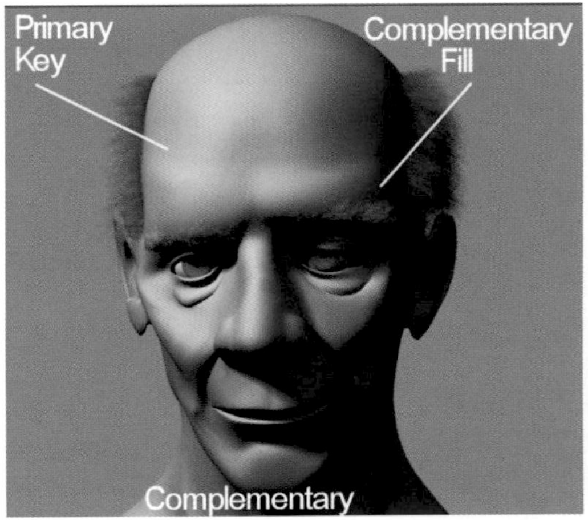

Key

Monochromatic

Figure 20.16

Complementary Fill

Primary Key

Complementary

Figure 20.18

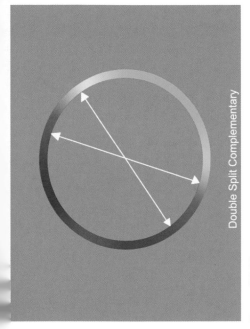

Figure 20.19

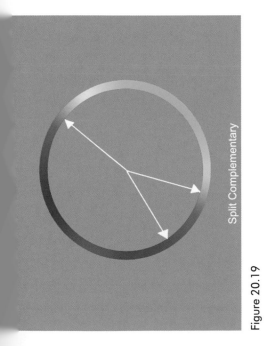

Figure 20.21

Split Complementary

Double Split Complementary

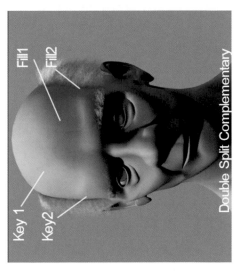

Figure 20.20

Figure 20.22

Split Complementary

Double Split Complementary

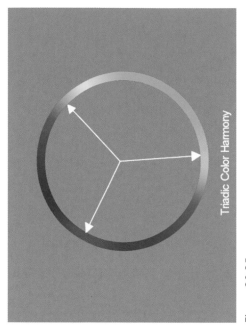

Figure 20.23

Related Tints (Analogous Color Harmony)

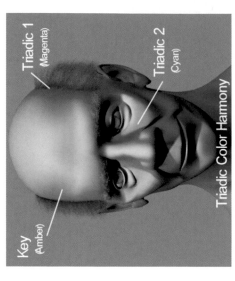

Triadic Color Harmony

Figure 20.25

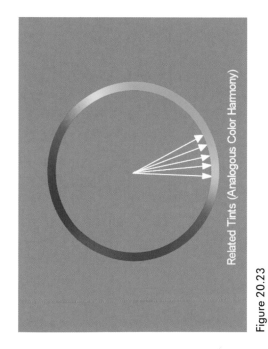

Key
(Amber)

Tint2

Tint3

Key

Tint1

Related Tints (Analogous Color Harmony)

Figure 20.24

Triadic 1
(Magenta)

Triadic 2
(Cyan)

Triadic Color Harmony

Figure 20.26

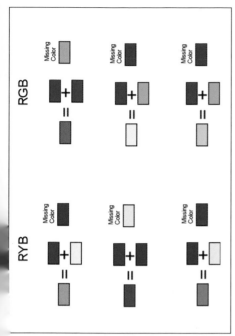

Figure 20.28: Determining "missing" colors.

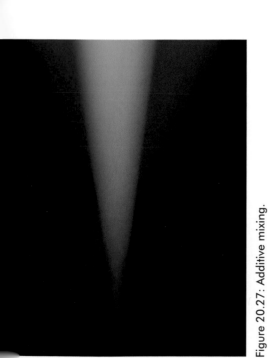

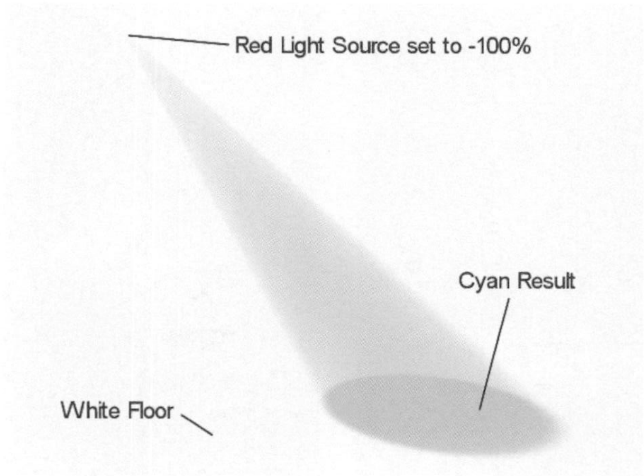

Figure 20.27: Additive mixing.

Figure 20.29: Subtractive mixing.

Figure 25.25: Using mental ray area lights.

Figure 23.5: Test render.

Using just the default settings, we get a pretty beautiful-looking render. The skylight with Light Tracer on and no bounces creates a very nice occlusion-based lighting solution that renders very quickly.

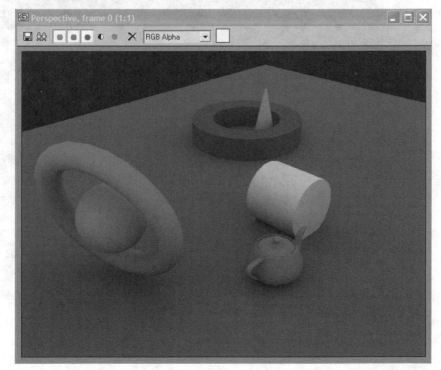

Figure 14.21

If we want to make it even more "outdoorish," we can add a standard distant light to simulate sunlight.

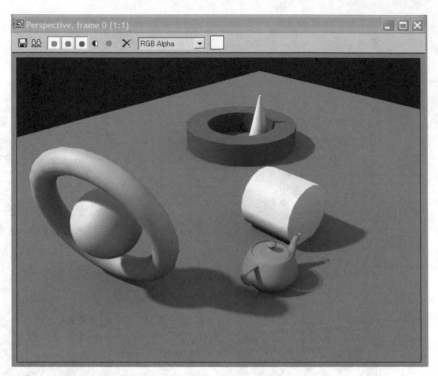

Figure 14.22

If you wish to see it, this scene is also saved on the CD as light_
tracer_2.max.

> **Note:** Photometric lights do not act physically accurately when
> using Light Tracer. If you need the correct physical representation of
> photometric lights, use Radiosity instead of Light Tracer.

mental ray Indirect Illumination

In MAX, direct illumination is the light that is emitted directly from light
sources. This is the light that reaches and illuminates the items in our
scenes. Indirect illumination refers to light that either reflects or refracts
from the direct light source after the initial illumination. In other words,
sunlight that shines on a white tablecloth will reflect off the tablecloth
and illuminate nearby surfaces, even if those surfaces are not directly
illuminated by the sun. This is called radiosity.

Caustics is another example of indirect illumination, except the light
is reflected or refracted into focused high-density areas of illumination,
such as when light shines through a glass of wine and onto the
tablecloth.

mental ray calculates its indirect illumination in terms of units called *photons*. These are samples of light that contain an amount of light energy. As the photons travel and bounce, the light energy is diminished, just as in the real world. mental ray uses two types of photons — global illumination photons and caustics photon — and requires photon shaders to be used in the scene. Simple ray trace materials will work fine.

mr Global Illumination Tutorial

Here's a quick and simple tutorial that will help you get up and running with mental ray's radiosity solution.

First load the scene mr_global_illumination.max from the companion CD. A basic render should look like Figure 14.23.

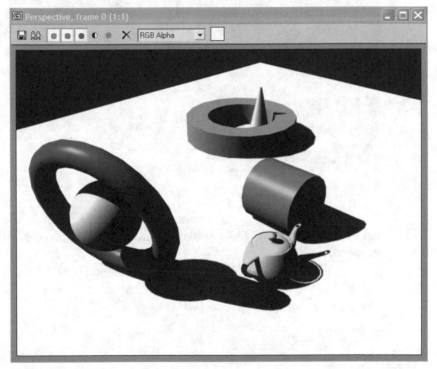

Figure 14.23

This is quite similar to the Light Tracer tutorial scene with one exception: Ray Trace material has been added to each item in the scene. This is because radiosity solutions in mental ray need a material that will recognize mental ray photons. These materials are known as *photon shaders*. We'll just start with simple Ray Trace materials, but there are others to choose from, some that will only render with mental ray.

Now it's time to switch the renderer to mental ray. Open the Common tab of the render panel and select mental ray Renderer.

Now switch to the Indirect Illumination tab and enable Global Illumination.

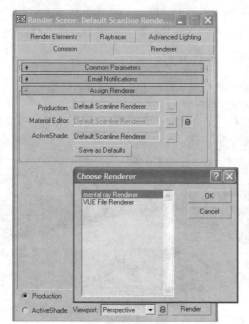

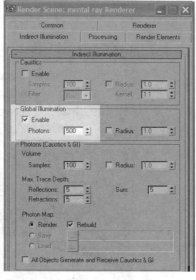

Figure 14.25

Figure 14.24

If you do a new render at this point, you won't notice much difference except that you'll see MAX calculate a radiosity solution and it will take longer to render.

Scroll to the bottom of the Indirect Illumination panel. In the Global Light Properties section set Decay to 1.0 instead of the default 2.0 and change Energy from 50,000 to 100,000.

Figure 14.26

At this point, a quick render should display nice light bounce and color bleeding throughout the scene.

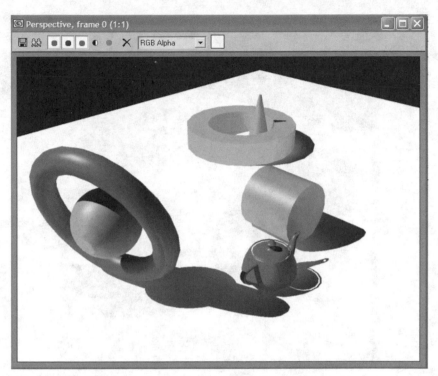

Figure 14.27: Scene with Global Illumination on (See color image.)

For final renders, quality levels will need to be increased, but that's the basic gist of how to get mental ray's Global Illumination up and running.

If you wish to use caustics, simply enable the caustics parameters and be sure you are using refractive or reflective materials.

Final Gather can help smooth out radiosity artifacts in the final render, so it's a good idea to use it. Don't forget to do test renders with Final Gather on before launching a full render, as your scene brightness may change.

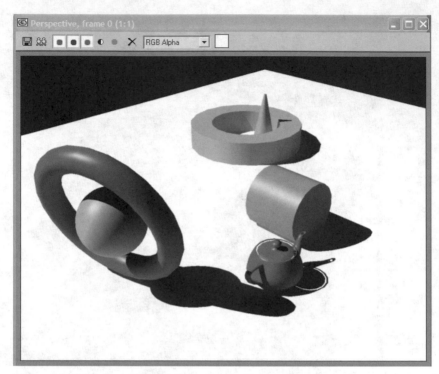

Figure 14.28: Scene with Final Gather on (See color image.)

■ ■ ■

This chapter should give you a basic grounding in how to get started with the radiosity tools in MAX. Once again, for detailed descriptions of the many tools and parameters, please consult the documentation or online resources.

Texture Baking and Light Painting

Texture Baking

Texture baking is one of the greatest ways to get cheap renders out of expensive lighting. What happens is you set up your scene, texture your objects, light the scene however you'd like it, and then apply a procedure called *baking*, which takes all the texturing, lighting, and shading and sandwiches it into one layer, then saves that layer as an image. You then remove your lighting, shading, and textures and apply the new image that has the textures, lighting, and shading "baked" in. Now your scene "looks" like it's carefully lit and shaded, but it really isn't. This technique works great as long as you don't have moving objects in the scene because the shadows will not move around. It is perfect for camera fly-throughs. On the other hand, if you are compositing CG elements post-render, you can render your entire environment texture-baked, and then add shadow layers at compositing time.

Following is a brief texture baking tutorial. Take it to heart. This simple technique can save you hundreds or even thousands of render hours and allow you to use some pretty sophisticated and otherwise-too-expensive lighting techniques.

Texture Baking Tutorial

Thanks to Matthew Mascheri for his ideas with this tutorial.

To begin with, open MAX and add a simple piece of geometry like a sphere.

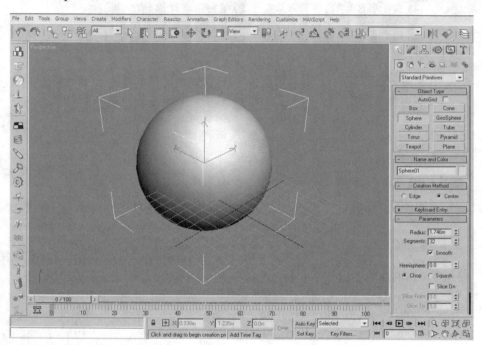

Figure 15.1: Add a sphere.

Now open the Material Editor and create a texture to apply to the sphere. Any texture will do.

I selected a simple checkerboard pattern, set the U and V Tiling values to 5, and changed the check colors to blue and yellow.

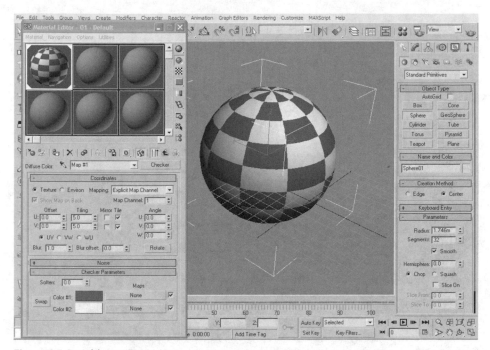

Figure 15.2: Add a texture.

Add a ground plane so the sphere will have something to cast shadows onto.

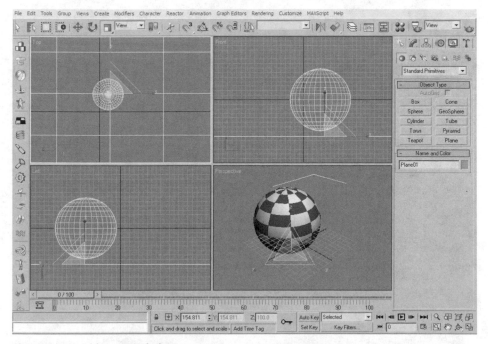

Figure 15.3: Add a ground plane.

Now add a skylight and a spotlight to your scene. Make sure the skylight is properly oriented and have the spotlight target your sphere.

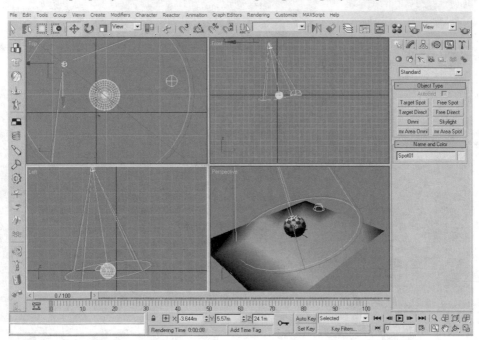

Figure 15.4: Add a skylight and spotlight.

Open the Light Lister and be sure the spotlight has Area Shadows selected.

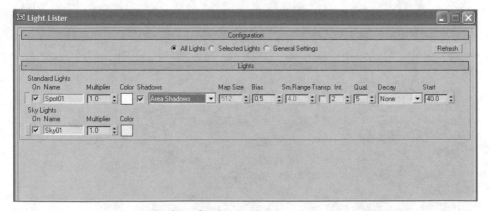

Figure 15.5: Choose Area Shadows for the spotlight.

Now open the render panel and add the Light Tracer plug-in on the Advanced Lighting tab. Leave all the settings at their default levels except for Global Multiplier and Bounces. Set Global Multiplier to 0.5 and Bounces to 2.

Figure 15.6: Choose the Light Tracer plug-in and change its settings.

Now do a quick render and have a look.

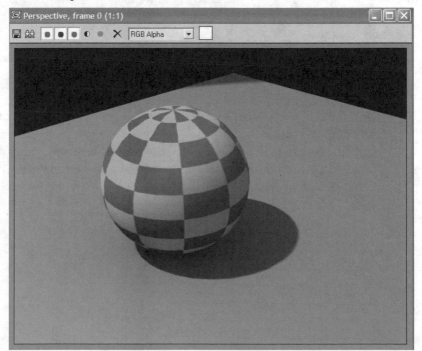

Figure 15.7: Render the image. (See color image.)

You can see the nice, soft shading and color bleeding from the light bounces.

You can really improve the light and shadow quality by increasing the light bounces to 10, although this takes quite a bit longer to render.

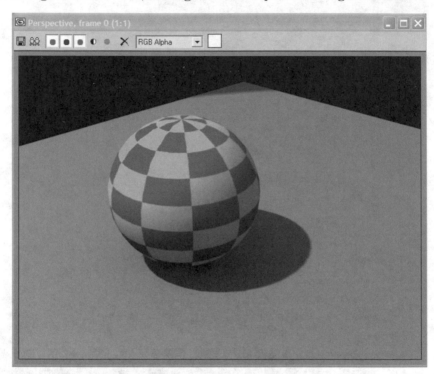

Figure 15.8 (See color image.)

Now that we're happy with the look, we can proceed to the next step: rendering to texture.

First, select both the sphere and the plane. Make sure you have both selected. Now, either hit the 0 button (zero) or, under the Rendering menu option, select Render To Texture.

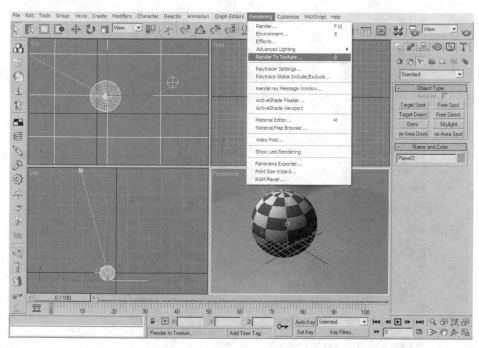

Figure 15.9: Selecting Render To Texture

The Render To Texture panel will open up. You'll see both your items selected at the bottom of the panel in the Objects to Bake list. We'll only bake one at a time, though.

Now set your output path. Click the Add button to bring up the Add Texture Elements panel. This is where we select which texture channels we want included in our final baked textures. Since we want everything included, click on CompleteMap and then click the Add Elements button.

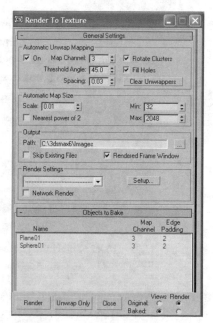

Figure 15.10: The Render To Texture panel

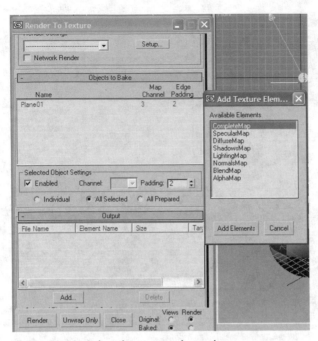

Figure 15.11: Select the texture channels.

Under the Selected Element Common Settings rollout, you can set such parameters as the name and resolution of the baked texture. I selected a resolution of 1024x1024 because I want a good quality image. Make sure the Shadows check box is checked at the bottom.

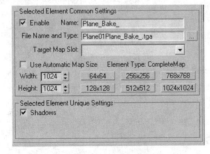

Figure 15.12: Select the texture parameters.

Now, click the Render button at the bottom of the Render To Texture panel. You should get a flat, rendered image something like Figure 15.13.

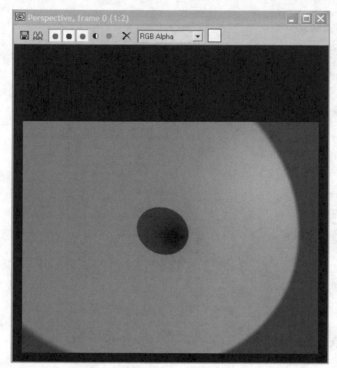

Figure 15.13: Rendering the rendered plane (See color image.)

Now, with just the sphere selected, go back and add CompleteMap again and render, basically repeating the steps we did for the plane. You should get an image like Figure 15.14.

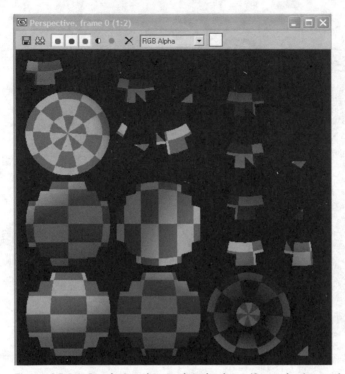

Figure 15.14: Rendering the rendered sphere (See color image.)

The two rendered "baked" images are saved as 24-bit TGA files. In our next step, we will apply the baked textures back on to the sphere and the plane. But first, we need to save the UVW coordinates of the sphere and plane so the images will align properly on the geometry.

Under the Modify tab at the right-hand side of the interface, you'll see that the sphere is selected and there is an Automatic Flatten UVs modifier in the stack.

With this selected, click the Save button in the Parameters rollout below. Save the UVW coordinates somewhere you will remember where to find them.

Figure 15.15

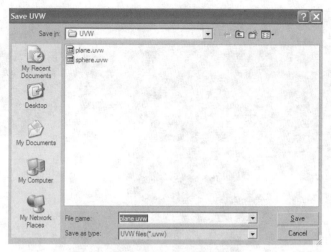

Figure 15.16: Save the UVW parameters for the sphere.

Do the same for the plane. We have baked textures to apply to both the plane and the sphere, so we'll need to save the UVW coordinates for each of these items individually.

> **Important:** Once you have saved the UVW coordinates for both items, remember to delete the Automatic Flatten UVs modifier. You won't be needing it anymore.

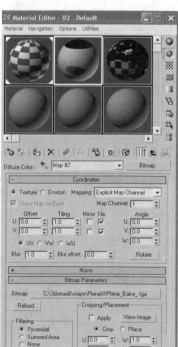

In the Material Editor, make two new materials, one with the baked plane bitmap we just created and one with the baked sphere bitmap we just created. See Figure 15.17.

Now drag the new baked sphere texture onto the sphere and the new baked plane texture onto the plane. A quick render looks like Figure 15.18.

Figure 15.17

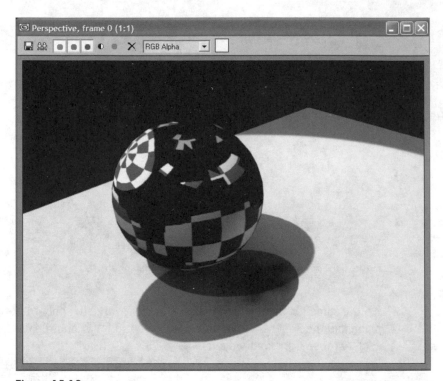

Figure 15.18

Not only does the render take just as long as before, but also the textures are out of place. Let's fix these problems.

First we need to reapply the UVW coordinates we saved.

With the sphere selected, choose the Unwrap UVW modifier on the Modify tab. See Figure 15.19.

Now under that modifier's Parameters rollout, click the Load button. See Figure 15.20.

Figure 15.19

Figure 15.20

When the file dialog is displayed, go and find the saved UVW file for the sphere that we saved earlier.

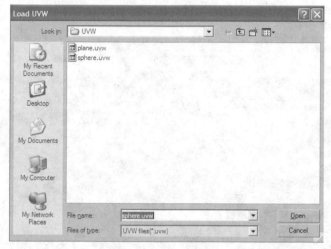

Figure 15.21: Choose the UVW file for the sphere.

Now do the same for the plane. Select the plane, choose the Unwrap UVW modifier, and load the plane UVW coordinates file you saved earlier. Now your baked textures will line up correctly on the geometry.

Before rendering, however, let's remove Light Tracer and all the lights from the scene. This will really speed things up. We'll also need to enter the Material Editor one more time to make both the sphere texture and the plane texture self-luminous. This step makes any scene lighting and shading irrelevant, which is what we want since we've baked all our lighting and shading into our textures.

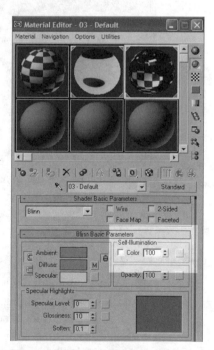

Figure 15.22: Make both the plane and the sphere self-luminous.

That's it. Now when you hit the Render button, you'll get an image that looks like it's using light bounces, color bleed, and area shadows, but it will take only seconds to render instead of minutes. Figure 15.23 shows my final render.

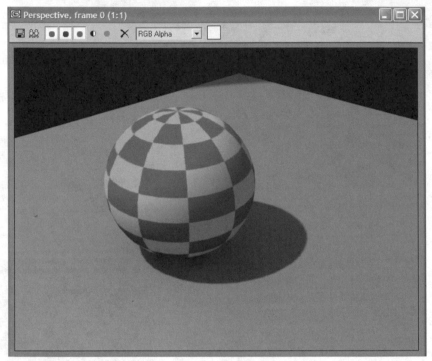

Figure 15.23: The final render (See color image.)

This technique can be of tremendous benefit where rendering time is at a premium but lighting quality must remain high. I urge you to learn this technique and keep it in your toolbox. It will almost certainly save your bacon some day.

Light Painting

The Light Painting options in the Light Painting rollout of the render panel allow you to touch up radiosity intensity levels after the radiosity solution has been calculated.

Sometimes, no matter how carefully you plan, the radiosity light and shadow just don't fall in exactly the spots you'd like. Sometimes you'd like a highlight just a little to the left, but finding exactly the correct light position and angle is troublesome, or the rest of the lighting is perfect and you don't wish to change it at all. This is where the Light Painting tool can become your very best friend.

Light Painting Tutorial

Here's a brief tutorial to show you how to use this very simple and intuitive tool.

First, create a room with some simple geometric shapes inside.

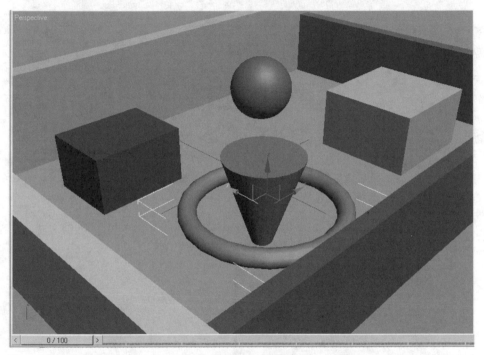

Figure 15.24: Create a room and some basic shapes.

Now throw in an omni light or two. I put mine behind the cubes where they are not visible from the perspective viewport. Don't forget to enable shadows for any lights you've added to the scene.

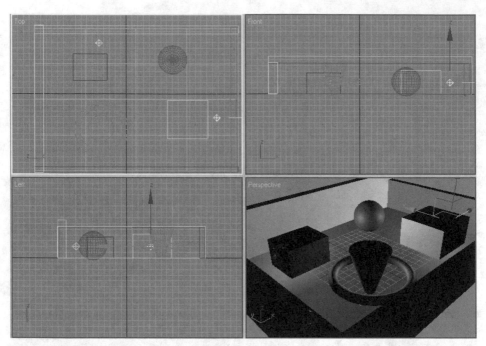

Figure 15.25: Add lights.

Add the Radiosity plug-in on the Advanced Lighting panel. Click the Start button to calculate a radiosity solution.

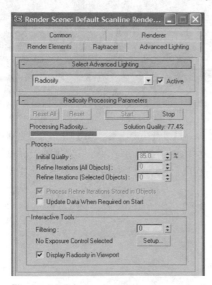

Figure 15.26

Now render out an image. See Figure 15.27.

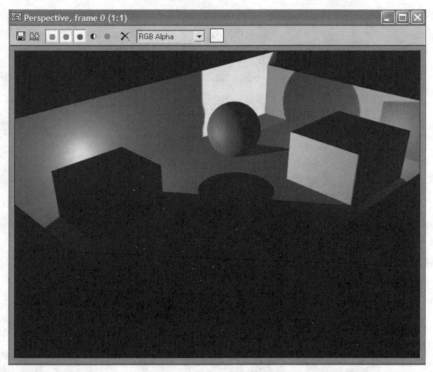

Figure 15.27: Scene rendered with Radiosity plug-in

This is too dark and definitely in need of some exposure help. In the Radiosity Processing Parameters rollout in the Advanced Lighting tab, down in the Interactive Tools section, you'll see a Setup button that will take you directly to the exposure panel.

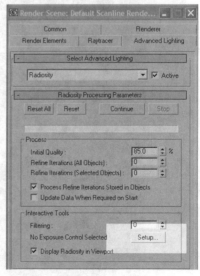

Figure 15.28: Choose the Setup button.

When the Environment and Effects panel opens, select Automatic Exposure Control from the Exposure Control drop-down. See Figure 15.29.

Don't change any other parameters. When you re-render your image, you should see much better exposure with light bounces and color bleeding. The quality isn't great, but you can save the higher quality settings for final render. See Figure 15.30.

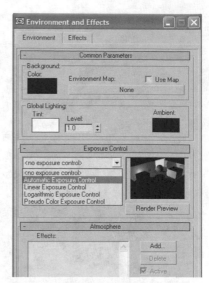

Figure 15.29: Choose Automatic Exposure Control.

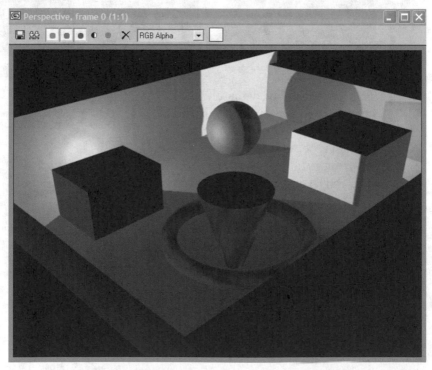

Figure 15.30: Radiosity with Automatic Exposure Control option

Now go back to the Advanced Lighting tab of the render panel and select the Light Painting rollout. See Figure 15.31.

Simply select one of the objects in your viewport, then use the add or subtract illumination tools to paint brighter or darker areas into your objects. The eyedropper tool will let you select an illumination level from somewhere on the currently selected object. The Clear button will remove all illumination changes from the currently selected object.

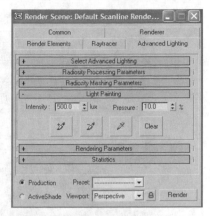

Figure 15.31: Open the Light Painting rollout.

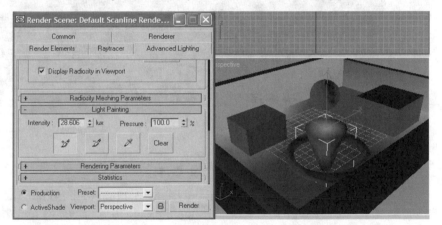

Figure 15.32

That's all there is to it. Once you have tweaked the illumination to your satisfaction, render the image and you'll see your changes in the render.

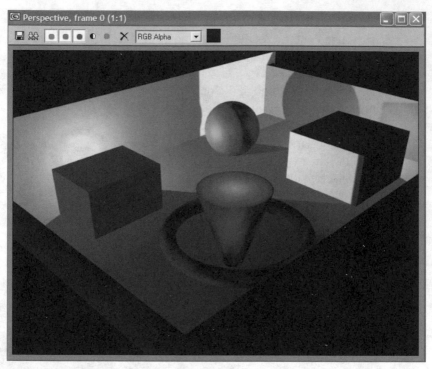

Figure 15.33

■ ■ ■

That covers texture baking and the Light Painting tool. Both of these tools are great time-savers and should reside in your permanent toolbox of favorite lighting tricks.

Go forth and bake!

Chapter 16

MAX Color Selection Tools

This chapter provides an overview of the color selection tools available in 3ds max. As light color is crucial to lighting design and CG lighting in general, knowing how best to obtain the colors is crucial. Understanding how the different color selection tools work will also help you understand color mixing.

MAX has a versatile and relatively feature-rich color selection tool called the Color Selector.

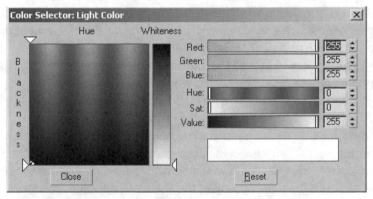

Figure 16.1: The Color Selector (See color image.)

The Color Selector is accessed by clicking on any color swatch in MAX such as the color swatch found in the Intensity/Color/Attenuation rollout on the Modify menu.

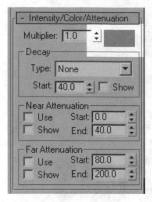

The color models represented in this Color Selector include the RGB, HSV, HSB, and HSW selectors. Each of these methods is just a different way of obtaining the same final color, so when you adjust the selector controls using one of the color models, the controls on the other models will automatically adjust at the same time.

Figure 16.2 (See color image.)

RGB

The Red, Green, Blue color selection model is probably the simplest to understand, and the easiest related to computer technology. RGB color has very little use in the real world, since RGB values determine the brightness of the red, green, and blue pixels on a computer monitor.

The computer monitor is composed of a grid of small illuminated dots known as picture elements, or *pixels*. In each grid position, there is a red element, a green element, and a blue element. If all the red elements were on and all the green and blue elements were off, the screen would appear red. If both the blue and red elements were all on and the green ones were off, the screen would appear magenta.

Each element has an illumination value ranging from zero (meaning off, or rather that no current is being applied to the element) to 255 (meaning that maximum current is being applied and the element is burning at full brightness). If all the picture elements were turned on to a value of 255, the screen would be white. This value would be represented as 255, 255, 255, where the R,G, and B values are shown respectively.

Below are some RGB values and their resulting colors:

Color	R	G	B
Red	255	0	0
Green	0	255	0
Blue	0	0	255
Cyan	0	255	255

Color	R	G	B
Gray	150	150	150
Orange	255	106	38

HSV

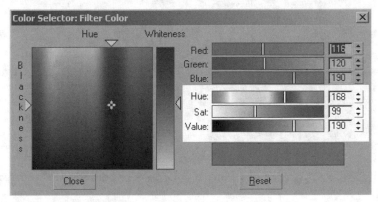

Figure 16.3

HSV stands for Hue, Saturation, and Value. This is a more "painterly" approach to color. Understanding these three color values will help you make exactly the desired changes you wish when your color is not exactly right.

Hue refers to the color. For example, blue, green, red, yellow, orange, and purple are all hues. If your color is blue and you'd prefer to have a little more green in the mix, change the Hue slider.

Saturation refers to how "deep" a color is. Crimson is a much deeper color than pink and is therefore more saturated. Sky blue is much less saturated than, say, cobalt blue. If you're happy with the hue but wish to have more or less of your hue in the mix, use the Saturation slider.

Value refers to how bright or dark a color is. Chocolate brown has quite a low value, while tan has quite a high value. If you like the hue selection but simply wish to make it brighter or darker, change the Value slider.

Remember, there are several ways to change your slider values. You can click on the spinner to the right and drag with the mouse, you can click in the numeric window and enter a numeric value, you can click and slide the sliders directly on the H, S, and V color bars, or you can even click around within the palette.

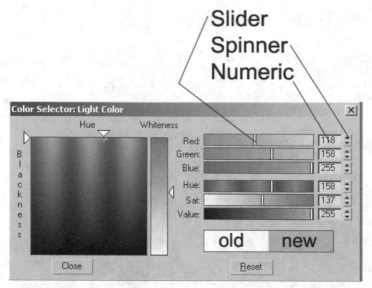

Figure 16.4: Changing values in the Color Selector panel (See color image.)

When you change a value in the HSV panel, you'll see the RGB sliders changing value and vice versa. This is because HSV and RGB are simply different ways of expressing the same thing.

HSB

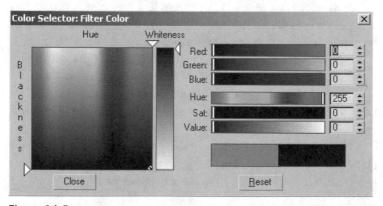

Figure 16.5

HSB means Hue, Saturation, and Blackness. Hue and saturation were covered above. Adding blackness to the color mix is the opposite of value. When you increase the blackness, you decrease the value. If you slide the Blackness slider up and down to the left of the color palette, you will see the Value slider at the right going back and forth at the same time.

Once again, this is just another way of looking at color selection.

HSW

To the right of the palette is the Whiteness slider. Adding whiteness is similar (although opposite) to adding blackness, except that instead of affecting only one primary color, it affects all three. Since white is composed of all three primaries — red, green, and blue — adding whiteness adds an amount of all three primaries to the mix. Just slide the Whiteness slider up and down and watch the RGB sliders move.

As a matter of fact, fooling around with the color picker is the very best way of becoming really familiar with the selection tools. Then you will be a color selection god!

Kelvin Color Picker (Photometric Lights)

Photometric lights are blessed with a Kelvin color picker in the Intensity/Color/Distribution rollout.

The real beauty here is that lights such as incandescent, fluorescent, HMI, and mercury vapor instruments emit light within the Kelvin color temperature range. Since photometric lights are supposed to simulate real lighting instruments, the Kelvin color picker will really help you create realistically colored light. It is unfortunate that this color selection tool is not generally available on the color picker, since skylight and sunlight all fall within the Kelvin scale, and you can use any light type you want to simulate skylight and sunlight; you don't *have* to use photometric lights. I would like to see this feature added to the MAX Color Selector.

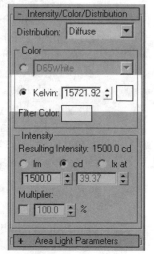

Figure 16.6

To select a Kelvin color temperature, simply roll the spinner until you have the desired color temperature. Of course, you need to know what color temperature a light should be first. See the "Kelvin" section in Chapter 12 for a table that lists some common light sources and their color temperatures.

Kelvin and Filters

Naturally, not all light color falls within the Kelvin range, which stretches from a deep orange to a pale blue. There are purple lights, green lights, pink lights, etc., none of which can be found in the Kelvin color temperature scale. How is this? If all natural light can be found on the Kelvin scale, how can other light colors exist? Very simply — with the use of colored filters. When you see a pink or green neon sign, for example, the light being emitted within the tube is not green or pink, but the tube is painted with a filtering color.

So the makers of MAX were clever enough to include a Filter Color control just below the Kelvin color temperature setting.

If you are extremely compulsive about creating physically exact colors, first set up the Kelvin color temperature of the light in question, then add any color filter on top of that.

The stark reality is that most of us (any artist with a brain, that is) are going to set up the lighting color by eye, according to what looks "right." The physically correct color temperature and filter color may satisfy some pencil-neck physicist's need for order, but certainly is not likely to satisfy the artistic requirements of the scene. So learn this, know it, and then forget about it. You're not likely to need it anytime soon.

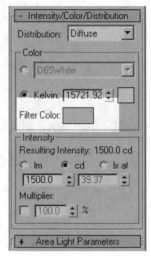

Figure 16.7

■ ■ ■

You should by now (since you have fooled around with all the tools) have a good understanding of how all the color selection tools work. Now you can color everything in your scene obtuse and clashing colors!

HDRI and Caustics

This chapter covers the definitions of HDRI, or High Dynamic Range Images, and caustics. In addition, you will learn some methods of employing these tools in your scenes.

> **Note:** Be aware that these are both advanced lighting options and are seldom used in a production environment due to the high rendering times and the fact that the technology requires further maturing. To date, HDRI cannot generally be justified by balancing the increased quality with the increased render times. HDRI lighting cannot create quality superior to other, less expensive techniques used by a skilled and creative lighting artist.

The universe contains a wide range of visible illumination. The human eye can detect extremely low levels of light but has an upper threshold. Light above this threshold can cause pain and even retinal damage. Enter the iris. The iris opens very wide under low-light conditions to allow as much light as possible into the eye. In brighter conditions, such as a normally lit office, your iris will close somewhat, allowing less light in so that the pain threshold is not exceeded. There is enough light so that you can see clearly, but not too much. If you step outside into direct sunlight, the iris will become very small, allowing even less light in. The sun produces much more light than the eye requires to see clearly, and the iris cuts out most of the light to prevent eye damage and pain.

If you step out of the sunlight and into a dark room, you will at first be unable to see. This is because the iris is contracted to a small circle and is allowing in very little light. Over time, the iris will open, allowing more light into the eye. As your eyes adjust, more detail in the room will become visible.

Now that we understand that the range of visible light in the universe is much higher than the range of light that the human eye can process, we can look at HDRI.

What Is HDRI?

HDRI refers to High Dynamic Range Images. These are images that contain more illumination information than is within the human visible range at any one time — more illumination information, for example, than can be displayed on your computer monitor, which has an extremely limited, or "clamped," range. The *range* is the difference between the lightest and darkest points in the image, also known as the *contrast* of the image. *High dynamic range* means that the range from the lightest to the darkest point in the image is greater than a human eye or a computer monitor can process at any one time. This high range of information rendered out in an HDR image is available to the user through image manipulation and post-processing. The extra information cannot be stored in regular RGB image file formats, however, and requires its own formats such as Paul Debevec's .hdr format or ILM's great new OpenEXR format. The full range of HDRI illumination information is not viewable on standard output devices.

So if you can't see the information, what's so great about HDRI? Well, the most obvious advantage comes when you render out your CG elements in an HDRI format and hand it over to a compositing artist. That compositing artist now has much more flexibility when it comes to manipulating the image. For example, if the CG element is rendered very dark, and there are areas of complete darkness, the compositor would not be able to "pull up" any information in the black areas. With an HDR image, however, all the geometry information is still in there and can be accessed. This means that the compositor does not have to ask the CG artist to re-light and re-render the CG element brighter. The compositor can brighten the image without any image loss or "clipping."

Let's take a look at a normal RGB format like a TGA image. Each pixel is colored within a range from 0 to 16 million. The RGB (red, green, blue) information is stored as ranges from 0 to 255. So an RGB color of black is 0, 0, 0, and an RGB color of white is 255, 255, 255. Red is 255, 0, 0, Green is 0, 255, 0, and so on. This is a fairly accurate way of mixing colors. The problem is that in the real world the high range of natural light acts on colors more broadly than is possible in a straight RGB image. Colors appear to shift in saturation and value when subjected to high or low lighting conditions. For example, the visual perception of a sunlit scene is completely different from the visual perception of a moonlit evening. The color of the ground is the same at night as in the day, but the illumination environment changes that perception.

If, for example, you had a bright spotlight shining on a white wall, you would conclude that the wall is colored 255, 255, 255, or pure white. What if we then shine some sunlight on that wall? Clearly the sun is much brighter than a spotlight, so the illumination conditions should change, but we have already "maxed out" our RGB values. What we need is a higher range of values. That is why HDR was invented. Artists needed a way to deal with the widely variable lighting conditions that they came across in photo-real work. The simple coloring and texturing of surfaces requires only the colors found in an RGB image, but lighting a scene brings in a whole new level of reality. HDR images allow us to tap into that reality by using floating-point values instead of the old, limited RGB value range of 0 to 255. Floating-point values are equivalent to RGB values in that 0 in RGB is the same as 0 in floating point (FP), and an FP value of 1.0 is the same as an RGB value of 255. But FP is not limited to an upper maximum value of 1.0; you can go higher if you like, as high as you want. This is where the higher range comes into play, providing you with virtually unlimited lighting levels.

Now for the really good news. The very fine folks at www.splutterfish.com have provided a free plug-in for OpenEXR I/O. Just go there, download the plug-in, install it, and you're rendering frames your compositors will like. One caveat, of course: Your compositing software must also support the OpenEXR format.

Why Should I Use HDRI?

There are many good reasons for using HDRI file formats, not the least of which is that all the lighting information is retained in the file, regardless of whether most of the image is in black shadows or blown out with blinding light. This means that an artist, be it animator, compositor, graphic designer, whomever, can brighten up or darken down the image *after* it is rendered to bring out the detail that would have been completely lost in a regular RGB format file. How many times have you rendered a sequence, then wished it were a touch lighter, or had the client come and ask for an intensity change that made you have to re-render the sequence? No more. Post-render image manipulation is now the answer to most of these problems.

Lighting a Scene with HDRI

As far as lighting a scene, HDRI has pros and cons. The great thing is that you can load an HDR image into your scene as a spherical environment map and use it to illuminate your scene. Since HDR image formats contain a very high level of lighting information, that information is used to emit light into the scene from the environment. This is known as *image-based lighting*.

When you enable Light Tracer or radiosity, the color and High Dynamic Range illumination information is used to light the scene. If you can imagine that each pixel in the HDR image is a different color and illumination value, HDRI is somewhat like placing a spotlight at each pixel with the right color and illumination value. So if you have an image of a blue sky with a sun on one side, the key light will be the sun that is illuminating the scene, and the fill light will be from all of the blue sky in the image. There are no actual lights, but the camera has recorded the illumination of the sun very high on the scale, so a majority of the scene's illumination will be coming from the area of the image where the sun is located.

The result is very complex and theoretically very realistic lighting. In feature production, this method can only be used well if HDRI Light Probe (360-degree) images are taken on set so that your CG lighting will closely match the real lighting used there. However, if you are doing all-CG work, you can use whatever HDR images suit your fancy, since you're designing all the lights rather than trying to replicate someone else's lighting.

In Figure 17.1, the tiger head and a complex surface were lit using HDR images only. The only difference between the two renders on the left is the HDR images to the right. Note that the HDR images are "fish-eye." This is to compress the entire 360-degree world into the image so that the whole environment is retained without stretching when the image is placed in your spherical environment.

Figure 17.1: Render on left with HDR image on right (See color image.)

How Do I Use HDRI to Light a Scene?

To light a scene using HDR images, you first need some HDR images. There are a number of HDRI references on the web. Using your favorite search engine, type in "HDRI" and you should get several pages of listings. Not only is there a selection of free HDR images available, but you can also find free tools to build your own HDR images such as HDR Shop.

Using LightGen

There is also an HDR Shop plug-in called LightGen. Both HDR Shop and LightGen are available on the web at http://www.debevec.org/HDRShop/. According to the documentation, LightGen "generates a list of directional light sources to approximate the lighting from a Light Probe image." A MAX script called LightGen Importer then takes the data from the list and converts it into an array of lights within MAX using the appropriate positional, directional, intensity, and color data for each light. LightGen2 Importer is available on the Internet. Just do a search; you'll find it. I found it in about 15 seconds at Scriptspot.com.

It probably sounds more difficult than it is, but if you follow the instructions on the HDR Shop web site, you'll find yourself creating colored light arrays in no time. It took me about ten minutes to locate and download an HDR image, locate and install both HDR Shop and LightGen Importer, and create a text file. A few minutes later I had a nice light array in MAX's Layout and rendered the following image.

Figure 17.2: LightGen render (See color image.)

This technique renders in much less time than HDRI and radiosity; however, it is unlikely that you will achieve the subtle complexities of image-based lighting unless you add a very large number of lights. The image in Figure 17.2 used 20 direct lights. The drawbacks to this method are as follows:

- Direct lights mean you'll have directional shadows, while HDRI and radiosity provide soft, diffuse global lighting, and you can use any light type you wish. I would recommend using shadow maps or area shadows with soft shadows.

- Multiple lights mean multiple shadows. Most lighting environments do not cast multiple shadows, unless you are in a room with multiple competing light sources. Outdoor lighting rarely exhibits multiple shadows except the relatively hard shadow from the sun and the soft shadow from the sky. If you are using 20 or more lights, as I did, you will end up with 20 or more shadows. To my eye, this just doesn't read correctly.

As with any technique, there will be situations where these points are moot. Shots with high motion blur, for example, can hide the stepping effect of multiple shadows. It is a cheap way to achieve more complex lighting than you will get from basic lighting techniques, and sometimes it will be very valuable to you. If I had the choice, the reference images, and the render power, though, I'd use HDRI and radiosity all the time.

> **Note:** You don't have to use HDR images to add illumination to your scene. You can use any old images you like, but because they don't have the higher range of illumination information, you may need to crank up your radiosity intensity to get decent illumination. Also, you don't have to use the "fish-eye" images. Again, any old image size or shape will do, but you will, of course, get stretching when you put the image in your background. This may be unimportant if the backdrop is not visible in the scene. Sometimes I will just place some interesting image in the backdrop for backdrop only radiosity just to get the complex colors and shapes.

Using an HDR Image

Occasionally, you will have the opportunity to light a scene using real HDRI lighting. Achieving this within MAX is actually quite easy since MAX loads HDR format images inherently.

First, open up the Material Editor, select a material slot, and click the Get Material button. See Figure 17.3.

In the Material/Map browser, select Bitmap. See Figure 17.4.

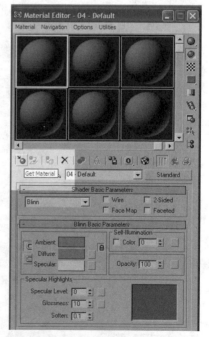

Figure 17.3

Figure 17.4

This will open a file requester in which you can select an .hdr format image. Click on the image and then click Open.

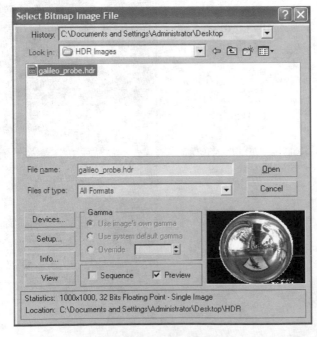

Figure 17.5:
Select Bitmap
Image File panel

You'll see the HDRI Load Settings panel. Accept the default settings and click OK.

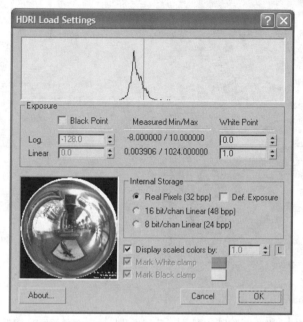

Figure 17.6: HDRI Load Settings panel

In the Material Editor's Coordinates rollout, change the material from Texture to Environment. See Figure 17.7.

Then, in the Mapping dropdown, select Spherical Environment. See Figure 17.8.

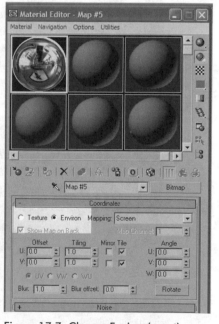

Figure 17.7: Choose Environ(ment).

243

Figure 17.8: Select the Spherical
Environment mapping.

Now open the Environment and Effects panel. In the Background section of the Common Parameters rollout you should see "Environment Map" with a button below it that says "None."

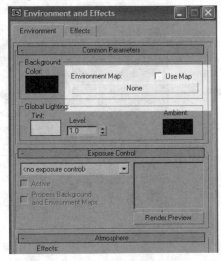

Figure 17.9

Drag the new material from the Material Editor onto the Environment Map button.

When the Instance (Copy) dialog comes up, select Instance and click OK.

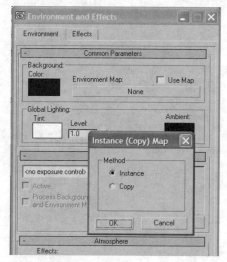

Figure 17.10: Choose Instance from the Instance (Copy) Map dialog.

The Use Map check box should check automatically when the map is loaded.

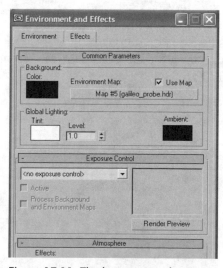

Figure 17.11: The button now shows your selected material.

Placing the image in the environment will provide a reflection source for any reflective materials in your scene.

Now add a skylight to your scene. See Figure 17.12.

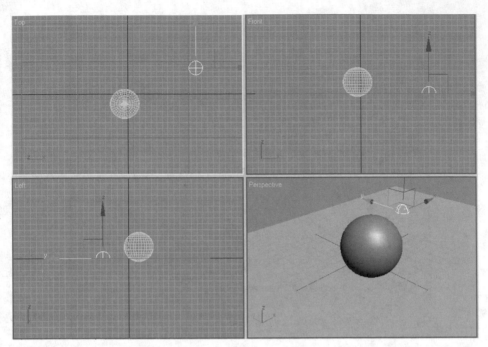

Figure 17.12: Add a skylight.

You can place your skylight anywhere you like in your scene, just as long as it is oriented dome-up as in Figure 17.12.

In the Skylight Parameters rollout, under Sky Color you'll see another button that says "None." See Figure 17.13.

Drag the new material to this button and make sure the Map check box is checked. See Figure 17.14.

Figure 17.13

Figure 17.14

Tip: Use a regular HDR image in your environment for reflections. To smooth out lighting artifacts and speed up render times, take your HDR image into HDR Shop, blur it, and resize it smaller.

In this case, I chose to use mental ray and Final Gather with its default settings to make my lighting calculations.

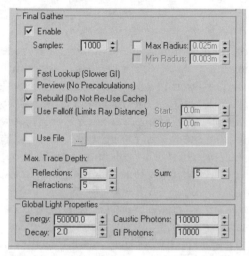

Figure 17.15: Using Final Gather options

Figure 17.16 shows my final render.

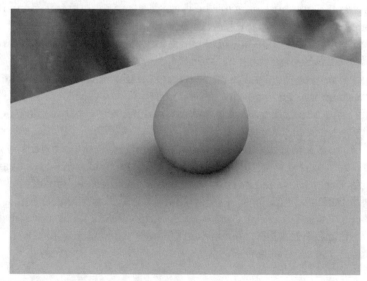

Figure 17.16 (See color image.)

247

Using HDR images as light sources for image-based lighting is really quite simple, as you can see, and provides unparalleled variation and subtlety to environmental lighting. This type of approach does come at a cost of increased render times, but when and where you can afford the time will be up to you.

Caustics Defined

Caustics in the real world refer to substances that burn or corrode in a certain way. Like so many other words of our profession, an entirely new definition has been devised to describe a new effect that does not exist in the real world. This is not to say that the visual effect we call caustics does not occur. It does. It is just not a fancy, render-expensive, and luxurious frill that is separate from the rest of the lighting.

Caustics is the focusing of light due to reflection or refraction onto another surface so as to cause areas of intense illumination. Let's examine how this occurs.

When light is reflected from a curved surface, and the curved surface causes light to focus and intensify onto another area, we call that caustics. But we also call it specularity because that is exactly what happens for specularity also. The only difference is perceptual. In the case of specularity, the light is focused and concentrated from whatever our point of view is. In the case of caustics, the light is focused and concentrated onto another surface. The principles are exactly the same. In the real world, in fact, caustics, specularity, reflection, and diffuseness are all pretty much the same physical effect. But here in the wonderful world of CG, we can separate and individually adjust each element of that effect to save render time and to make our materials behave as we'd like them to without having to go through all the trouble of creating and rendering physically accurate materials and environments — that would take a very long time, indeed. See Figure 7.17.

Caustics also occurs when light enters a material of a density higher than air and is refracted in such a way that the light focuses onto another surface. For those not familiar with refraction, here is how it works: Light bends when it passes from a substance of one density into a substance of another density, provided the light reaches the new substance at an angle. If the light approaches the new substance squarely, it will not bend.

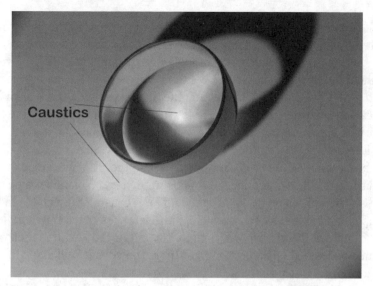

Figure 17.17: Example of caustics

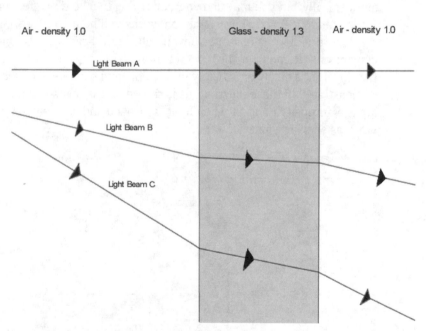

Figure 17.18: Refraction

In Figure 17.18, we are using glass as an example of a substance with a higher density than air. The same principles apply to water or any other transparent substance, although the diffraction value may be different. You can see that as light approaches a substance of higher density at a more obtuse angle, the angle of refraction is also more obtuse. If both the entry and exit points of the substance are parallel, the light will exit at the same angle that it entered, but the position will be altered.

This is the effect that occurs when you stand knee-deep in water and it looks like your legs are bent.

To remember which direction the light rays bend, think of an SUV leaving a paved road and driving into a muddy countryside. If the SUV drives straight into the mud, the angle will not change, but it will be slowed somewhat. If the SUV enters the mud at an angle, the side that enters the mud first will slow down first so the SUV will angle in that direction. The same principle applies to the exit. Whichever side of the SUV exits the mud first will speed up first, causing the vehicle to speed up on that side first. For example, if the left tires reach the mud first and slow down, the vehicle will angle to the left. If the left tires then exit the mud and speed up before the right tires, the vehicle will angle to the right.

Why do you care about this? It's true that MAX calculates all this automatically, but you may find yourself trying to fake this effect one day. Understanding exactly how refraction works will help you.

Figure 17.19 demonstrates how parallel light beams are affected by a convex lens. Remember the truck-in-the-mud analogy and you will see that the light's behavior is highly predictable and obvious. The focusing demonstrated in these illustrations is the effect that causes the caustic areas of intensity to occur when light is focused and intensified by a convex lens such as a glass of water.

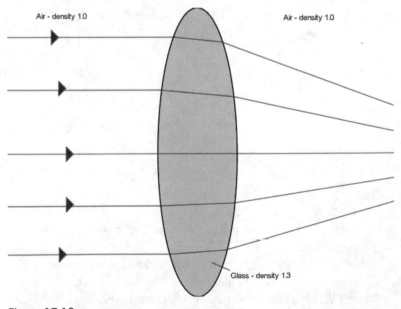

Air - density 1.0   Air - density 1.0

Glass - density 1.3

Figure 17.19

When and Where to Use Caustics

As attractive as caustics sounds and as physically accurate as it may be, I have found little practical use for this effect in production. To be sure, artists can create beautiful still images with glowing caustics, but the caustic calculation seems to differ with each frame, making it impractical for animation.

Caustics is a relatively new tool, however, and will no doubt undergo refinement until it becomes yet another strong, predictable tool in our MAX toolset.

Still, it is a beautiful effect once you have sorted out the settings for your particular need. This effect is probably currently confined to use in still images, but don't let that suggestion stop you from trying to make it work in animation. And if you have success, I would love to hear about it.

Since caustics is more of a special effect than actual scene lighting, I'm not going to dedicate much time to it in these pages. If you're bent on learning and using caustics in your scene, I encourage you to seek out tutorials on the Internet. There are lots of great resources out there. My favorite resource is cgchannel.com.

■ ■ ■

You should now clearly understand what HDRI and caustics are and have an idea of how to use them in your scene setups.

Carry on.

Chapter 18

Rendering

This chapter is intended as a brief overview of the rendering engines and panels available in order to get you started quickly rendering with your new lighting skills. If you are a seasoned MAX expert, this chapter probably won't be of much use to you, so I suggest you skip ahead. If you are a MAX beginner, this chapter will help you understand the location of key rendering controls and features. For a detailed description of every control, please consult the documentation that came with your software.

With 3ds max, you're going to decide early on what rendering engine you'll use. Mainly this is because your lighting instruments will require the use of either the Default Scanline Renderer or the mental ray Renderer. If you're going to use any mental ray specific lights, you'll certainly need to use the mental ray rendering engine.

For speed and ease of use, the Default Scanline Renderer is your friend. When using standard lighting, the scanline renderer will produce easy, predictable results most of the time. If you want to go for more complex lighting and a superior-looking final render, however, you'll want to take a serious look at mental ray.

Default Scanline Renderer Panel

First, let's take a look at the Default Scanline Renderer panel. This panel is split into five tabs: Common, Renderer, Render Elements, Raytracer, and Advanced Lighting.

The Common Tab

On the Common tab you get to select what frames to render, what size they are in pixels, and a number of options you can enable or disable. You can also set the render file location and format from here. Each of these settings is pretty self-explanatory. If you don't find them so, please consult your MAX documentation.

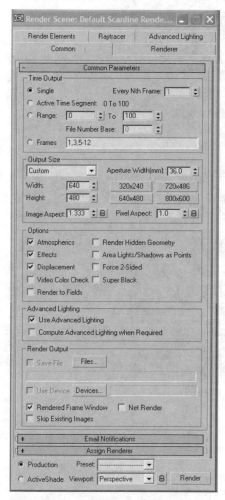

Figure 18.1: The Common tab

At the bottom of this panel are the Email Notifications rollout and the Assign Renderer rollout. Within the Email Notifications rollout you can instruct MAX to send you an email at desired intervals. This is useful if you are going to be away from your workstation, say at home for the weekend, and you want to be informed if and when a render completes.

The Assign Renderer rollout, naturally, lets you select which renderer
you are going to use to render your images.

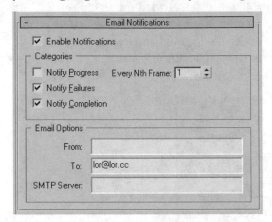

Figure 18.2: The Email Notifications rollout

If you have MAX right out of the box, you'll have a choice between the
Default Scanline Renderer and the mental ray Renderer for your production renders.

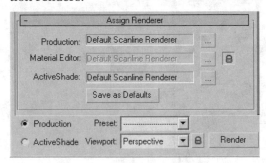

Figure 18.3: The Assign Renderer rollout

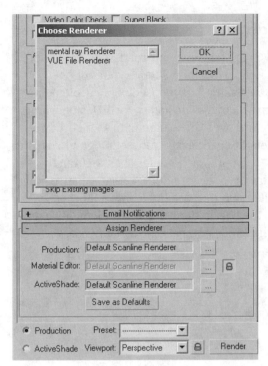

Figure 18.4: Notice that the mental ray
Renderer and the VUE File Renderer are
available in the Choose Renderer window. You
won't be using the VUE File Renderer for
production, so it won't be covered here. Further
information is available in your documentation.
The Default Scanline Renderer is not in the list
because it is the currently selected renderer.

The Renderer Tab

The Renderer tab is used primarily
to enable or disable some of the
many features available in the
Default Scanline Renderer. A quick
glance at Figure 18.5 reveals that
you would use the options in this tab
to enable or disable such features as
shadows, antialiasing, and motion
blur.

Figure 18.5: The Renderer tab

The Render Elements Tab

For production work where you are passing your rendered CG elements to a compositing station, the Render Elements tab is your very best friend. You see, each image you render is composed of many elements such as specularity, reflection, shadow, color, and so forth. Compositing artists like to have minute control over these elements so that they can make the rendered CG element fit seamlessly into a photographed plate. By using this panel, you can "pull out" each render channel from the final image and send it to its own render directory so that a compositing artist has a stack of render elements to reassemble into a finished image. This saves CG artists the hassle of re-rendering elements over and over to achieve exactly the look a compositing artist needs.

Figure 18.6: The Render Elements tab

The Raytracer Tab

Just as the name implies, the Raytracer tab is where you enable or disable the global ray trace settings for your scene. Such settings as whether to calculate raytracing for reflections, refractions, and atmospheric effects can be found here.

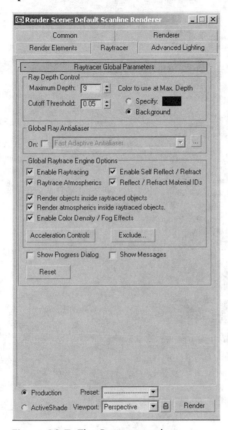

Figure 18.7: The Raytracer tab

The Advanced Lighting Tab

The Advanced Lighting tab is my favorite panel, because here is where I choose which radiosity solution I will use to beautify my lighting. I get to choose between Light Tracer, which is a sort of fake, hack radiosity, and Radiosity, which will calculate real light bounces in the environment.

Figure 18.8: The Advanced Lighting tab

Light Tracer Parameters

The Light Tracer Parameters rollout contains the general quality and property parameters for using Light Tracer. This is also where you enable Light Tracer for use in your scene. You may only select one of the Advanced Lighting plug-ins at a time, so if you have selected Light Tracer, the Radiosity panel will not be available to you.

Figure 18.9: The Light Tracer Parameters rollout

Radiosity Parameters

The Radiosity Processing Parameters rollout is where you'll find all the control parameters for rendering with radiosity as well as the Light Painting tools. For details on the radiosity controls, see the manual or consult Chapter 14, "Radiosity." For details on Light Painting, see Chapter 15, "Texture Baking and Light Painting."

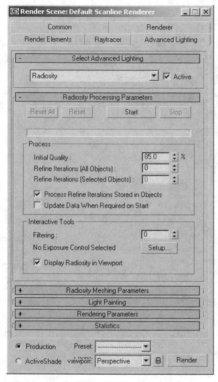

Figure 18.10: The Radiosity Processing Parameters rollout

mental ray Renderer Panel

If you select the mental ray Renderer instead of the Default Scanline Renderer, you'll be presented with a different selection of tabs in the render panel.

The Common Tab

The Common tab is the same for the mental ray Renderer as it is for the Default Scanline Renderer. This is because you still need to set render output paths, image sizes, aspects, and so forth just the same.

The Renderer Tab

The mental ray Renderer tab contains quality and property options such as sampling quality, rendering algorithm, depth of field, motion blur, shadow, and displacement controls.

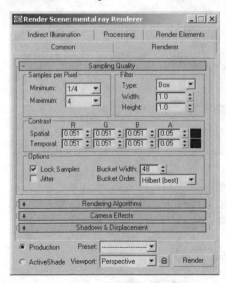

Figure 18.11: The Renderer tab

The Indirect Illumination Tab

Use the Indirect Illumination tab to enable features such as caustics, global illumination, and Final Gather, as well as to set the properties and parameters for each. For more information on mental ray Indirect Illumination, please see Chapter 14, "Radiosity," or consult the documentation.

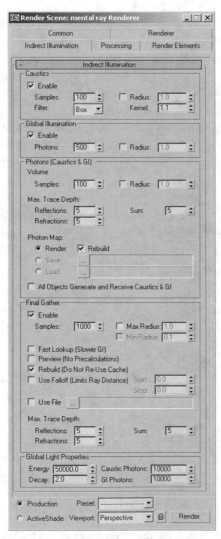

Figure 18.12: The Indirect Illumination tab

The Processing Tab

The Processing tab contains a number of advanced features not directly related to the subject matter of this book. Please consult the documentation for a full description.

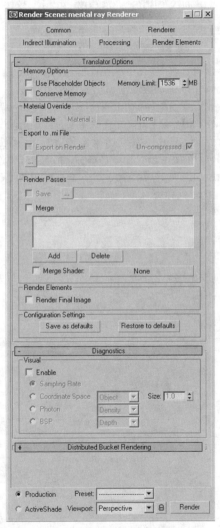

Figure 18.13: The Processing tab

The Render Elements Tab

The Render Elements tab here is identical to the one used for the Default Scanline Renderer. Once again, if you are rendering CG elements for compositing, this panel is a great asset, allowing you to extract render channels such as specularity, diffuse, shadow, and RGB to save as distinct file sequences.

■ ■ ■

Hopefully this brief overview of the render controls gives you an idea of where to find the most commonly used controls and parameters. If you want to delve deeply into render controls, and you probably do if you're serious about great, efficient renders, I suggest you learn from the documentation and the many fantastic online resources. Remember, there are thousands of MAX artists out there who have gone before you, who know the software inside and out, and who are only too glad to help you out in your quest to create great renders.

Part III

Creating Lighting

One of the great things about working in 3D is the instant gratification you get from creating and rendering something cool. No doubt if you are just starting out in the world of 3D, you will spend a lot of time making cool creations, showing your friends, boring your spouse or partner, and forcing your family to say "cool." Whether you are on the path to an animation career or you are already a professional, you probably know that mere "cool factor" doesn't usually make the cut anymore. If you are a serious artist, you know that the best creation comes with hard work and a great deal of patience. This means it's time to forget about instant gratification. It's time to realize that your very best work is going to take your very best effort and a substantial chunk of time. But when you're done, the "cool" you hear from friends and family won't be obligatory; it will be genuine. Your mother will start telling her friends about your successes. Your father will tape the first TV series you work on so he can pause the tape on the credits and show his friends your name.

Becoming a professional CG artist is not an easy road. Being a world-class artist is not for the lazy or impatient. But if you have patience and the drive to make it, you will count yourself among the top names in CG.

Design Considerations

Designing lights for a shot requires both technical and artistic considerations. If you are lighting a CG element for compositing onto a photographic background plate, your considerations are likely to be more technical than artistic. In other words, you are likely required to simply analyze and simulate the lighting in the plate. But if you are lucky enough to be designing lighting for a full CG scene, everything you know about lighting and art will come into play.

Technical considerations include placement, direction, and color of the lights. You must also take into account such things as:

- Camera placement
- What lighting is used in a background plate
- How tolerant the CG element is to lighting cheats
- How long you have to complete the shot and its render
- What, exactly, the supervisor or director is looking for in your CG element

These topics and more are covered in the following chapters. It is my hope that you will come away at the end with not only technical expertise but also an understanding of the process. This understanding will make you a more valuable artist, enabling you to foresee problems, plan your actions, and bring in your work on the project on time and budget. You see, there is much more to being a good artist than creating good art. We all work in business environments where we interact with many other people from many different departments. Your competence as a communicator and a problem-solver are as important to your success as your talent.

This part of the book contains a wealth of information about using light to set mood, creating a style, and designing lighting, along with a number of exercises explaining a variety of techniques. My hope is that the exercises do more than merely teach techniques but that they enable you to see the underlying principles of the techniques. If this is successful, you will be able to design your own techniques as need be. If you can walk away from this book with that skill, then I will consider this work a success.

Chapter 19

Intent and Purpose

This chapter deals briefly with the artistic concepts of intent and purpose. These are less esoteric and more obvious than such concepts as "style" and "art." Intent refers to both the intent of the script or scenario and your intentions to the story as a designer. Purpose refers to the practical justification of your lighting design. Each lighting tool and technique must have a specific design purpose. By the time you finish this chapter you should have a good grasp of the importance of both intent and purpose in your lighting designs.

In a production environment, the first step to lighting design is script analysis. In other words, you read the script, try to find out what story the author is telling and how it is told, then decide how you want to interpret that story or, if you are not the director, find out how the director wishes to interpret the story. Any good lighting designer is going to go into a meeting with a director having some idea of the direction he or she wishes to go with the lighting. An even better designer will enter the meeting with two or three completely different design concepts for the project. Having multiple ideas for the director to choose from is often a good strategy for heading off complete rejection. If a director is only given one lighting idea, you can almost guarantee major changes. If the director has two or three ideas to look at, there is a better chance that she will select one of your directions rather than taking a completely different one.

If you are lucky, you will have a director who wants to hear your ideas before making any final decisions. The obvious bonus here is that you will have real artistic input into the final look of the shot. In another scenario, the director may already have a vision of the final product. You may end up simply providing the technical expertise to accomplish someone else's artistic vision. But you still need to know how exactly to do that.

Understanding Artistic and Emotional Intent

When you first read the script, you will need to break it down into scenes, if it is not already done for you. Scenes are all the individual measures of the script, each of which tells a small part of the story. Scenes usually consist of individual time spans during which a specific kernel of information is revealed about the story. For example, the three witches in *Macbeth* have their own scenes, each of which occurs in its own locale during its own time period, and is separate from the other scenes. Each delivers specific information to the audience. Each begins and ends logically and ties to the next and previous scenes in some way. Within each scene there may be a number of different shots. It is likely that most of the shots in each scene will have a similar emotional tone. You will want to make note of whether a scene is happy or sad, gloomy or foreboding, exciting or disgusting. These are the cornerstones of your lighting design. It is your job to assist the storyteller and the audience in experiencing the story as fully as possible.

After you understand the feeling of a scene, your next job is to look at the technical requirements of the scene. Back to basics. Is it interior or exterior? Is it in a basement or on the roof of a 100-story skyscraper?

Now that you have the two key elements of lighting in your grasp — the emotional and the technical — it is your job to find a way to convey the first, without upsetting the second. For example, if I had a very sad, morose scene and I wished to make the audience feel the despair of the characters in the story, I would probably first think of using muted colors, low lighting levels, and perhaps some odd angles to make the whole scene uncomfortable. But what if the scene takes place at midday at a carnival? What if it is on a California beach? I seem to be stuck with the light provided by reality, and there seems to be little I can do to help the story with lighting. But if I put on my thinking cap, I will discover that there are many subtle changes I can make to these two scenarios, especially the carnival scenario, that will add surrealism to the scene. This surrealism will support the negative emotional intent of the scene. If you have ever experienced a real crisis, you will remember the feeling of surrealism that accompanied the event. This is easy to accomplish in a carnival. I can choose unusual colors and angles. I don't have to mute colors and intensities. In fact, I can counterpoint the emotion by adding brighter, more colorful lights, creating a deeper gulf between the environment and the tone of the scene. Sometimes going in the opposite direction will have a deeper effect on the scene than trying to create lighting of the same tone as the scene.

The key element here is that you, as the lighting designer, are purposeful with the placement and settings of your lighting tools. You must grasp the emotional intent of the script and implement your lighting deliberately in a way that you feel accomplishes or helps accomplish the goals of the storyteller.

What Is Your Light's Motivation? (Justifying Choices)

The objects in your scene are illuminated by one or more light sources. Each of those sources must be justified. Now in the world of photo-realism, this usually means each light source must have a real-world counterpart. In other words, if you're making sunlight the key light in your scene and blue skylight the fill, then the background image should be illuminated primarily by the sun and secondarily by a nice blue sky. The angle of the sunlight on your CG elements should also be the same angle as that in the background image. If there are no additional light sources in the background plate, then there should be no additional lighting sources in your CG scene. Every simulated light source must be justified by the existence of a real light source.

> **Note:** Probably the most common mistake among CG lighting artists is the tendency to always use a rim light to highlight the upper edges of the subject. Believe me, if you are facing the camera and the sun is shining on your face, there is no rim light in your hair. Don't use this easy, cheap, and very fake-looking trick unless you can justify a light source that would create the rim illumination. This is one of the worst and most obvious lighting mistakes you can make. You have been warned. Now back to our regular broadcast.

In the world of practical reality, however, there are numerous problems with such an exacting and unforgiving rule. Often we receive background images (plates) where the existing lighting will not allow us to illuminate our CG elements in a way that will present the story elements we wish to present. Sometimes we need to "beautify" the shot by adding subtle highlights and areas of focus without the physical justification for those light sources. Sometimes your director or VFX supervisor will just tell you to darn well do it (that's justification). Not everyone is concerned with whether or not something is physically possible. And sometimes, it's just not a good idea to argue with your boss.

So, as artists who are paid to do what our overlords wish, we will find ways to stretch reality in an attempt to provide the desired effect without completely rewriting the laws of physics. In general, and where possible, a lighting artist should, however, make every attempt to place light sources only as justified by the plate. Failing that, try to get creative with your justification: "There *could* be a light over there, or up there, even though we don't see it in the plate." That's justification too.

If, on the other hand, you are designing lights for an all-CG scene, then you have a world of possibilities. As the lighting designer, you should have access to the other designers and to the director to discuss, beforehand, where lights will be placed for the best possible lighting. You will likely be able to discuss with the scenic designer, for example, just where a window might be placed behind the action so you can adorn the foreground objects with that magic halo of light (the evil rim light) that almost never happens in reality. Or you might contribute to the story in ways that enhance lighting. Take, for example, a scene on a stormy day. It's raining hard. "Here's a perfect opportunity for effect lighting," you think to yourself. "How about some lightning outside!" you spout. Lightning can be used in a variety of ways to load the scene with tension and foreboding or to surprise us with the skeleton in the dark closet that we didn't see before.

Designing lights for all-CG scenes is a lighting artist's playground. If you are ever fortunate enough to have this opportunity, let loose. Throw ideas in every direction. Sure, lots of them will get dropped and some will evoke looks of horror — but that's half the fun! Some of your ideas will stick, some will go through minor changes, and others will need complete rethinking. That's all part of the challenge. Don't expect your first idea to be the best one. Be flexible and be willing to consider new ideas, even if they aren't your own.

Chiaroscuro: The Use of Light and Shadow

Chiaroscuro is a method of painting invented in Italy during the Renaissance. Artists such as Leonardo da Vinci and Raphael used this method, a defined set of rules really, to determine how light affected the objects in their paintings. The rules were based on light approaching the object from a predetermined direction. The word "chiaroscuro" comes from two Italian words: *chiaro* meaning bright or clear and *oscuro* meaning dark or obscure. My favorite master of chiaroscuro is Rembrandt, whose paintings are made deep and foreboding by the deep shadows and dark backgrounds that make his human subjects nearly leap off the canvas with life. In my opinion, it is Rembrandt's mastery of light and shadow that defines his breathtaking style.

Your use of light can define the entire style of your CG artwork too.

Think about a brightly lit room. Sunlight streams through the tall windows and radiates from the high ceiling. The air is warm and still. The room is silent. Leather-bound books line the walls and an old oak desk sits at an angle in front of a stone fireplace.

Picture this same room at night. Moonlight streams through the high windows. There are no lights on in the room, but the oak desk is in silhouette from the dying embers of an unattended fire. The room is nearly black but for the silver-rimmed, moonlit furniture and the pale, orange glow silhouetting the desk.

Both of these scenes offer interesting lighting challenges. Lighting alone can give strong feelings to these scenes; the day scene makes me think of ages of dust, perhaps particles in the air creating a volumetric effect to the light streaming in the window. I see yellowish, amber radiosity as the light bounces off the natural wood floor and the oak desk. In my mind the room is silent in the afternoon, unused, but warm by the day's sunlight. By night, the room is still warm from the dying fire. The fire tells us the room is not derelict, the house is occupied, and the inhabitants are probably now asleep. The moonlight tells us that the weather is clear and may be a hint as to the time of year. There is a sense of activity here as we survey in the moonlight the papers strewn across the desk, the work left unfinished, to be completed another day.

Do you see how easy it is to enhance a story with a few simple lights using basic colors?

Some Examples

The following examples demonstrate the most basic interpretation of these scenes. This is by no means the only way, nor the most interesting way, of accomplishing these lighting objectives. My purpose here is to provide a basic understanding that you can use to grow and develop your own much more interesting ideas. Besides, if I wrote down *all* my good ideas, then everyone would probably get to be a better lighting artist than me. And *then* where would I be?

A Pleasant Scene

Typically, a pleasant scene will strike the audience with its warmth,
brightness, gentle mood, and familiarity. Take a look at the following
image and see if you can pick out the lighting techniques used to make
the image more pleasant.

Figure 19.1

Here we have a toy horse sitting in front of a fireplace. The scene is illuminated by a soft glow from the flames. A highlight has been added to
both sides of the toy, one side to represent illumination from the fireplace, and the other to represent moonlight entering from the window
above the couch to the left. (If this were a color image, you would see
that the fire highlight is amber and the moon highlight is blue.) It is a
simple scene utilizing only three lights. Both highlights are spotlights
and the fireplace light is an area light.

The room feels warm and welcoming. The moonlight adds a sense
of magic to the scene. The additional highlights add subtle form and
color to enrich the scene.

A Sad Scene

Let's take the same scene and apply a few changes to make it into a sad scene.

Figure 19.2

First, and this is not a lighting thing, I changed the camera angle. Instead of the previous shot, which had a more "toy" point of view, I've raised the camera and pointed it downward for a more "human" POV. This makes the toy seem more alone and lonely in the middle of the floor.

As for the lighting, I removed the warmth from the scene by turning off the fireplace and enhancing the cool moonlight. Now the only lights in the room are the cold, lonely moonlight from outside and its radiosity source, which is softly illuminating the surrounding room. I think it gives a real sense of sadness and loneliness.

A Frightening Scene

Perhaps the simplest way of making a scene tense, strange, or frightening is to use colors, angles, and intensities that immediately strike the audience as unnatural, unusual, or strange.

Figure 19.3

In this image, I added a gobo to the moonlight source to create a window
shadow with overexaggerated, or forced, perspective. This, coupled with
the long shadows created by the low angle and also by the banking or
"Dutch" angle of the camera, serves to make the scene seem quite
strange and perhaps even frightening. It is difficult, without the context
of a story, to look at this image and find it frightening, but what if the
light through the window had been a flash of lightning revealing something other than a toy horse? It could quite easily jolt you out of your
seat.

■ ■ ■

Any artist, before laying brush to canvas, intends to create a specific
image. Within that image, each element has a purpose. Consider these
as you are designing your lights and you will sidestep the many pitfalls
of lighting design such as clutter, overdesign, and the inappropriate use
of light.

If you design with both intent and purpose, your design is likely to
be streamlined, elegant, and simple, not to mention illuminating. Good
luck with your search for lighting perfection. Let me know when you get
there — I hope I won't be far behind!

You should now have at least a basic understanding of the importance of intent in your work and purpose for each of your design
elements. While these concepts may not be clear to you yet, they will
become so as you begin to tell your own stories with your design work.

Chapter 20

Color Mixing

In this chapter we discuss what makes colored light and what makes colored pigments. We also look at the relationship between mixtures of light and pigment as well as the color wheel and principles of color mixing. By the time you are finished with this chapter, you should have a grasp of how color wavelengths interact to create the many colors available for our CG palette.

Two Types of Color

Understanding color mixing begins with understanding two distinct elements:

- Light such as the color of sunlight, neon signs, or fireworks. You must understand what makes a particular color of light appear to be that color.
- Pigments such as paints, dyes, fabrics, stone, and wood. You must understand what makes pigments appear to be the color that they are.

The Color of Light

Light is composed of a wide range of electromagnetic radiation from heat sources. Most light radiated by these heat sources is not visible to the human eye. There is a very small range of light between about 0.4 and 0.7 micrometers that is visible to the human eye. Light at the top of the visible range with wavelengths shorter than 0.4 micrometers falls into the ultraviolet range. Light at the bottom of the visible range with wavelengths longer than 0.7 micrometers falls into the infrared range. Neither ultraviolet nor infrared light is visible to the human eye. Below infrared light lie the ranges of microwaves and radio waves. Above ultraviolet lie the ranges of x-rays and gamma rays. Lower band radio waves can be found in the frequency range of 300 meters or more, while gamma rays are in the frequency range of 0.003 nanometers. So you can see that the range of light in the universe is incredibly large, and of that enormous range, the bit that we can see is very, very small.

Within the human visible range of light, the color spectrum extends from red to violet going sequentially through orange, yellow, green, blue, and indigo, respectively. Remember your elementary school lesson about rainbows? ROYGBIV: red, orange, yellow, green, blue, indigo, and violet. The rainbow is simply white light that has been refracted and split up into its component light frequencies. Or, to put it another way, when you take all of the frequencies of visible light and mix them together, the result is pure white light.

So what does this mean? Well, to start with, there are three primary colors in light: red, green, and blue. By mixing these three colors, you should be able to create any color shade visible in the world.

There is a very easy way to visualize why colored light is colored. First, think of white light as "whole" light. It is made up of a mixture of every color or wavelength in the visible spectrum. Any individual color like green, pink, or blue is that "whole" light with some wavelengths or colors missing.

Pink light, for example, is white light with most of the green ranges missing. Only red and blue ranges remain, and when you mix red and blue light, you get pink. If you were to put a red colored filter, or "gel," in front of that pink light, the light coming out the other side of that gel would be mostly red. The gel filters out most of the light in the blue range of the visible spectrum.

This is called *subtractive* color mixing. It may take you a while to get your head around exactly how it works, but once you do, you will be able to easily mix any colors you desire, not only on the color palette, but by shining the light from two or more lights together, including lights of both positive intensity (for additive mixing) and negative intensity (for subtractive mixing).

To create the image in Figure 20.1, I placed three spotlights over a white polygon and aimed them so that they would overlap. One light had an RGB value of 255, 0, 0 (pure red) and the other two were 0, 255, 0 and 0, 0, 255 (pure green and pure blue, respectively). Where any two of the colors mix together, a secondary color is created. In lighting, the three secondary colors are amber, cyan, and magenta. In the center area where all three primary colors overlap, the light is white because all the ranges of visible light have been mixed back together. Remember, we get closer to white by adding missing colors. We make a color more pure by subtracting colors.

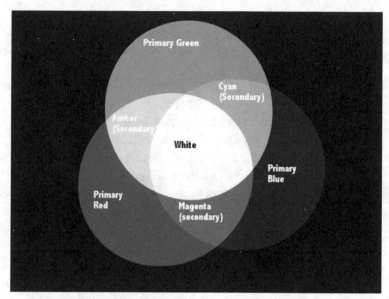

Figure 20.1: Primary and secondary colors of lighting (See color image.)

The Color of Pigments

Pigments are colors that apply to materials. Paint, for example, is a pigment. So is color dye and ink. Every material in the world — rocks, cloth, leaves, metal, paper, everything — has at least one pigment. Materials absorb some wavelengths and reflect others. Different materials absorb and reflect different wavelengths. This is why different materials have different colors.

Where light colors are identified by the light wavelengths *transmitted*, pigments are determined by which wavelengths are *absorbed* and which wavelengths are *reflected*.

If, for example, you shine white light onto a piece of white paper, the illuminated area of the paper will appear white. This is because the full spectrum of visible light is being shone on the paper and the paper is not absorbing any wavelengths and is, therefore, reflecting all of them. Materials that are white absorb very few or none of the visible wavelengths of light.

If, on the other hand, you shine a white light at a blue piece of paper, the illuminated area of the paper will appear blue. This is because the paper absorbs all or most of the green and red ranges of the visible light spectrum but reflects all or most of the blue range of the visible light

277

spectrum. Since only blue light is reflected, your eyes only receive the blue portion of the white light that is being shone on the paper.

If you shine a blue light at a white piece of paper, the illuminated area would, again, appear blue. Although the white piece of paper reflects all wavelengths, the only ones being shone on the paper are blue, and therefore only blue light is visible.

This means that different materials appear to be different colors to us because different physical materials tend to either absorb or reflect certain visible wavelengths. Our eyes perceive these different wavelengths and interpret them as different colors.

One would not expect that there are two kinds of pigments. But in fact, pigments in the real world behave one way, while pigments in the computer world behave a different way.

Pigments in the Real World

In the real world, pigments have three primary colors: red, yellow, and blue. If you mix red and yellow paint, you will get orange. If you mix yellow and blue paint, you will get green. If you mix red and blue paint, you will get purple.

In other words, pigment secondary colors are orange, green, and purple, where secondary colors in lighting are amber, cyan, and magenta.

If you have ever tried to mix paint colors, you are probably familiar with these simple color mixes.

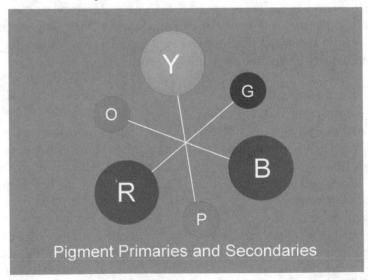

Pigment Primaries and Secondaries

Figure 20.2 (See color image.)

Figure 20.2 shows a color wheel displaying the three primary pigment colors (the large circles) and the secondaries that can be achieved by mixing the primaries in equal proportions. So we know that pigments in the real world mix very differently than light does. Take a look at both color wheels side by side.

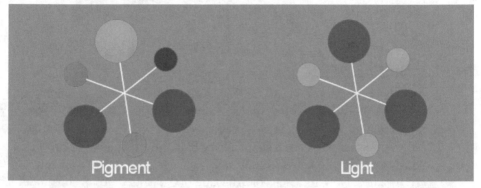

Figure 20.3 (See color image.)

Pigments in MAX

One might expect that mixing pigment colors and mixing lighting colors in MAX would adhere to the physical realities of the real world as much as possible. But there is a problem inherent in trying to mix pigment colors on a computer monitor. The problem is that computer monitors, and television monitors for that matter, create colors by mixing red, green, and blue picture elements, or *pixels*. So any color mixed on a computer is going to be created using the RGB lighting color model as opposed to the RYB pigment color model.

"Why then," you might ask, "bother learning about the RYB pigment color model?" Simple — because you will be mixing colors with pigments in the computer. You may be trying to mix colors to simulate a background plate if you are working in visual effects. It is essential for you to understand the physically correct relationships between light and pigment.

What you must keep in mind is that "real-world" pigment primaries are red, yellow, and blue, and "real-world" lighting primaries are red, green, and blue.

MAX's pigment primaries are red, green, and blue, and MAX's lighting primaries are also red, green, and blue.

It's a funny way of creating pigment colors, but at least this way you only have to think about one way of mixing colors and one set of primaries.

Those of you who have experience mixing paints will understand exactly why I feel this is kind of strange. Those of you who have only mixed colors using computer software will probably wonder what planet I'm from. The bottom line is that if you can mix the color you want for your surface textures, and if you can mix the color you want for your light, and if your light and your texture interact in the way you desire, then there's really no problem, is there?

RGB Values

Any color you choose in MAX's color picker, whether it is for a lighting instrument or for a texture, will be composed of three 8-bit values, one 8-bit value for each of the three primary colors: red, green, and blue. 8-bit values are used because, in binary language, a value of 1111 1111 is equal to 255. If you count from 0, an 8-bit range accounts for 256 discrete values. Now, for each color, a value of 0 means there is no amount of that color in the mix, while a value of 255 means all of that color is in the mix. When you account for all three colors, each with a potential value in the mix ranging from 0 to 255, the number of possible combinations is calculated by multiplying 256 x 256 x 256, resulting in 16,777,216 possible combinations of color. This is why modern computer monitors and video cards are advertised as being capable of displaying over 16 million colors.

Following are some typical RGB values and their associated colors:

R	G	B	Color
0	0	255	Blue (primary)
0	255	0	Green (primary)
255	0	0	Red (primary)
255	255	0	Yellow (secondary)
0	255	255	Cyan (secondary)
255	0	255	Magenta (secondary)

It is easy to see how so many different colors can be mixed so quickly using this method.

Hue, Saturation, and Value

Using the Hue, Saturation, and Value, or HSV, method of mixing colors can give us a different understanding or a different way of looking at color and how it mixes.

You can mix any color using the HSV method that you can mix using the RGB method. If you have taken some time to play with the MAX Color Selector you will notice that as you change any of the H, S, or V values numerically, the RGB values also change and vice versa. This is because HSV and RGB are linked together even though they are different types of values.

Hue

Hue refers to the pure color that is being chosen. Any color along the visible spectrum of light is considered a hue, whether it is a primary or a mixed color. Figure 20.4 demonstrates the range of hues available to the human eye.

Figure 20.4 (See color image.)

You can see all the colors of the rainbow in this spectrum. Each of these wavelengths is a component of white light. In other words, if we were to mix them together again, we would produce white light.

But we are able to mix much lighter and much darker colors than just those visible on this spectrum.

Saturation

When we think of *saturation* we think of how *much* of a color is incorporated. We think of a highly saturated color as being pure and deep. For example, if we say that the light coming from a lighting instrument is a highly saturated red, then we think of a deep red, perhaps even primary. We think of less saturated colors as being paler and closer to white. A very light pink, for example, would be considered a low-saturation red. This is exactly how saturation works in the HSV model of color picking.

This is a very interesting way of demonstrating saturation, since it is actually opposite to how it really occurs. We know, for example, that white light is "whole" with all the primaries at full saturation. If you remove all the green and all the blue, then you have primary red. Certainly the final color is a highly saturated red, but is primary red a more saturated color than white? White is actually a highly saturated mix of the primaries.

However, for the purposes of individual hues, we will accept that any color that moves toward white is less saturated.

High Saturation   Low Saturation

Figure 20.5 (See color image.)

Value

Value works similarly to saturation except that instead of the hue moving toward white, the hue moves toward black. A higher *value* color is considered to be closer to the pure hue. For example, a pure cyan is considered to be a color of a very high value. If that color were to become very dark, getting closer to black, then that color would be considered to have a very low value.

High Value   Low Value

Figure 20.6 (See color image.)

In the business of lighting, value is tied to light intensity, as we know that a light that is colored black emits no light. As a matter of fact, if you set a light to 1,000,000% intensity, set that light's color to a value of 0, 0, 0 and shine it on a white, 100% diffuse surface, there will be no illumination on that white surface.

So, in fact, there is more than one way of setting a final color value. You can set the value in the HSV color picker, you can change the light's intensity, or you can even change the diffuse value of the surface that the light is shining on. The diffuse value of a surface is a multiplier of how much illumination is applied to that surface. Less illumination means less color transmission to the surface. Less color transmission means a lower final value.

How Hue, Saturation, and Value Interact

Hue, saturation, and value are not completely independent values. They are interlinked through axes. Just like there are x, y, and z axes in MAX, there are H, S, and V axes in the HSV color selection model.

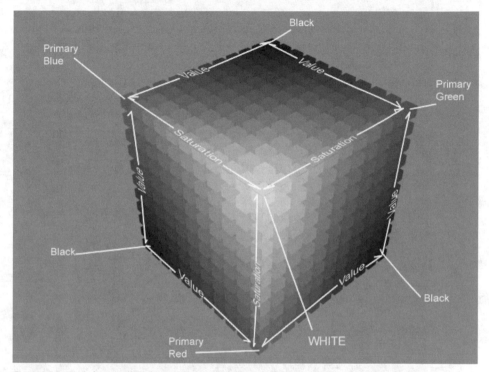

Figure 20.7: Color model showing the interaction of hue, saturation, and value. (See color image.)

As you can see in this "color cube" model, color hues that tend toward black have low values, while colors that tend toward white have low saturations. Colors that are closest to their original hues have high saturation and high value.

Recapping HSV

To be clear, hue is simply the base color, the pure wavelengths, whether it be orange, green, purple, or whatever. Saturation is how pale a hue is, with lower saturations being paler and higher saturations being more vivid. Value is how dark a hue is, with very dark colors having a low value and very vivid colors having a high value.

The Additive Color Wheel

There are a number of different ways of describing what is called the "color wheel." Some color wheels display only primary colors and their mixes, some display primaries and secondaries, and others run the full spectrum including variations of hues, saturations, and values.

The *additive color wheel* is a simple circle of colors in which a color mixture is created by adding light colors or wavelengths together. This is different from subtractive color mixing. Subtractive color mixing applies to pigments instead of light and refers to what light wavelengths are absorbed by the pigment. By adding pigments together, more wavelengths are absorbed and are therefore subtracted from the total reflected light. For more on this, read the sections on additive and subtractive color mixing later in this chapter.

Figures 20.8 to 20.10 show different examples of color wheels. Each displays the correct orientations and relationships between the colors.

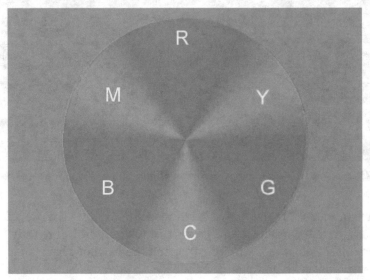

Figure 20.8 (See color image.)

The color wheel in Figure 20.8 shows the three primary colors — red, green, and blue — and the secondary colors — magenta, yellow, and cyan — that are created by mixing combinations of the primaries. Where red and green mix, we get yellow, where red and blue mix, we get magenta, and where green and blue mix, we get cyan. This is a good way to begin to understand how basic color mixing works when choosing different light colors for your scenes.

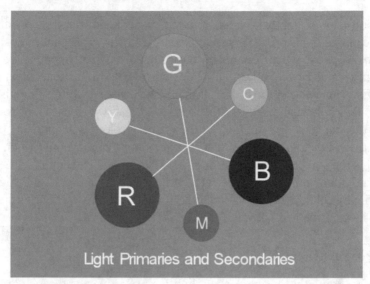

Figure 20.9 (See color image.)

A more traditional color wheel, like the one shown in Figure 20.9, also represents the three primaries and the three secondaries, although I prefer a color wheel that shows the mixing as it actually occurs.

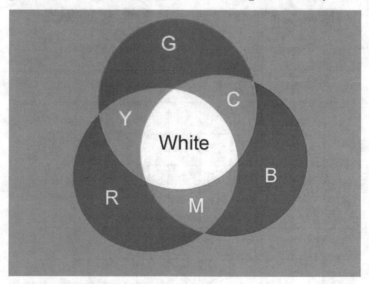

Figure 20.10 (See color image.)

For a color wheel that demonstrates all the primaries and secondaries, the one in Figure 20.10 is my favorite. This color wheel not only shows what happens when you mix primaries but also what happens when you mix secondaries together. This color wheel gets to the heart of what light is made of. In the center of this wheel, we see white. White is what I call "whole" light. White light contains all the wavelengths, or colors, in the visible spectrum. Each of the primary colors is an individual part of that whole. So if you mix a secondary color like magenta (which contains red and blue) with a secondary like cyan (which contains green and blue), then you have all three pure primary colors. Mixing all three pure primary colors will result in white, providing all three primaries are at full saturation and full value.

Primary Colors

Considering this is a book about lighting in 3ds max, and considering that MAX does not use the "real-world" RYB pigment model of primary colors, this section deals exclusively with the RGB color model.

Primary colors are those colors in the visible light spectrum from which all other colors can be derived through mixing. Primary colors are not divisible into other colors.

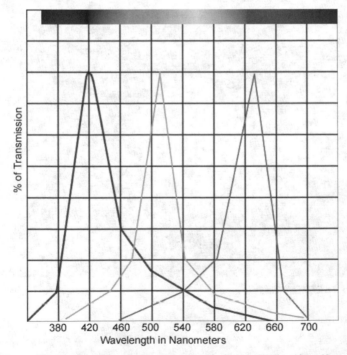

Figure 20.11: A graphic representation of all three light colors (See color image.)

The graph in Figure 20.11 illustrates the three primary colors in the RGB lighting model and how they might appear in a color transmission graph. The horizontal axis represents the wavelength, shown both in nanometers and as a color representation. The vertical axis represents the amount of all wavelengths that is mixed into the color.

In theory, primary red, primary green, and primary blue would be only a single spike exactly on a single wavelength; however, in reality it is extremely difficult to produce physically precise primary colors.

If you find yourself in a situation where you are mixing primary colors for a scene, be aware that "real-world" lighting and "real-world" pigments almost always have mixes of other wavelengths within them.

A typical wavelength transmission graph for a theatrical lighting filter (gel), for example, will look something like Figure 20.12.

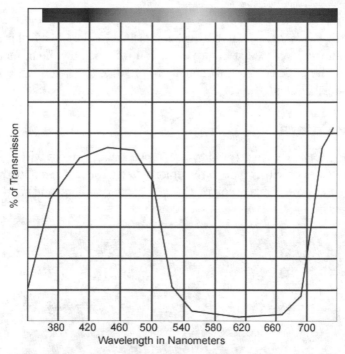

Figure 20.12: A typical wavelength transmission graph for a lighting filter (See color image.)

As you can see in this graph, primary blue is only one portion of all the light that is transmitted through this filter. There are related wavelengths such as cyan, violet, and even green. At the upper end of the spectrum, some red light is also allowed to pass through this filter. In the world of stage lighting, this is known as a primary blue filter. But how can it be primary blue if it contains so many other colors? There are two main reasons. One is that all the colors you use in your design are relative. They are relative to each other and to the scenery. Also, the human eye can easily be fooled into believing this is primary. This filter is close enough to primary blue and contains enough of the blue range of wavelengths to pass for primary blue by completely overpowering the traces of other wavelengths.

What it comes down to is this: One of the main problems with computer-generated work is that it often looks computer generated. You can add some error simply by taking care never to create colors, like primaries, that are practically impossible in the real world. Don't be afraid to fudge with the colors. You will find it adds a great deal of dimension to your lighting.

Secondary Colors

Secondary colors are created by mixing primary colors in equal proportions. If you look back at Figure 20.3, you will see how the primary colors (the large circles) mix equally to produce the secondary colors (the small circles).

Tertiary Colors

Tertiary colors can be created by mixing secondary colors with their primary colors on either side in the color wheel. You can see now that there are three primary colors, three secondary colors, and six tertiary colors.

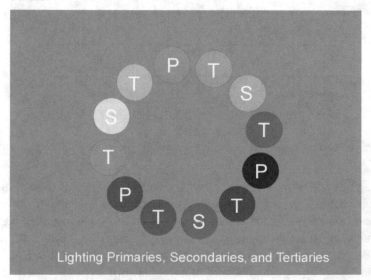

Lighting Primaries, Secondaries, and Tertiaries

Figure 20.13 (See color image.)

Intermediate Colors

Intermediate colors are all the other hues that come in between the primary, secondary, and tertiary hues on the color wheel.

Figure 20.14 (See color image.)

I find it much more natural and intuitive to view a color wheel like the one in Figure 20.14 as I work. This color wheel demonstrates color mixing in action, rather than displaying the individual colors arranged in a pattern, although those examples are good for illustrating the basic examples of primary colors and their mixed results. This color wheel also shows the full spectrum of hues rather than only specific mixes.

Color Harmonies, or Schemes

When we think of the word "harmony," we probably think first of musical notes that sound agreeable together. Color harmonies follow that logic. They are a way of finding colors on the color wheel that will work well together. There are a number of standard harmonies that you can use in your lighting design to create vivid, pleasing, and stylistically strong work. This does not, by any means, mean that you are confined to a set of rules for selecting your colors. These harmonies are principles that can help guide you in your color choices. If you wish, you can discard these completely. However, color harmonies are known as effective color selection tools that can greatly speed up your color choice process and at least get you into the ballpark of where you want your final colors to be.

Monochromatic Harmony

A *monochromatic color harmony* simply means that you have chosen to use a single hue alone. Any choice of only one hue constitutes a mono-chromatic color harmony. You may, for example, choose a single amber light as room illumination. If you have a basement room with no exterior illumination and only a single, bare lightbulb in the ceiling, a monochromatic color scheme may very well fit the bill. This is not a very exciting, vibrant, or interesting way of lighting, but that does not make it any less valid a color scheme. Your scene may call for drab, dull, boring. Mono-chromatic color schemes are an excellent way of conveying this sort of feeling to the viewer.

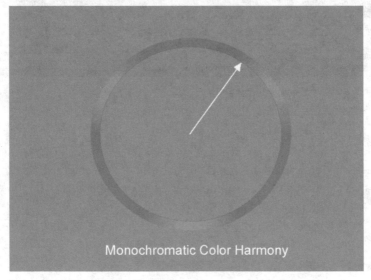

Monochromatic Color Harmony

Figure 20.15 (See color image.)

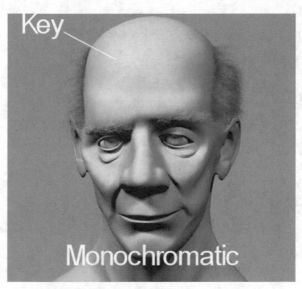

Figure 20.16 (See color image.)

Complementary Colors

Complementary colors are two colors from the color wheel that are directly opposite from each other. If, for example, you chose primary blue as one of your colors, the complement to that color would be yellow.

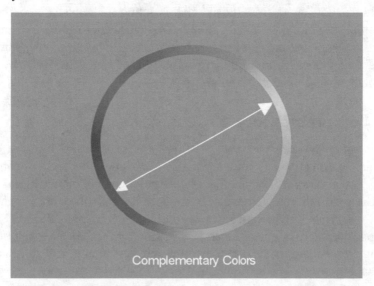

Figure 20.17 (See color image.)

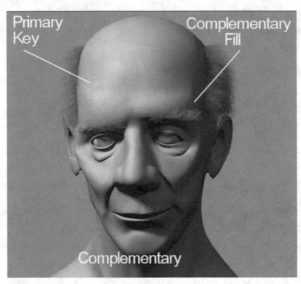

Figure 20.18 (See color image.)

Complementary colors have a high contrast that makes them vibrant and exciting. This system of color harmonies, along with split complementary, is, perhaps, one of the most used color selection systems used in lighting. If you are outside on a sunny day, you are lit with complementary colors. The sun has a yellowish hue that illuminates your face. Within the shadows of your face, however, there are blue hues. This blue illumination comes from the sky that is acting as the fill light source. So complementary color illumination exists everywhere and is extremely natural and pleasing. You are free to exaggerate this relationship by selecting more vibrant and more saturated colors if you wish or by selecting less saturated colors.

Split Complementary

One of my favorite color selection methods is *split complementary*. What this means is that one color is chosen as the key color, and two complementary colors are chosen that are the colors on either side of the color that is directly complementary to the key. Because the color scheme is based on a key color with a pair of complementary colors slightly off of opposite, there is a pleasant color variation rather than a garish or clashing scheme like triadic color harmony, which is mentioned later in this chapter.

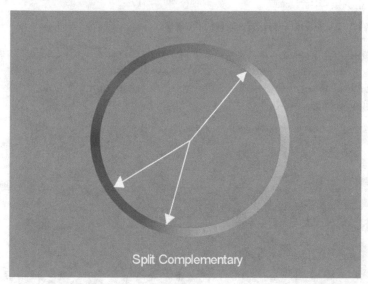

Figure 20.19 (See color image.)

Split complementary allows the designer to build a color highlight into either the key or fill light sources (or whatever light source you choose, really) by adding a second complement that is a related hue.

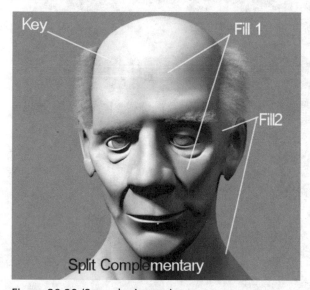

Figure 20.20 (See color image.)

Double Split Complementary

Double split complementary is simply two related hues with their respective complements across the color wheel. You can use this color selection method to find the appropriate color highlight for both key and fill sources, for example.

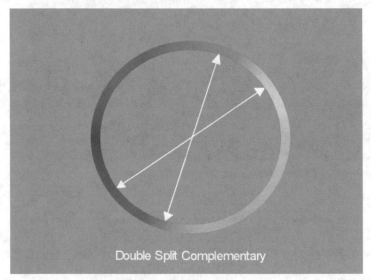

Figure 20.21 (See color image.)

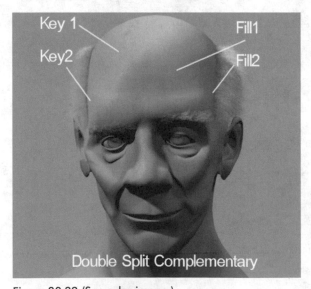

Figure 20.22 (See color image.)

In Figure 20.22, a key light and a fill light were added to the scene using complementary tints. A secondary key and a secondary fill were then added using the double split complementary tint color selection method. The secondary key and fill lights were used to create pleasing color highlights on the subject, adding a richer and more three-dimensional look to the lighting.

Analogous Color Harmony, aka Related Tints

Analogous color harmony, or related tints, means a selection of colors that are in a similar hue range. Orange and yellow, for example, would be considered related tints. So would orange and red or red and crimson. Red, magenta, and blue would not be considered related tints because, although red and blue are both related to magenta, they are not related to each other. Color selections must be closer to each other than the distance between primaries.

There can be any number of color selections in a related tints color scheme. Unlike complementary, which is limited to two selections, and split complementary, which is limited to three, related tints really has no such limitation. You can select any number of primary, secondary, tertiary, or intermediate colors, provided they all fall within a related hue range.

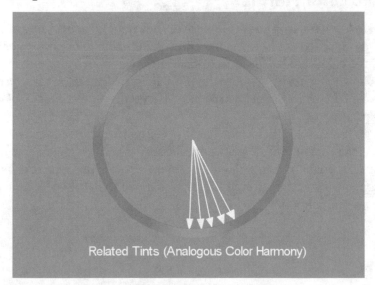

Related Tints (Analogous Color Harmony)

Figure 20.23 (See color image.)

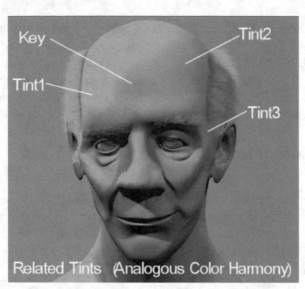

Figure 20.24 (See color image.)

Related tints tend to be more calming than the vibrant complementary schemes.

Triadic Color Harmony

Triadic color harmonies are similar to split complementary in that they are composed of three colors. However, in triadic color harmonies, the three colors are evenly spaced about the color wheel, rather than two colors being nearly opposite the third. If you selected the three primary colors, for example, that would be considered a perfect triadic color harmony.

Triadic color harmonies tend to be bright, vibrant, and rather garish and unsophisticated. If you were painting a child's playroom, you might select a triadic color harmony. You might also use this type of color scheme if you wish to grab attention or if you wish the scene to seem edgy and disturbing.

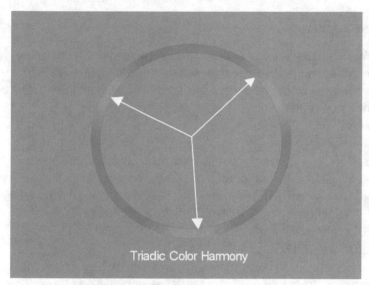

Triadic Color Harmony

Figure 20.25 (See color image.)

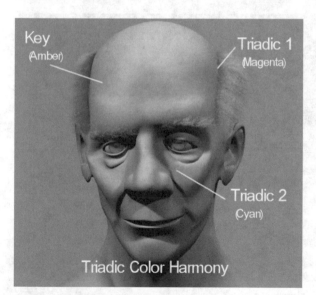

Key
(Amber)

Triadic 1
(Magenta)

Triadic 2
(Cyan)

Triadic Color Harmony

Figure 20.26 (See color image.)

Additive Mixing

Additive mixing refers to a color mixing method in which light wavelengths or colors from one light source are combined with light wavelengths or colors from one or more other light sources. The combined sum of all the wavelengths and intensities from all the light sources results in a final color.

The classic example of additive mixing is the combination of all three primary lighting colors at 100%. If you color three lights red, green, and blue, set them each to 100%, and aim them all at the same spot on a surface that is set to an RGB value of 1.0, 1.0, 1.0 or 255, 255, 255), and the surface is 100% diffuse, the resulting color on the surface will be white. The three primaries combine to make white on a surface that absorbs no light wavelengths.

Regardless of the surface color, however, the light from the three lighting instruments combines to create white light at 100%. This can be demonstrated if we can see the light beams by using volumetrics.

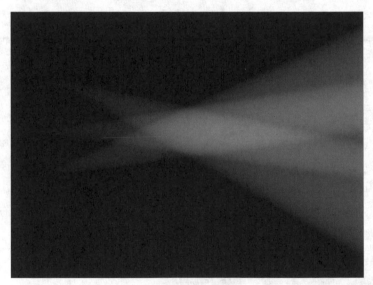

Figure 20.27 (See color image.)

Additive mixing occurs anytime you are using two or more lights of different hues on the same surface. Knowing, or at least being able to estimate, the final hue is critical to lighting your surface properly. Have you noticed how on a bright, hot, sunny summer day, the light seems very white? This is not because the sun emits a very white light. As a matter of fact, sunlight is rather yellow. But once you mix the blue from the sky into the sunlight, the light appears very white. Why is this? If you look at your color wheel, you will see that yellow light such as sunlight is composed of the primaries red and green. If you add blue light into this, you then have all three primaries — red, green, and blue — in the mix to some extent. Mixing these three lighting colors always results in a whiter light color.

By examining the component colors of any color you have selected, you should be able to guess what the final color will be if mixed with another light.

We are only talking about light color here. Once the light reaches a colored surface, there are many other considerations that can change your expected results. If, for example, you have a red light and a green light and you combine them by aiming them together at a blue surface, you know that you have a combined yellow light shining at the blue surface. But what will the surface color be when it is illuminated by the yellow light?

The following chart shows examples of some mixing results

Color 1 +	Color 2 =	Color 3
Red	Green	Yellow
Red	Orange	Bright Orange
Orange	Green	White
Blue	Magenta	Purple

Try throwing a couple of lights together, point them at a white surface, and start fiddling with the colors. If you don't already have a handle on light color mixing, you soon will.

Missing Color

One good way of estimating the final color of a lighting mix is to try to determine a "missing color." If you were to mix an orange-colored light with a green-colored light, for example, what would the missing color be? Well, we know that green is a primary and so it cannot be broken down into component primary colors. An orange light color is mixed out of red and green. So we now know that red, green, and green are the components of the two lights. The missing color is blue. We know that the final color of the two mixed lights will not contain any blue light. This tells us that the final color is probably in the yellow-orange range of the color wheel, nearly opposite the blue range.

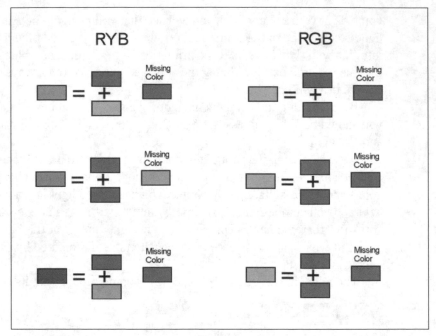

Figure 20.28 (See color image.)

Subtractive Mixing

In the real world, we usually refer to *subtractive mixing* when we are talking about mixing paints together. This is because, unlike lights which get whiter as you mix more colors together, paints get blacker as you mix more colors together. In theory, if you could mix true primary red, yellow, and blue paint together, the result would be black paint. In reality, paint pigments are never true primary colors. Primaries are extremely difficult to produce and impractical for paint pigments. Besides, most people will never be able to tell the difference.

But what is it that makes this *subtractive* color mixing?

Simply put, pigments appear to be a certain color because they reflect the wavelength's component to that color. Orange paint, for example, reflects red and green light wavelengths while absorbing blue wavelengths. The blue wavelengths do not reach your eye; they are absorbed into the paint and do not, therefore, mix into the reflected light that makes up the color of the surface. Blue paint, on the other hand, reflects mostly blue wavelengths and absorbs most red and green wavelengths. So what would happen if we mixed the blue paint with the orange paint? The blue paint would probably subtract most of the

reflected red and green light wavelengths that the orange paint had originally reflected.

By adding more colors to the paint, we are subtracting the number
of wavelengths that are being reflected by the pigment. This is why
paint mixing is called "subtractive mixing."

Subtractive Light Mixing

I know, I know. I just finished explaining how light mixing is additive and
pigment mixing is subtractive. Here is where we step off the tracks of
physical reality and into the world of computer-calculated light
intensities.

One of the coolest tools available to the CG lighting artist (which is
not available to real-world lighters, I might add) is the ability to create
negative lights.

You make a negative light by loading it up and setting its intensity
level to a negative number like –1.0. Not only will this make the light
decrease illumination intensity wherever you shine it, but it will also
subtract color from wherever you shine it.

Say, for example, you have a white floor lit by a white direct light. If
you shine a spotlight on that floor, make the spotlight intensity –1.0, and
set the color to red (255, 0, 0), that spotlight will remove 100% of the
red light from the white floor. This means that only green and blue light
will remain in the area where the spotlight is shining.

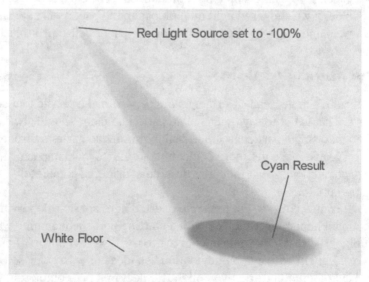

Figure 20.29 (See color image.)

Subtractive mixing can take many complex forms, resulting in unusual permutations. You can use subtractive lights to create negative shadow colors, for one. You can surgically remove intensity or color from specific areas. In short, subtractive mixing of intensity and color is a precision tool that gaffers world-wide wish they had at their fingertips.

Mixing Light with Pigments

Once you get down to lighting colored surfaces, you will have to understand exactly what light is absorbed and what is reflected by the surface. Lighting a yellow piece of paper with a blue light, for example, is not likely to result in very much illumination. Why is this? Yellow paper absorbs blue light and reflects red and green light. If you only shine blue light at the yellow paper, it will absorb the blue light. There are no other (or other) wavelengths left to reflect. The likelihood is that the yellow paper is going to appear black or, perhaps, very dark green, depending upon how close both the light color and the paper color are to their respective primaries.

Try to keep these simple rules in mind:

- Pigment reflects its color and absorbs all others. So red light on red paper will show red paper.

- Light is absorbed by pigments if it is a different color than the pigment. So if we shine a white light on pink paper, we will see pink paper. If we shine a blue light on pink paper, the paper will appear blue. If we shine red light on pink paper, the paper will appear red. If we shine green light on pink paper, the paper will appear black.

The Psychology of Color

It is quite simple, really. Certain colors tend to make people feel certain ways. That is not to say that a single particular color should always be used for a single particular emotional intent. In fact, artists throughout history have made yet more poignant statements by juxtaposing scenes with color choices that might, at first, be considered completely inappropriate.

It comes down to the first rule of art: There are no rules. With this section, I hope to provide you with a starting point, a beginning way of thinking, so that you can take your art to the next level. Don't hesitate to experiment with completely outlandish ideas or with color selections and lighting methods that you might think at first are completely wrong. Go for it. Sure, it might look awful, but you can always change it back.

Mixing color is partly about finding pleasing, relevant color combinations for your scene. The color mix must be relevant in that the colors are appropriate to the design and practical considerations of the scene. Red neon lights, for example, produce a red glow on nearby walls. If it's sunny, and the sun is the key light source, the light should probably be somewhere in the yellow range of the visible light spectrum. Relevance is the first technical consideration of your lighting design.

Following relevance, your lighting must be pleasing. I am not saying that it must be rosy and pretty. When I say your lighting must be pleasing, I mean it must please you, the designer. It must convey those meanings you wish it to convey. If you want a scene to appear morose, and you achieve morose lighting or some lighting effect that contributes to the feeling "morose," I imagine that you would be pleased. Understanding the psychological effects of certain color ranges and mixes can assist you in presenting a pleasing and effective lighting design

The following sections offer some basic ideas about how color selections tend to affect most people. Use this as a guide or a starting point. Remember, this is only the very basics. How much further you go is completely up to your imagination.

Warm Colors

Warm colors include those that are in the red, magenta, or yellow side of the color spectrum or color wheel. Colors that are warm tend to give us feelings of warmth and coziness because we associate reds, yellows, and oranges with heat, such as that from a fireplace.

Red

Red is one of the most powerful and aggressive colors. Among the things it can represent are blood, heat, fire, emergencies, warmth, love, and excitement. Alone, red can be overpowering. Using red as an accent can draw attention to specific areas of a scene.

Orange

Orange can represent strength, generosity, and warmth. Although not as powerful as red, it has a wider appeal and can be used to subtler effect.

Yellow

Bright yellows can be cheerful, but they can also be irritating. Because yellow reflects so much light, it can become tiresome for the eye and may lead to discomfort or even annoyance and distraction.

Cool Colors

Cool colors include those in the blue, green, and cyan side of the color wheel. We associate these colors with ice and water. These colors can also be associated with feelings of peace and serenity or even sadness and withdrawal.

Green

Green has long stood for renewal and rebirth. For thousands of years, primitive tribes initiated the rites of renewal at the winter solstice, half of the tribe blackened with charcoal, the other half adorned with green leaves. The two halves of the tribe fought in mock battle, the green side always winning. This sympathetic magic was used to ensure the return of spring and growth to the world. Since those ages long past, green has always been strongly associated with fertility and life.

Blue

Blue can be a calming and trustworthy color. Blue is the favorite color of most people. But it also denotes sadness and depression. Have you ever felt "blue"? In its purer forms, blue can indicate wisdom and trustworthiness. In its paler forms, it can give a sense of loss and helplessness.

Purple

Purple is often associated with royalty and wealth. Royal purple is one of the favorite shades of purple. It indicates wealth and sophistication, containing both the loyalty and trust of blue with the power and excitement of red.

Black

Black can be associated with evil such as black magic and fear, or it can denote strength and power. Many people prefer black clothing because it gives them an air of control and serenity, others because it can be intimidating. On the other hand, black is often associated with personal loss, death, despair, and mourning.

White

White is often associated with cleanliness, purity, chastity, innocence, honesty, and other human traits that are thought to be good and desirable. A bride may wear a white dress to denote virginity and/or chastity, while an angel is clad in white to represent pure good. And we all know who the good guy is if he is wearing a white cowboy hat.

Other Colors

Of course there are millions of other colors distinguishable to the human eye. Most of them fall into a range near at least one of the colors discussed above. These definitions are only part of how color can be interpreted. How you choose to use colors in your design is up to you. Whether or not your color choices work will be up to the judgment of hindsight. But you've got to start somewhere. Let's now take a look at how some colors may mix to create emotional responses.

Related Tints

Related tints is also known as an analogous color harmony. It refers to two or more colors selected from a similar range of the visible color spectrum. Olive green and forest green, for example, are considered related tints. So are pink and purple. Sand and orange are related as well.

Related tints tend to have a calming effect. This is true not only of lighting colors but of pigment application as well. If you wish your viewer to maintain a serene vision, avoid clashes or strong complements and go with a key and its relatives.

Complementary Colors

Complementary colors refers to colors that are opposite or close to opposite on the color wheel.

At this point, we must bear in mind and understand the key difference between primary pigments in the real world and primary pigments in the computer world. In the computer world, the three primary colors are red, green, and blue, whether you refer to lighting or pigments. In the real world, however, pigments have a different set of primaries. (For more details on this, see the "Primary Colors" section earlier in this chapter.) The "real-world" pigment primaries are red, yellow, and blue.

This is an extremely important distinction when mixing colors because even though computer-generated pigments are mixed using RGB primaries, you must mix them *as though* their primaries were RYB.

In the RGB world, the complement of red is achieved by mixing the other two primaries, in this case green and blue. The complement of red, therefore, is cyan.

In the RYB world, however, the complement of red is achieved by mixing the other two primaries, yellow and blue. The complement of red, therefore, is green.

So when you are creating complementary colors in your lighting design, you must consider that the complement to your key is achieved by going across the RGB color wheel. If you are creating pigment complements, however, you should mix using the RYB primary system for pigments; otherwise your complementary, secondary, and tertiary colors will come out differently than they would in the real world. MAX does not support RYB color mixing, so you'll just have to keep an RYB color wheel handy or make one up yourself. There are also many color mixing references available on the web that will help you understand pigment primaries and color mixing, if you don't already have a handle on them.

That said, let's get to the psychological effect of complementary colors, regardless of the primary system you are going to use.

A key color next to its complement can be very vibrant and exciting. If you wish to maintain a vibrancy to your scene, using a complementary color scheme is a good place to start. Standard McCandless key-fill lighting uses complementary colors. Even a sunny day uses this color scheme. The sun is your key light in the yellow range, while your fill light source, the sky, is blue. Blue is directly complementary to yellow in the RGB system that we use for lighting.

Complementary coloring is arguably the color selection method used most often in lighting, and perhaps in pigment selection as well. It is very simple and very effective, producing interesting and usually visually pleasing results.

Triadic Colors

Perhaps the first, most obvious use of a triadic color harmony is the use of all three primary colors in a coloring scheme. How many children's toys have you seen that make use of red, yellow, and blue, or of red green, and blue? Triadic color harmonies tend to go beyond the vibrancy of complementary coloring schemes and take the excitement to a new level. Some selections can be shocking or even odd.

Imagine what your scene would look like lit with three-point lighting using one each of the three primaries.

Monochromatic Colors

Monochromatic lighting designs are usually used with the express purpose of conveying boredom, drabness, and plainness. Monochromatic
color schemes, using one and only one lighting color, have been used
many times to denote unpleasant office environments, poor, shabby
homes, or drab, boring, rainy afternoons. They're also used effectively in
real-looking space shots, as the only light source often is the sun.

While it seems at first that this would be a very strange and mainly
useless design tool, one must consider the viewer reaction if such a
drably lit scene were juxtaposed with a scene lit using bright complements or even triadic color selections. One may use this tool to
counterpoint a severe disparity between two peoples' lives or between
two environments.

Monochromatic design is really a very powerful design tool and can,
if used effectively, punch home a design concept.

High-Saturation, High-Value Colors

High-saturation, high-value colors tend to be more vivid and exciting
than those of lower values or saturations. Toys for infants and children
often use these colors in order to stimulate the less-developed optical
senses of the child. We understand, then, that these colors tend to be
more noticeable and tend to hold attention longer than the softer, gentler
colors created by using lower saturation and value.

Low-Value Colors

Lower value colors, as discussed earlier, are those colors that tend
toward black. A dark crimson, for example, is a lower value shade of red.
These colors tend to have mysteriousness about them. They can also be
interpreted as having a "rich" quality as in the colors dark emerald and
royal blue. Dark wood such as mahogany, cherry, and walnut are considered to be more expensive and luxurious than light wood such as pine,
fir, and maple.

Low-Saturation Colors

Colors with lower saturation tend toward white. Pink, for example, is a
lower saturation shade of red. Many low-saturation colors are referred to
as *pastel* colors, named after the oil chalks. These low-saturation colors
are often associated with serenity, calm, and softness.

High-Contrast Color Combinations

High-contrast colors are those usually found on opposite sides of the color wheel. Whether you are mixing with light or pigment, pick a color, find the color on the opposite side of the color wheel, and you will have a high-contrast color. Yellow contrasts highly with blue, for example. If you use high-contrast colors together in your design, you are likely to come up with a vibrant, exciting result. Here are some other high-contrast combinations:

RGB

Red	←→	Cyan
Green	←→	Magenta
Orange	←→	Aqua

RYB

Yellow	←→	Purple
Green	←→	Red
Orange	←→	Blue

Low-Contrast Color Combinations

Low-contrast colors tend to be near each other on the color wheel. They usually offer the viewer a sense of calm and order as opposed to the vivid excitement of their high-contrast counterparts. Lower contrast examples include:

RGB

Magenta	←→	Blue
Green	←→	Yellow
Red	←→	Orange

RYB

Green	←→	Blue
Purple	←→	Red
Yellow	←→	Orange

Designing with Color

There is no way to set out ABCs of color use in your design. The attempt of this chapter has been to give you a theoretical background and basic understanding so that you can use whatever colors you wish to achieve your desired effect.

You do not need a tutorial to explain where to place a light, what color to make it, and what intensity to set. You need to equip yourself with a base understanding of color and the effects it has on your scene. You need to understand how the light plays in your scene and what a colored light does to a colored texture. You should have an understanding of what different colors and intensities do to your scene to bring about a desired psychological or emotional response from your viewers.

There is only one way to achieve this knowledge and understanding and that is by practice. Practice your lighting and trust your eye. When you choose a color, look at how it plays on the scene and ask yourself how it makes you feel, what, if any, emotional response you have to it, and what sort of mood you think the light brings to your scene.

If I were an audience member and was shown a scene brightly lit with warm hues of pink and orange, I might expect that the scene will be happy, invigorating, joyful, or even comedic. If the scene were lit dimly, on the other hand, using the cool hues of blue and green, I might be expecting a darker tone to the scene, a morose theme, or perhaps black comedy.

This is not to say that you might not light a death scene very brightly with highly saturated colors and multiple highlights. Such a contrary set of color choices may serve not to dilute the emotions of loss and grief but to enhance and complement them, perhaps even to punctuate them by virtue of their complementary and contrasting nature.

You are the designer. The choices are yours.

■ ■ ■

Now that you have come to the end of this chapter, you should have at least a basic understanding of color primaries, secondaries, and tertiaries as well as how light and pigment interact and relate to each other. As an exercise, you might try imagining what color will result if you shine a spotlight of color "A" on a surface with color "B." Fill in the A and B with whatever color you like. Once you get every answer right, you've pretty much got color mixing down.

Chapter 21

Mood Setting

This chapter describes yet another esoteric and debatable topic: mood setting. It may very well be that you disagree with everything written here. Storytelling does, after all, take infinite forms. But I hope, at least, that this will help you think about how you set the mood of your scene and how you can accomplish this intentionally and with planning and art.

Every scene has a mood. Every mood can be defined by any number of criteria, not the least of which is lighting. Design style can set a mood; so can music, characters, scenery, or even odor.

What is it about lighting that helps define a mood? Some say that millions of years of evolution are to thank (or blame) for our emotional response to certain lighting qualities. Some say that it is social conditioning or even traumatic experience. The truth probably involves some or all of these for each of us, and our specific reactions tend to differ depending on our cultural, social, and personal backgrounds and experiences.

There do seem, however, to be general trends that apply to most people. If, for example, we choose to illuminate a scene with blue lighting, the audience is likely to presume a morose scene, a nighttime scene, or a very cold scene. If, on the other hand, we choose to illuminate the scene with bright, white light from below, our audience will likely experience a sense of foreboding, evil, or drama. If we light with green, the audience is likely to become ill at ease or, in the absence of any other signals, presume the setting is in a forest or under water.

These responses occur because we, as human beings, make certain associations with certain lighting properties. Predominantly dark blue lighting, for example, is never experienced during the day. A hot fire is not blue. Happy evenings at home are not generally experienced in dark blue environments. These may seem like obvious statements, but they are key to understanding why dark blue lighting makes us react a particular way.

Lighting a scene from beneath seems dramatic or evil simply because the primary natural light in our world comes from above. It has always come from above, even since long before life graced our little blue marble. Our response, therefore, is that lighting from beneath is odd, off, strange, unusual, unnatural, and weird. This response has been used to great effect by artists of every ilk for millennia.

Angle and color are only two of the lighting properties that can evoke an emotional response from the audience. Let's look at some others.

Angle and Shadow

Angle and shadow, like many light properties, are linked together. Certain lighting angles produce certain types of shadows. Sometimes the shadow is dependent on the orientation of the light relative to the object, and sometimes it is dependent on the orientation of the light relative to the camera.

Let's go back to our head model and look at a few examples.

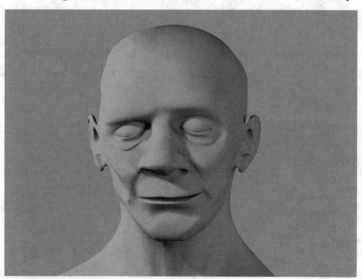

Figure 21.1: Typical key and fill lighting

This is a fairly typical render, one in which we use a variation of a simple McCandless lighting setup. Key and fill lights coming in at roughly 45-degree angles illuminate the full figure with additional highlight instruments placed for warmth and, of course, highlights. These angles are selected because they represent a natural light source. They make the viewer feel at ease and familiar. We can change that very easily simply by applying an unnatural or unusual angle to our key light.

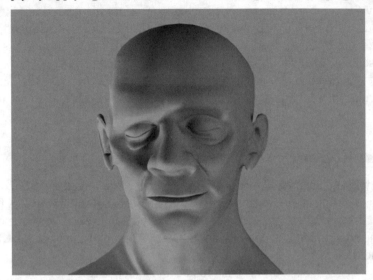

Figure 21.2: Key light from below

All the other lights remain where they were. Only the key light has been moved to a position in front of and below the subject, yet the image already looks a little odd. What happens if we turn the other lights off and leave only the single light from below?

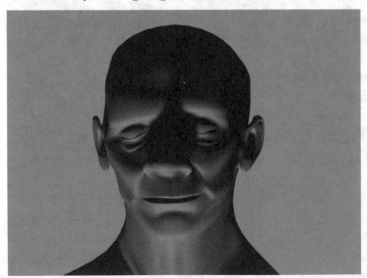

Figure 21.3: Fill light removed for more dramatic effect

The image in Figure 21.3 is very strange and unnatural, even frightening if the context makes it so.

We can also light the subject from directly above, providing deep, unusual shadows.

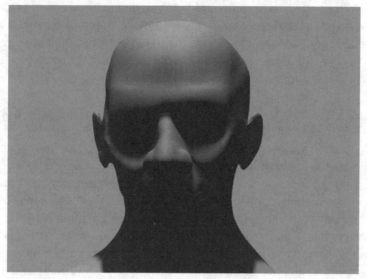

Figure 21.4: Top light only for dramatic effect

These deep shadows provide the figure with a sinister appearance, hiding the eyes and making the subject seem untrustworthy.

Lighting subjects from the side can help define subtle shapes in the subject.

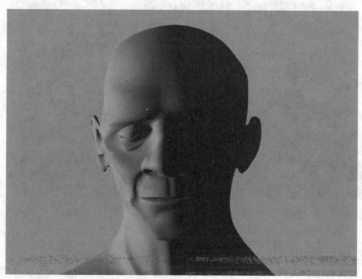

Figure 21.5: Side light only for dramatic effect

This angle is serene, yet still hides part of the subject. It can be used to great effect for many different scene types, primarily where the artist is interested in drawing attention to shapes and forms in the scene.

Mixing these lighting angles with each other, with fill lights, with anything your heart desires will help you define the mood of your scene. Your lighting angles are an easy way to make your audience either comfortable or ill at ease. Play with a bunch of lights and angles. When you render out a frame, look at it and ask yourself how it makes you feel. Chances are your audience will feel the same.

Contrast

Contrast in your scenic lighting can help set a mood for your scene. Where low-contrast images tend to give viewers a serene, low-energy feeling, higher contrast lighting is likely to energize your shot. Imagine how you feel on a cloudy or rainy day. On those days, the sun is hidden. The clouds are diffusing most of the light, which results in a low-contrast lighting environment. People feel down and tired. On a sunny day though, bright sunlight and dark shadows result in a high-contrast lighting situation. People generally feel energized and happy on sunny days.

Figure 21.6: High-contrast image

Figure 21.6 is a high-contrast shot. Notice that there is a high range between the whitest and the blackest points in the image.

Figure 21.7: Low-contrast image

Figure 21.7 is a low-contrast shot. Notice that there is a low range of difference between the whitest and the blackest points in the image.

Intensity

Light intensity is another of the more subtle ways of weaving mood into your scene. Subtle variations in light intensity from one scene to the next can serve as a dynamic thread leading the viewer through a range of moods or over a gradual change from one mood to another.

Very dim intensities are usually associated with night or evening and can be associated with somber, serene, or unhappy events. Very bright intensities are usually associated with high energy, happiness, activity, and heat. Intensities of medium or "normal" levels tend to make an audience feel relaxed, at home, and familiar.

Of course, that is not to say that you are forbidden from using very bright lights for a very sad scene or very dim intensities for a very happy scene. Once again, sometimes lighting a scene exactly opposite of what is expected can serve to silhouette and intensify your mood message.

The best thing as a designer is for you to experiment, render out frames, and see how they make *you* feel. Trust your instincts.

Motion

Motion is not usually associated with the mood of a scene, but I have observed that it can have a profound effect on an audience's mood. Take, for example, the typical mirror ball. It produces tiny illuminated reflections that move in graceful arcs throughout a room. This lighting gives a sense of wonder and magic to most environments. On the other hand, the rushing lights of speeding traffic tend to heighten stress and awareness, giving an edge of fear and chaos to a scene.

Motions can vary from nearly imperceptible to wild and seemingly uncontrolled. It is up to you to use motion in your scenes as you see fit. It is up to you to decide whether or not lighting motion achieves your objectives or obscures them. The best way to find this out is to experiment with motion.

Weather

In the world of CG, weather is definitely considered to be a lighting condition. Take, for example, lightning. These intensely bright flashes of light can bring fear or even panic into your scene very easily depending on the proximity, and therefore the intensity, of the lightning. Distant lightning can be foreboding, brooding, broiling, and forewarning, while immediate lightning can signal imminent disaster and complete chaos. Mother Nature can be an extremely powerful way to evoke emotions in the viewer. Use it wisely and do not overuse.

Rain on the windowpane can also be considered a lighting effect. I would probably find some footage of a rainfall and project it through a spotlight. This is more of a special effect than a regular lighting effect but can be quite persuasive in lending mood to the scene.

■ ■ ■

Setting the mood in your scene is not about a single light source, a single color, or a single effect. It is about the web that you weave to draw your audience into the story. The most successful web is woven of multiple subtleties tied together with a thread of style. If you are new to lighting design, your immediate challenge is to know the tools and understand what they can do. Subsequent to that, you should experiment with your lighting as much as you can, as much as you have time for. If you are intimidated by the thought of weaving these careful webs of illusion, my best advice to you is to just throw caution to the wind and do it! Forget about criticism. Be wild. Sooner or later you will get the feel for setting moods. And most of all, observe the world. Reality is, after all, far more strange and unlikely than our best-told stories.

Hopefully by now you have some idea of the importance of deliberately setting the mood of your scene. Certainly you could light a shot simply based on the technical requirements of the scene. But with a little forethought, planning, and imagination, you can change the lighting from mere illumination into a tool that illuminates the story line as well.

The clever artist will now build some scenes with specific emotional intentions in mind, then ask their bored friends, mothers, aunts, or whomever for an emotional response. Hopefully it will be more constructive than "You're such a geek!"

Chapter 22

Style

This chapter briefly discusses the rather esoteric concept of style. You may or may not agree with some of the discussion here. That's okay though, because if you already have your own concept of style, you don't even need to read this chapter.

Style. There really isn't that much that can be unequivocally defined about style except that it's a very important part of lighting design. The problem is that style can't really be taught. Furthermore, that which one person considers style may not be considered style by another. It's a slippery concept, yet it exists.

So I can't teach you style, yet it is very important for a lighting designer. What, then, to do? In the absence of any empirical fact, I'll include herein the few tidbits I have learned about style over the years. Maybe they will help you in some way to find your own style.

What Is Style?

Style can be defined as a distinctive combination of features, either in literature or in visual or performing arts. These features can be characterized through design, execution, performance, or expression and define a particular era, person, or school. In other words, there are a number of different ways to define style. In our case, we are discussing the execution and look of the final lighting as defining a style that is distinctly yours.

Sooner or later, if you find yourself designing, you will discover that you wish to explore your own creativity, combining elements from the works of artists you admire, and adding your own ideas and interpretations into the mix. You will try many new things, adapt the old tricks of the Masters to your own use, and mix in the technical requirements of the shot or the show. One day you will be able to look at your work on a television monitor as you walk past it in a mall and instantly recognize it as your own. You will recognize it not because you worked on it tirelessly into the wee hours and the shot is burned permanently into your retinas but because you can immediately see that it is decisively *yours* in a way that transcends technical requirements. You will discover that you know your own style.

Your style is not about the show. It is about you. You are an individual with individual experiences and interpretations. You bring these experiences and interpretations to the design table with you because when you read the script, you react to the dramatic situations of the script in a certain way. Your emotional reactions to a scene or to the script in general are based on your life experience, your opinions, and your interpretations. You anthropomorphize non-living characters on a page. You make notes about your reactions and feelings. After you have read the script a couple of times, you have to start thinking about how you are going to make the audience experience those same feelings and reactions.

So What Do I Do?

First you must ask yourself what you want your work to say. Do you want your audience to be shocked or delighted? Do you want to disgust them or please them? Would you prefer to grab attention with a shock or allow your audience to slowly discover your messages? Do you wish them to be comfortable and familiar or uneasy and on edge?

Each of these decisions will have a direct impact on the lighting you choose for your scene. Exactly how you choose to implement those lighting goals is where style comes into play. You can carry a single style through many different types of scenes, or you can choose to vary it, drawing on many different resources and styles.

Style is really a method of making aesthetic choices. For example, a designer may prefer muted earth tones. There is no reason the designer can't use muted earth tones in joyous scenes as well as depressing ones, thus giving the lighting elements a common tonal thread throughout. The scenic designer, however, may handle these scenes in any number of very different ways.

If you wish, every scene can have a completely different look, a completely different style, but exactly the same message. Are you starting to see? There are no rules to style. You can mix and match as you please, provided that in the end you have attained your goals. If your goal was to confuse and upset your audience but they leave angry and want their money back, you may have to revisit your methods or your goals. If your goal was to frighten and delight your audience and they are frightened and delighted, then nobody has an argument with your methods and style, whatever they may be. Beware, however: It is easy to clutter and obscure the story with too much style, too many different elements, or too many changes.

Less Is More

If we examine great works of art throughout history, whether it be a marble sculpture, a painting masterpiece, a classic automobile, or a great work of architecture, we see that these great works have one thing in common—simplicity; simplicity of line and form, of design and function. You have probably heard the expression "Less is more." In the world of art, nothing could be more true.

I have heard CG lighting artists brag about using 72 lights to illuminate an exterior shot as though more lights are better, as though an immense amount of work and a huge number of lights somehow characterize the technical prowess of the artist. Let's be clear about this: A massive number of lights do not guarantee a superior result.

It's not how big your array is, it's how you use it.

While there will indeed be situations in which you will need to employ large numbers of lights for practical or technical reasons, you will find over time, if you don't know already, that the best lighting solution is usually the simplest and the most elegant. Too many light sources are unnatural and unnecessary. The results are likely to be less than satisfactory.

Consistency between Shots

If you are the director, the piece is experimental, and you wish to create a completely different look for each shot, that's your prerogative. Chances are that your audience will be confused and spend so much time struggling to understand your wild changes and design choices that the real story will be lost. That may be your intention. Probably not, though.

As storytellers ourselves, we usually don't want our lighting to be so intrusive that it detracts from the story. We want a smooth, flowing design style that assists the story from behind, never quite getting in the audience's face. Lighting should usually be like the steel or wooden piles deep in the ground underneath the skyscraper. They're there for support, to help keep the building level and straight. Without them, the building would fall down. But nobody who enters the building ever sees them or thinks about them.

By maintaining some sort of style consistency between shots, the audience is less likely to notice the lighting, which means they are more likely to be thinking about the story. I call that a success. Not everybody does, but I do.

■ ■ ■

Style can be a slippery topic to talk about. Debate often rages about what is considered style and what is considered technique. An artist may consider that he has a wildly successful and distinctive style. His art may speak to him, portraying the precise message he wished to portray. On the other hand, others may consider the very same work to be trash, perhaps self-indulgent and meaningless. That certainly does not necessarily validate either position.

This is the subjective nature of art and style. The only advice I can offer is this: If you set out to achieve a particular look for a set of particular reasons, and you achieve that look, then you have been successful. Whether or not others respond to the work in the way you would prefer is not necessarily relevant. You have demonstrated that you can achieve the look you desire when you desire it. It means that you know how to get what you want out of the tools. That's a success in anyone's book.

All that is required is that you simply keep doing that over and over. One day you will realize that you have developed a style all your own.

If you wish to understand style in greater detail, there is no better way to learn than to study the work of great artists throughout history. When you hear a particular piece of music, you may be able to identify the composer. When you see a painting, you may know right away whose masterpiece it is. These are the paths that lead to understanding style.

If, after this chapter, you don't have any clue what style is, don't let it bother you too much. Most people don't. It's such a personal and subjective thing, that its definition can be argued from many different perspectives. On the other hand, style may be completely unimportant to you, in which case congratulations for reading all the way to the end of the chapter!

Chapter 23

Designing Lighting

The Design Process

We are artists. Most of us became CG artists because the computer environment affords us the ability to be every kind of artist we ever dreamed of. We can be sculptors, architects, painters, directors, and designers, to name but a few. Many of us would rather stay away from really structured processes. If this is the case with you, you may be disappointed, annoyed, or downright shocked to discover that design can be a rather administrative process with many steps. Each of these steps has a specific order and a specific purpose. That's not to say that there is only one process and everybody must use it. Over time you will, if you have not already, develop your own process, a method that works best for you. No matter how you go about it, however, your process is going to include several key steps. Among these steps will probably be:

- Script analysis
- Research
- Discussion
- Planning
- Implementation
- Evaluation

Script Analysis

Script analysis conjures images of college literature classes, stuffy professors, and long, boring essays. You could get the Coles Notes (or Cliff Notes) or ask someone else what the story was about, but that wouldn't really provide you with the immensely detailed information you will need to successfully complete your lighting design. The best way I have found to analyze a script is a method used by designers for the stage. It's a systematic analysis of the script for story elements, technical requirements, and other considerations such as mood and foreshadowing. It is not as boring and drawn out as you might expect, especially considering you will have direct artistic input into the final look of the project. It's an exciting time filled with possibilities, but it begins with a bit of background work that prepares you very well for the tasks ahead.

Understanding the Story

The real key to an attractive, successful, and cohesive lighting design is the ability of the designer to understand what story is being told by the author and then how to interpret and re-tell that story using lights. This begins at the beginning, when you are first handed a script and asked to read it. With that unopened script in your hands, your design is a carte blanche, an empty page. How you fill in that page depends on how you approach the script. There are many ways to analyze a script and derive a deep understanding of the story. I prefer the method outlined in the following sections.

First Reading

The first time I crack open a new script, I like to find a quiet, relaxing space where I can indulge myself and enjoy the story. There is no work to be done here. The goal is to familiarize yourself with the story, to gain a general, overall understanding of all the elements before you get into the nitty-gritty, before you start trying to answer all the questions that will inevitably come up during the production and design process. Of course, just because you are reading for pleasure doesn't mean it might not be a good idea to keep a pen and notebook handy just in case a brilliant idea pops into your head. If one does, take the time to jot it down. There is little more infuriating than having a great idea but deciding that you want to finish reading the scene first, and then when you've finished reading the scene, the idea is gone. Design ideas can come out of nowhere or can be triggered by the simplest things. Sometimes the inspiration can be a few words by a character or a brief setting description by the writer. Sometimes it is where you were on vacation last summer. Sometimes unrelated ideas just click with something in the script. I have often found that first reading, spur-of-the-moment ideas tend to be the strongest and clearest of all the design ideas I have. It is, after all, the first impression that holds the longest. Chances are that if an idea really catches you it will really catch your audience as well.

Second Reading

It is probably a good idea not to do your second reading immediately. Put the script away for a day or two and let the story percolate around your brain for a while. Once you've had plenty of time to think about the story, about things you liked or did not like, find that quiet spot again to begin your second reading.

This time, with the story under your belt and a few glimmers of ideas brewing in the back of your head, try to find ways to build up concepts for scenes. Jot down quick notes either on a notepad or, better yet, in the margins of the script where you won't get notes from Act 1 Scene 4 mixed up with notes from Act 4 Scene 1.

While you are reading, take time to stop and think about scenes and make note of technical requirements for each scene such as time of day, weather conditions, and light sources. Make quick notes and move on. Try not to lose the momentum of the story. Don't forget to jot down any other thoughts or ideas you may have about a scene's mood or foreshadowing opportunities.

Third Reading

When you read the script for a third or even fourth time, you are looking for all the minute details that may come up in the course of your design. If the apartment is messy, for example, you might want to know something about that mess. Are socks hung on the floor lamp? Is the window grimy? Are there burned-out lightbulbs in the hallway? All these elements are lighting design considerations.

There will be specific technical requirements such as placement of lighting sources like lamps and windows and placement of foliage or a clothesline full of clothes that may have an effect on light sources. There will be specific design elements and ideas such as the light shining through a stained-glass window in a cathedral, or the light through a high, small barred basement window and the volumetric light shining into the dusty basement.

Each scene is likely to be loaded with these details, each one of which must be taken into account while creating your lighting design.

The margins of the script are not likely to be sufficient to house and keep organized all the notes and ideas you are likely to come up with. It is time to do some administration. Get a binder and some page separators. Make a section for each act and, within that, a section for each scene. Keep the right notes with the right scene. You'll be adding a lot more information to each of these sections later on.

Research

Any designer worth her salt is going to take the production seriously enough to engage in some research. How much research is done depends upon the nature of the project and also upon the tenacity of the designer. It's pretty tough, for example, to research the lighting properties on the surface of Planet Xargon Seven or to find photo reference for the size and shape of the rocket flame from the good ship *Rescue Team Alpha*. On the other hand, there is a good deal of reference material on real planets and real rockets. You don't have to make your scenes look the same as the real thing, but they could trigger a few interesting ideas way in the back recesses of the brain cavity, and they could help you add a sense of realism to your design work, fantastic as it may be.

Research can take a number of forms. These days most research seems to take place on the Internet. There is an immense variety of written and visual information that is available to the web searcher. You'll want a high-speed connection, though. The quantity of irrelevant information you're likely to have to sift through is not for the faint of heart.

There are also libraries. Remember libraries? Local libraries are a great place to do fairly run-of-the-mill research; however, for more obscure topics you may have to find a large regional library. Colleges and universities generally have good book selections as well. If you are researching period looks, your best bet is to find a college or university with a theater and film design program. These programs maintain large selections of tomes specifically for the use of their design students.

Historical

If you are doing a period piece (a work in a historical context), you are going to find yourself knee-deep in some serious historical research. What if you find yourself lighting a foggy London street in 1849? Do you know what gaslight lamps look like? Do you know the real qualities and properties of the light they produce? Probably not. But there is plenty of reference material available on that era.

What about life in Egypt in the twelfth century B.C.? Do you know how Egyptians illuminated their hallways at night? Better find the answers to these questions if you're doing a piece on Pharaoh Ramses III. How about the reflective properties of the material used in pyramids? Pyramids were very large structures covered with white limestone. No doubt there was a great deal of diffuse reflected lighting nearby.

Visual

When we talk about visual research, we are referring to the setting and its surrounding environment. What does the place look like? Is it a smoky bar? Is the only sunlight through cracks in the window shutters? Is it afternoon or nighttime? Is the setting filthy or antiseptic? Are the lights fluorescent or are they candles? What about the scenic textures? At some point any lighting designer is going to get involved in certain aspects of surface textures. Visual elements will include such items as specularity, glossiness, diffuseness, and reflectivity. Is the toilet seat highly specular? Is it plastic or porcelain? Is it stainless steel? Is it highly polished oak or does it have one of those furry covers? If you are trying to light a scene and you don't see the specularity you think you should, there may be some surface tweaking to be done. You may find yourself having to correct some of the other surface attributes as well. The artist who built the model, even if it was you, could not know exactly what the model would look like within a particular lighting environment. It is probably a good idea to save scene-specific versions of your model, as the surface attributes may change from scene to scene.

Technical

Technical research, also referred to as R&D, is the research you will have to do to develop the specific lighting techniques you will need to accomplish all the fancy-pants ideas you have conjured up with the director and the other designers. The design of lighting techniques ensures not only that the look you are seeking is achievable, but also determines early on what sort of render power you are going to require to get all the frames rendered on time and on budget. If you have planned an effect that is going to take ten hours per frame to render, you might want to consider either finding a way to pare down the render time or scrapping and redesigning the look or the technique. Some techniques are just not practical.

Technical research takes place primarily during the early phases of a project. However, ideas change, mature, and evolve as the project grows from an idea into reality. Research and development is likely to continue in some measure until near the end of production.

As an example of R&D, imagine that your project involves a cataclysmic event on the earth such as a comet striking the planet or a massive volcanic explosion. What are you going to do to accomplish the obvious pyrotechnical lighting effects required for the hero shots? A comet shooting through the atmosphere overhead is burning up and is sure to cause some sort of lighting effect. The impact and subsequent explosion of billions of particles of molten rock will certainly be a serious lighting consideration. Many of those molten particles are raining down around your characters. What effect will this have on the local lighting environment? Next, how are you going to accomplish these effects? What light types will you use? Or perhaps you will not use lights. Perhaps you can project an image sequence on the background and use global illumination. That sounds very render intensive, but it might be worth a try. It might look great enough to justify the extra render time. It might make all the difference between your film and some other film. It is probably a good idea to sketch out a number of approaches to each problem and try them out. You'll come to the right balance sooner or later, or perhaps during the course of experimentation you will discover an entirely new, untried technique. Either way, you can see that technical research will be a keystone in your design and development phase.

Dramatic

Dramatic research goes to the very heart of the story and characters. By striving to understand the story, by seeking the emotional truths that lie at its heart, and by endeavoring to understand all the characters in their fullness, you will be better able to make decisions about how to light specific scenes. Many well-written stories contain much more than the surface story elements on the page. They are also filled with metaphor and symbolism, perhaps pointing from the veneer of the story to an underlying social, political, or emotional truth. By analyzing the story and the characters, the designer is much more likely to understand what the writer is really trying to say. That understanding will bring you, the designer, to a new level of consciousness regarding the story. You will find yourself understanding symbols in the story in a way that is separate from the base story itself. You will be better equipped to provide a more truthful interpretation and, therefore, more truthful lighting.

Take the time to know the story. Discuss it with the other designers and with the director. It may be that the story is a simple, light comedy. If you are lucky, however, you will find yourself working on a project with much deeper meaning that requires a much deeper understanding on your part.

Discussion: Working with the Design Team

Art is often a solitary business. Many artists prefer to work in complete seclusion, never showing their work until it is complete. There is no reason you can't maintain this attitude with your own CG stories, but it may take you a while to complete all the work yourself. If you are working with a design team, on the other hand, you must realize that there is automatically a teamwork approach to the project. Sometimes a headstrong director will have a single vision and will work toward that vision with little or no regard for the creative processes of the rest of the design team. Sometimes this results in a single, unified look to the finished product, but more often it simply results in a narrow vision of a much broader story and disgruntled artists who have not been allowed to exercise their creativity. A director is wise to listen to the ideas of the design team; whether or not she chooses to incorporate them is something else entirely. However, many brilliant ideas have come out of brainstorming sessions with all the designers throwing wacky, strange ideas onto the floor. If you have ever been in one of these meetings and been witness to the birth of a brilliant idea, it is likely that you have never forgotten it. It is one of those memorable moments when everybody stops and stares at each other with excitement. They all know that *this* is the idea that will make everything work. Every person is on the same page, everyone is thinking the same thing. All the designers leave the meeting excited, ready to build on the foundation that has just been laid. All the designers are now working toward a common goal. Where I previously believed that my artwork was always solitary and that others had little or nothing to do with my artistic successes, I have found team experiences like this to be the most creatively fulfilling of my life. It doesn't always happen, to be sure. Sometimes the director and all the designers remain at cross-purposes from one end of the project to the other. Sometimes even this tangled mess creates stylistically and dramatically strong work. Some artists are driven to excellence through harmony, others through tension and strain. In any case, each production team is unique and the interrelationships within that team are certain to be interesting to observe.

What it comes down to is that you can never tell at the beginning of a production if that magical team is going to form, if the diverse ideas are going to form into a collective whole, or if the whole thing is going to be a disaster. For the record, very few projects turn into disasters as long as each member of the creative team is willing to do a good job.

The best you can do is review the script and come to the first meeting with as many different ideas and with as open a mind as possible. Bring your best ideas to date and present them like a salesman trying to sell a car. You have got to sell your ideas to the rest of the design team. There is a possibility that you will be outvoted, that the rest of the team has completely divergent ideas. On the other hand, if your ideas are really good, the rest of the team may be willing to look at new ideas themselves.

Bear in mind that, as part of a team, it is your duty and obligation to marry your design ideas with the work of the scenic and costume designers, whatever those ideas might be. Holding onto a single design plan is a disservice to the project and will most likely get you fired. Pride hath no place on a team.

Once you have some experience under your belt, you will probably discover that the challenges of working with a team, of building a collaborative whole, is just as challenging and creatively interesting as solitary work—perhaps even more so.

Planning

Once you're on the same page as the other artistic brains on the team, you have the task of planning just how you will achieve the lighting goals you have set for each and every shot. This means it's time to create a lighting bible.

Depending on the size and scope of the project, the lighting bible may be a few pages attached with a paperclip or a three-inch binder with separators. If you are talking about a feature-length project, you are definitely going to have to be organized. That means you must keep sketches for each scene in addition to storyboards, magic sheets (described later in this section), and, if you have a team of lighters implementing the show for you, probably some sort of drawn lighting design and lighting schedule.

Sketches and Drawings

Whether you are the sole lighting artist implementing all of the lighting yourself or the lead lighting artist coaching a team of artists with widely varying skills and experience, it is probably a good idea to plan out your lighting design scene by scene, not only with notes, research, and discussions but also with sketches and drawings. If possible, get a hold of the scenic design drawings. Make sure you can keep them and scribble all over them. Plan out each light position and purpose. You might even work out a lighting schedule for each scene if your design becomes complex enough to call for it. You don't have to start out at a drafting table. Start with scribbles on napkins. Take some serious time to forget about the whole project and relax — it might help the ideas flow. When the ideas come, write them down, sketch them out, tell them to someone — just don't let them get away from you. All these scraps of paper, napkins, and whatnot go into your bible for later conversion into useful information such as the magic sheet.

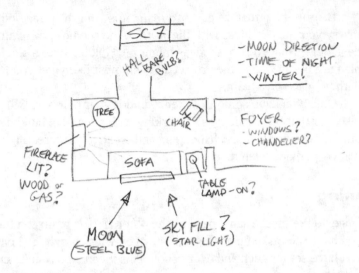

Figure 23.1: Quick sketch of a lighting design

For this particular sketch, I just did a quick drawing of what I thought the set might look like for the scene, then added elements I thought would affect my lighting design. I had a number of questions about the scene such as whether or not certain lights in the house would be on.

- This scene takes place late at night. There is a child sleeping in the house, so the parents might leave a light on. If so, which light?

- Perhaps the parents have only just gone to bed. Did they leave a fire burning in the fireplace?

- Is it a wood-burning fireplace or a gas one?

- Is the fireplace ablaze or does it hold dying embers?

- Which direction should the moonlight come from?

- Has the moon's direction been established in previous shots?

- Is the light in the foyer off? There might be moonlight if there are windows.

- If there is no moonlight, will we be filling with ambient starlight?

- Does the camera see the foyer during this shot? (Make a note to check the storyboards.)

The Magic Sheet

A *magic sheet* is a representational sketch or drawing of a lighting intent. Initially there is no need to be specific about light types, specific colors, or specific techniques. Just take a plan view of the scene and sketch in general directions and purpose. Take the following drawing, for example:

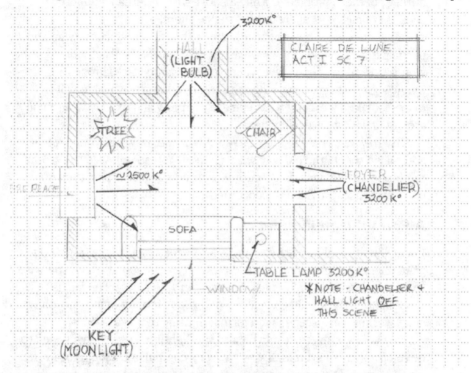

Figure 23.2: Magic sheet reflecting a more formal version of the sketch in Figure 23.1

The magic sheet is a more formalized version of the napkin sketch. This is drawn once all the questions from the first sketch have been answered. In this drawing, I have roughed in some color temperatures as a guide to the lighting TD (technical director). Actual placement of lighting elements such as lamps and lightbulbs will be a collaborative decision between the scenic and lighting designers and the director. All three are striving to achieve the most effective look with as few compromises as possible. There are likely to be disagreements along the way. If, for example, the scenic designer called for an ornate and detailed chandelier and the modeling department spent a long time building it, the modelers might not be very pleased to discover that it spends most of the time in the dark and is almost unseen. The lighting department, on the other hand, which spent a month researching how best to simulate light from a roaring fireplace, may be annoyed to find that the fire is mere glowing embers. While it is likely that many of these details will be decided upon before the serious work begins, the likelihood of this type of communication snafu is directly proportional to the scale of the project. A production with hundreds of scenes is almost certain to have any number of these problems, while a short with less than a hundred scenes is much less likely to experience them.

Having regular meetings with the rest of the production team and participating actively in your department's updates and activities discussion is crucial to keeping everybody on the same track. Presenting magic sheets at these meetings as soon as they are available will let everybody know exactly what you are planning and exactly where you are going with your design ideas.

By the way, you don't have to sit down and draw out your sketches and magic sheets the old way with a pencil. You are allowed to use any medium you like, including drafting or drawing software or even crayons, if you like, provided the documents are legible.

A Formal Lighting Plot

Formal lighting plots are by no means a necessary part of your production, unless you find yourself saddled with a huge job in which you wish to convey large amounts of information very precisely. The fact is that most lighting TDs will be tweaking and repositioning lights once they start working on a scene, but a formal lighting plot is a good way to convey your complete design data to the lighting TDs. You will need to develop a symbol system. If you are very compulsive about cross-referencing your information, you can even write up a lighting instrument schedule, although I have not found this document to be very useful once the lighting implementation has begun since so much of the information becomes obsolete as soon as adjustments begin.

A formal lighting plot is not as stuffy as it sounds. It can be as simple as a set drawing with specific light placement and general direction sketched and notated over the plan.

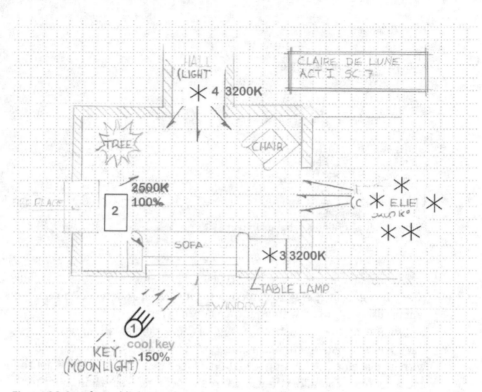

Figure 23.3: A formal lighting plot

Symbols and Notations

You will be working with a number of different lighting instrument types. Rather than writing in longhand what each light type is on a plot or magic sheet, it is much easier to have a symbol system for your light types. It doesn't matter what the symbols are, just as long as you and the rest of your team can identify and understand them. Here is a list of symbols I like to use:

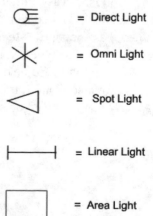

Figure 23.4a: Lighting symbols

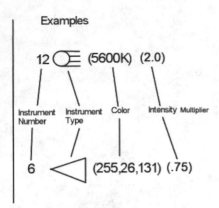

Examples

Figure 23.4b: Lighting symbol examples

In 23.4a, I have listed all the light types I'll be using. I find these symbols easily recognizable, easy to remember, and quick to sketch, although you will probably come up with your own set of symbols.

Figure 23.4b demonstrates usage of the symbols with notations. Each lighting instrument has an instrument number that corresponds with its place on the lighting schedule. Once again, if you choose not to use a lighting schedule, you will not really need to assign a number to each light, although if you are manipulating a large number of lights it might be very useful.

While you are assembling the paperwork, you will not likely know the exact color or intensity you need a light to be. In cases like this it is just as easy, rather than writing in a color or color temperature, to write in "C" for cool or "W" for warm, or you can write in a color name such as "orange," "steel blue," or "hot pink."

The type and number of symbols and notations you use is entirely up to you. Some designers use very little paperwork, while others are manic about it. It is your choice. Whatever works best for the production team is what you should use.

A Formal Lighting Schedule

A formal lighting schedule is a numerical listing of all the lights in your scene or act. The page includes a number of columns or fields containing data for each individual lighting instrument. A lighting schedule is a good idea if you are dealing with a large number of lights or a very large lighting project. It is also particularly helpful if you are reusing one setting in many different scenes. You can create a single lighting plot, if you wish, and turn the lights on and off as you require them. A lighting schedule is very helpful, in this case, for keeping track of all the various lights for the various scenes, although it seems to be more efficient and easier to work with a scene if it is pared down to include only the lights required for the scene. Once again, the choice is yours. The best method is the one that works best for you and the rest of the production team.

Instrument Number or Name

Each lighting instrument needs to be identified in the lighting schedule either numerically or with a unique descriptive name. If you choose the numeric method, you will simply list all the lights in your scene and then number them. If, for example, there are 26 lights illuminating the scene, your lights will be listed on the page from #1 to #26. Finding a numbered instrument on a lighting plot is much easier than finding a descriptive name among 25 other descriptive names. Further, you may run out of really unique descriptive names if you have a large number of lights in the scene. I would recommend descriptive names for scenes with few lights and a numbering system for scenes with many lights.

Descriptive names might be something like *Key, Sunlight, Floor Lamp*, or *Chandelier.* If your chandelier has 20 individual lightbulbs or candles in it, you might give them a descriptive name followed by a number, such as: *Chandelier #12*. Whichever method you choose, you should name or number your light in MAX the same way you have them in the lighting schedule.

Light Type

Light types need to be identified in the lighting schedule as well as on the lighting plot. It would certainly not do to place a point light where there ought to be an area light. In this column you simply write the type of light such as *omni* or *spot.*

Intensity

Naturally, light intensity is key to the final look of the shot. When designing lights, you are likely to have a "ballpark" idea of what you think the intensity of the light is going to be. Write that number in this column.

Color

Once again, you may not know the exact color. You may simply know whether you want a light to be warm or cool, or you may know roughly where on the color wheel you want to start. On the other hand, you may know the exact color temperature. Color temperature is a very precise way of determining the color of a light source. We know, for example, that most incandescent lightbulbs burn at around 3200 degrees Kelvin. So if you have a lightbulb in your scene, that's a good place to start. You may have to adjust that color later due to the relative color of the other light sources in the scene or because the director wants a dirtier, warmer look, but it can't hurt to start with physically correct measurements.

Position and Angle

You may wish to record the exact final position and direction of the light for archiving and record-keeping purposes. If this is the case, you can include a column for position and angle. Leave these columns blank, however, until the lighting artists have finished lighting the scene.

Notes

If you are an adamant record-keeper, chances are you will want some additional space to keep notes about each light. Notes as to the light's purpose are often helpful when leafing through a long lighting schedule looking for a particular light. Notes are especially helpful if you have chosen to number your lights rather than give them descriptive names. It is a good method of cross-referencing your lights.

The chart on the next page is a sample lighting schedule. You don't have to do it this way. You don't have to include all of the columns given here, and you can certainly add your own if you like.

Notice that the first three lights have intensities and colors listed as "E." This means that the color and intensity is *enveloped*, changing over time, as one would expect for light emitted from the ever moving and lapping tongues of firelight. The position is listed as "A," which means *animated*. "TBD" is shorthand for "to be determined."

Inst#	Type	Int	Col	Pos	Angle	Notes
1	Area	E	E	A	0,90,0	Fireplace 1
2	Area	E	E	A	0,90,0	Fireplace 2
3	Area	E	E	A	0,90,0	Fireplace 3
4	Direct	175	Steel	5.277,5.07, 1.2877	56.3,54.8,0	Moon
5	Omni	100	3200K	0,756mm,0		Table Lamp
6	Omni	45	3200K	TBD		Chandelier1
7	Omni	45	3200K	TBD		Chandelier2
8	Omni	45	3200K	TBD		Chandelier3
9	Omni	45	3200K	TBD		Chandelier4
10	Omni	45	3200K	TBD		Chandelier5
11	Omni	75	3200K	TBD		Hallway

Implementation

If you are working in a small production environment or if you are a lighting TD in a large production environment, you are going to be the one implementing the lighting design. There are several steps to implementation, usually beginning with a rough "blocking out" of light placement and direction, followed by the roughing out of light intensities and colors. After this, you can start rendering out frames to see exactly what the lights are doing, then move on to the last stage, which is fine-tuning. If you are working in consultation with a director and/or lighting designer, you will be presenting frames for evaluation and further implementing lighting changes as directed by the designer and/or the director. This final phase can go back and forth many times, sometimes indicating that a new approach or an evaluation meeting may be necessary.

Block Placement

When you are in the *block placement* phase of implementation, don't worry too much about exact position. Get the light somewhere you know it's going to roughly do the job. You can fine-tune it later. Make sure the light is not behind any geometry that will prevent it from illuminating the scene once Ray Traced Shadows or Shadow Maps has been selected. Other than that, it's just placement by eye.

Roughing Out

During the *roughing out* phase, you will look at the properties of each light in your scene and assign it a base intensity and color. The intensities and colors you choose to start with may very well change in the *fine-tuning* stage, but you have to start somewhere, so make your best guess. If the designer has given you a lighting schedule, you should apply any color and intensity data available to you from that resource.

Fine-Tuning

Now that you have your lights roughly in place and you have a starting point for lighting intensities and colors, you can start making test renders to evaluate the lighting in the scene. You would be very lucky indeed to have the lighting work out perfectly the first time around. If you are a meticulous artist with a very specific image in mind, you may find yourself spending a good deal of time going through the evaluation loop of adjustment-render-evaluate again and again until the lighting is satisfactory. Sometimes this process will reveal basic flaws in the lighting design. Don't be afraid to suggest major changes to the design if you think it will provide a major improvement to the scenic illumination. If, however, you are a lighting TD and not the designer, it would be best to seek approval before making any major changes to the design, as your alterations could impact other design elements of which you are not aware.

Figure 23.5 (See color image.)

Figure 23.5 shows an early test render for a shot from an animated short. You can see that there have been some scenic design changes since the original sketches and drawings shown earlier in this chapter. The hallway has been moved out into the foyer and a rocking chair has been added in the corner by the fireplace. This early test render is not yet textured. This is one frame of a fireplace R&D sequence.

Working with Materials

At some point, you will have to start working with material attributes since lighting and material attributes are inextricably linked together. Alteration to the materials will depend on a number of factors including how segmented the production departments are. In my opinion, the best, most efficient relationship between modeling/texturing departments and the lighting department is for the model to be provided built and shaded. Then when the lighting department takes over, a new scene is made so that the lighting department can make shading changes as necessary without altering the original "master" model created by the modeling and texturing departments.

If your level of experience and expertise does not include shading and texturing, you should consult with the texturing artist who originally shaded the model. As a lighting artist, it is your responsibility to learn the craft of shading so that you can make informed decisions about making material alterations without seriously impacting other departments or design considerations.

Evaluation

CG lighting designers have an enormous benefit not available to stage, video, or film lighting designers or gaffers. On the stage or the sound stage, lighting designs are implemented at immense cost. Equipment is rented, the crew is hired, the lighting plot is hung and focused. Usually evaluation is the last step — the step where the designer critiques her own work and tries to learn from it, to remember the design elements that really worked and to scrap or rework elements that may not have been entirely successful. Evaluation for stage lighting designers begins with technical rehearsals where the designer gets to see the lights in action, to see how they affect the scenic elements and the performers. The designer then has a limited number of days to make changes, alterations, and additions and to continue evaluation until opening night. There is an enormous cost associated with these changes, revolving mainly around union wages for the lighting crew and possibly including lighting rental and materials costs.

But in the beautiful, versatile world of CG, usually a single operator or artist implements the lighting design, tweaks and adjusts it, and examines the results within a rendered frame — and all this before lunch! A single rendered frame can provide enough feedback about whether it is necessary to tweak the design or even to completely redesign a scene if necessary (provided the artist time is available and within budget, of course). Regardless, it is much, much simpler to relight a CG scene than it is to relight a stage. Once you have rendered a test frame, you will probably know right away whether or not adjustments are required. You will likely spend time working in the render-evaluate-adjust loop before moving on to the next scene.

Balancing the Scene

Balance can mean a lot of different things. For example, when thinking of balance, one may envision a set of scales that is perfectly level, balancing perfectly. This is the classic image of balance, perfect and very, very cliché. When you are designing lights for your stage, whatever that stage may be, you may want your lights to be balanced in that way, or you may wish them to be balanced in an entirely different way. You may have your lights heavily emphasizing one side of the frame. This is also balance. It's just not balanced in the center. Balance refers to a lighting design that embodies illumination, style, and interest while enhancing (but not overpowering) the story. Choosing the balance can also mean choosing to be unbalanced. Unbalanced lighting can seem odd or off to an audience. It can set them on edge and give them the sense that something is not right. Look at the two following images. One of them appears to be right and the other appears to be wrong. But who is to say which is right and which is wrong?

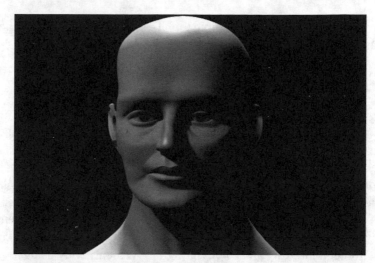

Figure 23.6

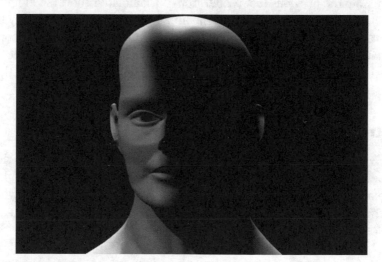

Figure 23.7

Figure 23.6 appears normally lit, as one would expect, while Figure 23.7 seems somehow mysterious. The character may be hiding something or hiding from something. We suspect that there is more to the story than we know, and we wish to know more.

Do you see how a simple tool like this can either bore or excite your audience? You choose whether your stage is balanced or unbalanced, whether your lighting will be shocking and outrageous or subtle and keen. You decide whether the audience will be comfortable in their seats or crawling out of them. A simple tool like this can bring an audience laughter, anticipation, horror, fear, or any other emotion.

Focus and Emphasis

You get to decide where the audience looks.

When you are designing lights, there are certain things you and the director wish the audience to notice. There may be things you wish to remain unnoticed at first. With lighting levels and a few simple tricks, you can lead your audience's eyes from one shot to the next and place them exactly where you wish them to be in the frame.

It is not necessary for you to be obtrusive in focusing the attention of your viewers onto a particular area of your scene. You can add emphasis through intensity and color, through movement, or by using an unusual lighting angle that makes a particular area stand out from the rest. In the previous test render from our animated short (see Figure 23.5), our eye is first drawn to the fireplace. It is the most brightly lit area of the room. Our eye follows a sweeping curve around the room, noting the sofa and window, the rug, and finally the Christmas tree. The picture is painted, the scene has been established in just the way the artists desire.

Designing with Light and Shadow

Everybody knows about designing with light. You place a light so that a desired area is illuminated in a certain way. It may be a soft key light playing across a face, or it may be a brilliant rim light that makes your character stand out from the background. This is a given. Lighting designers design light.

There's more, though. We must also know how to design with shadow. If we can learn where to strategically place shadows just as we instinctively know where to place light, we have effectively doubled our lighting toolkit, for shadows are just as useful, just as good at telling the story, as lights are.

Designing with Light

By illuminating one area more brightly than another or by applying a more vibrant color in one area than another, we can shift focus. We can spread the visibility homogeneously around the scene if we wish or we can punctuate certain symbols or moments within the scene. We can offer clues as to the time of day, the atmospheric conditions, and the setting by use of color, angle, and intensity of light. We can change the lighting during the scene to signify the passage of time or the change of environment. In essence, anything that happens on the stage can be punctuated, supported, or counterpointed by the deliberate and artistic use of lights in the scene.

Designing with Shadow

Designing with light is only half of the toolset. You can design with shadow as well. That which we choose *not* to light is equally as important as that which we choose to light. We may wish to hide some information until later, perhaps only allowing information to leak subconsciously into the scene. We may wish to be more deliberate than that, excluding important information so that the viewer will wonder why and will focus more on that missing information. There is little that draws a viewer into your story better than genuine curiosity.

Take a man standing half in the shadow of a dark, dead-end alley.

Now that you have that image in your mind, what are you seeing? Are you seeing the half-illuminated face of a man or are you seeing the dark, silhouetted shape that resides in shadow? Certainly the illuminated half tells us that there is a man in the alley. We are given that piece of the story up front: There is a man in the alley. Then the questions start to rise: Why is there a man in the alley? Why is he half in the shadows? Is he trying to hide from something? Or maybe he's stepping into the light on purpose, trying to make himself more visible so the old lady walking home won't be frightened of him.

There are many different ways you can use shadow to accentuate elements in your scene, to draw the audience's eye toward, or away from, scenic elements.

Lighting a Scene vs. Lighting an Object

In the world of visual effects, CG artists often find themselves creating and illuminating individual elements to be composited onto photographic background plates. In a case like this, the artist will be attempting to simulate the lighting environment found in the plate. If, on the other hand, you are the designer and your scene is entirely, or even largely, CG, then the design becomes infinitely more complex and infinitely more rewarding.

Lighting a scene means understanding the story and the technical requirements. It means being able to interpret the emotional intent of both the writer and director. It means being able to implement a lighting design that supports that intent. If you are a lighting TD or a lighting art-ist with experience in visual effects and you wish to move on to lighting all-CG scenes, be aware that lighting individual CG elements for visual effects composition bears very little resemblance to all-CG lighting design. If you have read this chapter in full, you have a good idea of what can be involved in lighting design for computer animation. Don't be dis-couraged. There is no better way to learn the process than to work your way through it. If you are not lucky enough to be assigned such work, I would recommend taking some time to create your own short. Once you have demonstrated your design abilities, it won't be too long before a suitable opportunity arises.

Putting It All Together (Making a Pleasing Picture)

If you started thematically, with a single vision, then you should not have too much trouble inserting all the various elements of your design and having them work together reasonably well. You can tie your elements together very simply by choosing a color palette at the beginning and sticking to it. If you alter it, be sure to alter it for everything. This does not mean that all key lights have to be the same color. It means that you pick your main colors, decide how far you are going to vary those colors through hue and value variations, then go with it. If you have decided to stick to earth tones, for example, and one scene is lit with purple and yellow, it is going to stick out. It won't belong to the scenes around it and will seem out of place. That's not to say that you can't make a scene appear out of place if you want. This is a great tool that can be used to keep your audience off balance and uncomfortable if that's what you wish.

Maintaining a thematic view is not going to be very difficult if you are working with a team. There are many other artists and designers working with you, discussing your ideas and offering their own. You are likely spending a great deal of time trying to sort out how to incorporate your own design ideas with the concepts of the other artists. This pro-cess is conducive to thematic work since a group of people all working together on the project are much less likely to go far off track than a sin-gle artist or a very small production team that doesn't meet often enough.

The main idea is that you should be thinking about making a pleas-ing picture — one that is pleasing to you because it conveys the messages and feelings that you want it to convey. It doesn't necessarily have to please your audience.

Art should not always be beautiful. Sometimes it should be ugly and horrible.

Saving and Reusing Lighting Rigs

Perhaps one of the most magnificent advantages of having your lights as nothing but a mess of pure data inside a conglomerate of plastic and metal is that you can save, copy, cut, and paste your lighting design together from previous designs as though you were copyediting a paragraph. I like to do this by stripping out all the objects in the scene and then saving the scene as a lighting rig. When you want to use this rig again within your scene, simply choose File>Merge. When the Merge dialog box comes up, select the lights and other items you want to bring into the scene and click OK.

■ ■ ■

I have said it before and I'll say it again: "There are no rules!" If you are a new lighting designer, you can expect to have to gain some experience before you get some really great gigs. There is only one way to get experience. Get lighting! Think about light and observe light all the time. Every day is filled with uncountable opportunities to learn something that will help your lighting some day — maybe tomorrow. You can't learn lighting from a book. You must observe light in the real world and you must then attempt to simulate that light in the computer environment. Sooner or later you will gain an understanding of how light works. This understanding will make you a force among your peers. They will throw adulation and bottles of champagne in your direction, offer you ridiculous raises, and fall at your feet with gratitude for saving their show. Or at least they'll say, "Yeah, that looks pretty good. I could do that."

Identifying and Recreating Light Sources in a Plate

This chapter deals with how to analyze the lighting in a photograph and recreate it in MAX so that your CG elements will be lit appropriately on top of the background image. Analyzing and recreating lighting in this way is perhaps the single most crucial skill in creating 3D visual effects. By the time you have finished this chapter, you should understand how to go about this process.

About Photo-real Lighting

There is nothing in the manual and no button or plug-in in MAX or anywhere else that will create appropriate and photo-real lighting for your shot. The only way to do this is through your understanding. Your understanding of the light types and properties, of the shadow types and properties, and of the lighting instruments, colors, and diffusion gels used on set is the only thing that will enable you to do a world-class job of lighting (or in this case relighting) the shot.

Furthermore, it is crucial that you understand the textures and materials that you are lighting. You need to know the properties of those textures. Are they highly specular or matte in finish? Should they be highly reflective or glossy? Your understanding of how the textures *should* be reacting to your lights will let you know whether or not your lighting or textures are appropriate. If one or the other is too far off, either the element will be unsuccessful or the compositing artist will have a great deal of work to do to make it a success. As a lighting artist, you should take pride in providing lighting and shading that requires little compositing alteration (other than color correction; there's always color correction). If nothing else, this makes you a valuable asset because you are saving your company money in compositing time.

About Plates and Light Sources

A *plate* is usually a photographic element (either a still or an image sequence) onto which we want to add some sort of computer-generated element. Take, for example, the dinosaurs in the movie *Jurassic Park*. The dinosaurs themselves, of course, were CG, but the background *plates* were filmed on location. This is what we mean when we talk about compositing a CG element onto a *plate* or *background plate*.

Now, how do we identify light sources? And how do we recreate them for CG elements that will be added to the plate?

Well, if you're lucky, an experienced and resourceful visual effects supervisor will have brought back from set a load of reference images including gray ball and mirror ball still frames that provide valuable lighting position and quality information. The gray ball really helps you see the color and quality of the light sources, while the mirror ball seriously helps you pinpoint the position of each lighting instrument.

In many cases, however, there will be no reference of any kind, and you'll need to analyze the plate to discover the light positions and properties by eye. That's okay; you can learn this skill.

First, learn how to look at light and shadow. Understand the qualities and properties of light. Know the color temperature, angle, size, and everything else about every light source. It is very helpful to understand the type of luminaires, or lighting instruments, along with gels, flags, and diffusion filters used by the lighting crew on set. Second, learn how to use the tools in MAX. Know what all the different light types can do. Know how to make a hard shadow and a soft one. Understand inverse square falloff and how to create real soft shadows and everything else there is to know about the lighting tools in MAX. Part II of this book and the MAX documentation both deal extensively with how to use the toolset.

Probably the very easiest way to learn how to match CG lighting to a plate is simply to look at some photographs, identify the light sources, then proceed to set them up in MAX, compositing the two at the end. We will look at a few different lighting scenarios to see how to do this.

After you have lit a few hundred CG elements to match plates, you will probably get a feel for the lighting just by looking at any old photo. But to begin, it may help to look at a couple of tools that can help you identify light sources, their direction, and other properties. Perhaps the most used lighting analysis tool is a matte ball. Just any old Styrofoam ball will do, although it should probably be at least 12" across to give you a good look at the lighting. Some prefer to use a gray ball. In this case, I managed to get my hands on an 18% gray ball used in a feature film and a mirror ball (no, not the kind used in discos and high school dances), which we will discuss later.

If you need to light CG elements to a plate and you are lucky enough to have someone on set who will stick a ball in the shot and shoot a few frames in exactly the same lighting context, your life will be made easier. Rather than guessing at what the lighting might be, you will have a better visual reference. Of course, a well-organized shoot will include several feet of film containing nothing but the clean plate (empty set with no performers) and a gray ball or mirror ball. If the footage is shot through the same camera that is used to shoot the film, you'll be much more likely to accurately match the lighting. Below is an image of a gray ball in a studio setting.

Figure 24.1

In this context, the direction and relative intensity of the key lighting source is completely obvious. We can see by the shadow on the ball that there is one key light source and that it is above the ball to the left and slightly closer to the camera than the ball. If the light source were behind the ball, more than half the ball would be in shadow. But more than half the ball is in the light, so we know that the light source is closer to the camera than the ball is, thereby illuminating more of the ball facing the camera.

Take a look at the next image and see if you can clearly identify the light source.

Figure 24.2

This time, it is easy to see that the light source is above and behind the ball. We know that a direct light source pointing at a spherical shape will illuminate half of it. If we see less than half of the ball illuminated, the light source must be shining on the side of the ball that is facing away from us.

This is why using a ball is so simple for identifying light direction. If you choose to use a white ball, and you have the benefit of color images, you can also use the information in the ball photos to help you determine the color of the light sources as well. Be aware, however, that the colors on your computer monitor, your digital camera (if you are using one), and a television monitor are all likely to be quite different. While you may do your best to match colors in the plate with your CG lighting colors, the likelihood is that color adjustment will have to take place during final compositing. So while it is important to try to match the plate's light colors, to at least get in the ballpark, it is a waste of time trying to be completely precise because the color palette is almost certainly going to be adjusted by someone with a different monitor calibration anyway. So get it close, but don't waste time trying to get it perfect.

Replicating the Light Source

Let's take a look at one of our "ball in a studio" shots and see how easy it is to replicate within MAX. The first thing we'll need is a ball. So open up MAX and make a simple ball.

Once in Layout with the ball, open the Environment and Effects panel either through the Environment menu or by pressing 8 on the keyboard.

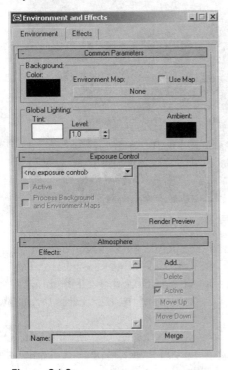

Figure 24.3

Under Common Parameters, the button below "Environment Map" is currently labeled "None." Click this button and you will be presented with the Material/Map Browser.

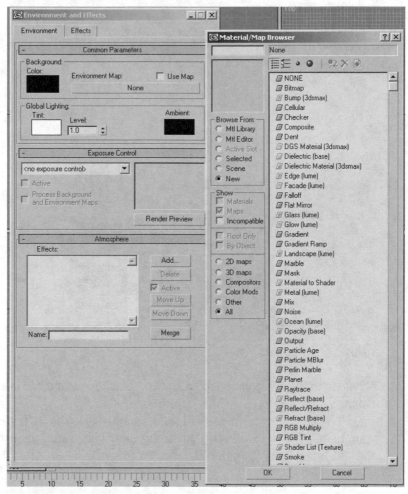

Figure 24.4: Select Bitmap.

Double-click on Bitmap and you'll get a file selector dialog.

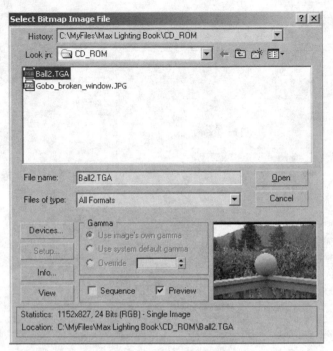

Figure 24.5: Load Ball2.TGA.

Navigate to the companion CD to find the Ball2.tga image and click Open.

Now the reference image will render in the background. If you don't want to take the time to set up the background image and ball, just load the ball2.max scene from the CD.

Figure 24.6: The ball2.max scene

One thing is immediately obvious: The lighting direction is completely wrong. As a matter of fact, the lighting in the plate is so soft and wide, my first inclination is to use a sky light.

I'll use an IES sky light this time. You can find it in the Photometric list. Orient it so that the half-globe is open-side down.

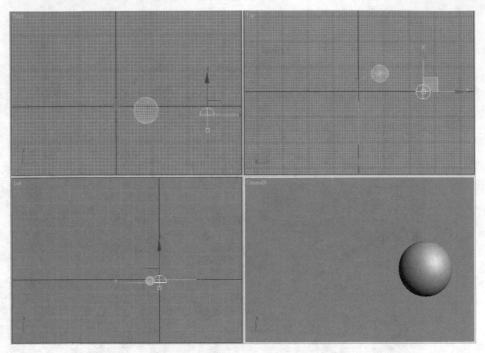

Figure 24.7: Add an IES skylight.

Then, in the IES Sky Parameters rollout, I set Coverage to Cloudy and rolled the intensity multiplier back to 0.64. I changed the sky color to white, since it was an overcast day and the clouds were pretty white that day.

Figure 24.8: Set IES Sky parameters.

The result was immediately much closer to what I needed for the shot.

Figure 24.9

Now all we need is a little fill light, since the bottom of the ball is a little too dark.

The simplest way to accomplish this is to add a touch of ambient intensity. Under the Rendering menu, click the Environment entry or simply press the 8 key to bring up the Environment and Effects panel.

In the Global Lighting section, Ambient is set to black by default. Pick a middle gray color such as HSV 0, 0, 77. That's all there is to it. This adds a slight ambient intensity so that no area of the image will be completely black, even those areas completely out of light. This is because the ambient color is

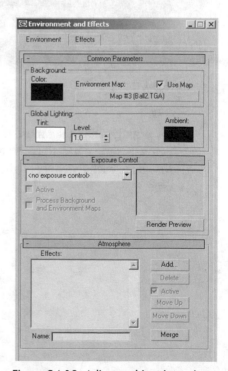

Figure 24.10: Adjust ambient intensity.

added evenly to every pixel in the image. Beware though; adding too much ambient intensity will flatten out the image and will brighten all areas, so you may have to balance the image out by bringing down other lighting levels in the scene. Here's what my render looked like:

Figure 24.11

It certainly didn't take more than one or two minutes to sort that out. See how simple it is to recreate real lighting within MAX? The trick is to recognize each individual light source and then build each one, one at a time.

The Mirror Ball

Another way of analyzing light sources is to get a big shiny mirror ball and photograph it in the environment. You'll get a reasonably good look at the surrounding light sources, although I find this method tends to skew reality a little. Take a look at the following image and you'll see what I mean.

Figure 24.12

You can see most of the environment, but I find this method inferior to the gray (or preferably white) ball method. I prefer a white ball because you'll have a pure color mix. Using a gray ball affects the color saturation. I prefer a matte ball instead of a mirrored ball because a matte ball will have obvious shadows demonstrating the direction of the key light source. But that is not to say that the mirrored ball provides no useful information. As a second source of information, I'd use a mirrored ball so I could see the whole environment. If used on set, the mirror ball can give you valuable information about lighting placement, type, color, and intensity ratios. If you are having trouble identifying the light sources, this information could be quite valuable. But most of the time you should be able to get all the information you need from the matte ball. The gray ball has the advantage that it is not likely to look "blown out" if the illumination is too bright, which a white ball might. After you become experienced, you will find that you don't even need a ball, as most of the time you can extract the lighting information from any old photo just by looking at how the lights play across the objects and textures in the shot.

It's always wise to acquire as much data on set as possible, so if you have the option of getting mirror ball and matte ball photos under the lights and from the camera position, definitely do so. Ideally, the reference images will be taken with the same camera used for the principal photography, using the same lens, under the same lighting conditions, and on the very day and time of the shoot.

A More Complex Lighting Environment

The following figure is a photo of a typical sunny winter day in Vancouver. (Note the magnificent North Shore Mountains freshly dusted with snow — skiing just half an hour from the city core!)

Figure 24.13

Although this image is black and white, it demonstrates a lighting environment with three discrete lighting sources. The primary source, or *key*, is the sun. The two secondary, or *fill*, sources are the diffused skylight and the bright reflection from the wooden roof deck in the foreground. We can approximate the angle of the sunlight not only by the shadow terminator on the test ball but also by the direction of the shadows on the ground.

Recreating this lighting requires an understanding of the nature of each of these light sources. So what do we know about them?

We know that our key source, the sun, is the brightest of the three, produces the hardest shadows of the three, and is somewhere in the amber range of color. We know from our environment that this is a winter scene. We know that it's in the Northern Hemisphere above the 49th parallel, so the sun is fairly low in the sky. The length of the shadows on the ground confirms this. We know the mountains in the image are to the north of the city (hence "North Shore"); therefore the sun is in the west, indicating an afternoon timeframe. We know that the sky, one of our two fill sources, is very large and therefore creates very soft shadows. We know that the sky's color is somewhere in the blue range of the color spectrum. The second fill, the light that is being reflected off the wooden roof deck (this light is also known as a "bounce" light), is probably a light grayish or brownish color since it is mainly yellowish sunlight reflected from the gray-brown wood of the roof deck. (This is sometimes called "color bleeding," but what really describes it is reflection. The wood absorbs certain color wavelengths and reflects others.) It is also a fairly large diffused light source, although not nearly as large as the sky.

My first inclination is to use a distant light for the sun, even though the shadows will not be perfectly accurate, and two area lights, one for the sky fill and one for the bounce light. The sky fill light will be considerably larger than the bounce light.

Now there are a number of different ways I could approach this lighting problem using any number of lights and any number of combinations. There are methods that will render more quickly and there are methods that will render more slowly. (Believe me, there are always methods that will render more slowly!) I have selected this method as being a sort of "middle-of-the-road" solution. Quality is likely to be fairly high without monstrous render times.

Let's take an object and throw it into the scene, then load up the background image as we have done in previous sections.

The first thing to do is start a fresh scene and load an image into the environment. We'll need to see the image in the viewports so we can line up our geometry.

Hit the Alt+b keys to bring up the Viewport Background panel.

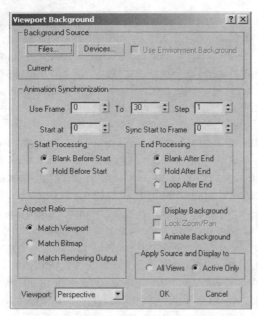

Figure 24.14: The Viewport Background panel

Click the Files… button to open the file requester and navigate to the vancouver.tga image on the companion CD. Select the image and click Open.

Figure 24.15: Load the vancouver.tga file.

You can choose to Apply Source and Display to all viewports or only the currently active one.

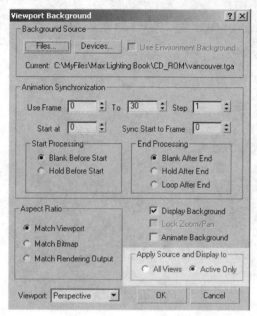

Figure 24.16

I've expanded the perspective view a little to get a better look at the grid orientation. I see I'll need to rotate my view a little to get the world perspective lines close to the perspective lines in the background image.

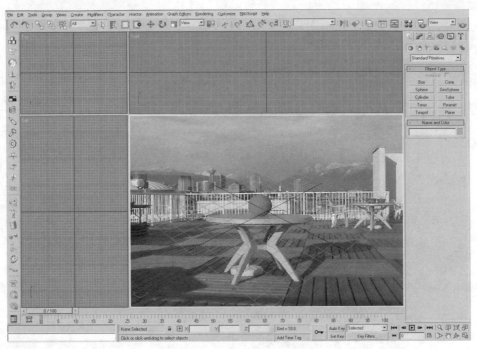

Figure 24.17

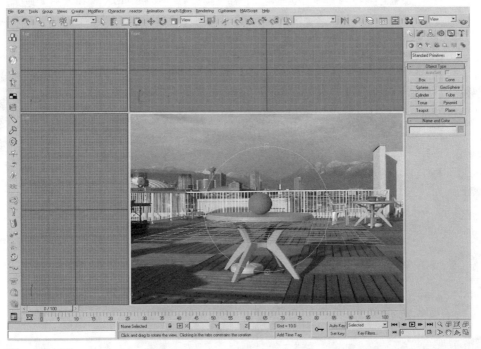

Figure 24.18

There, that's a much better lineup. Now to add some geometry to the scene. The first thing we'll need is a ground plane to receive shadows from any items we put in the shot.

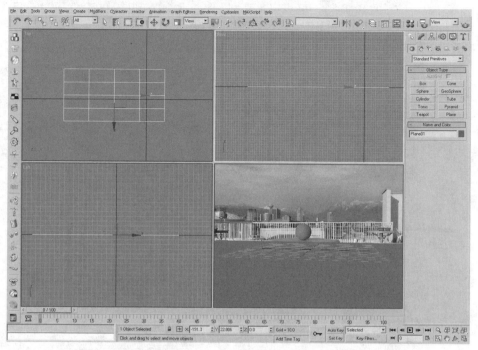

Figure 24.19: Add a ground plane.

We will need to project our background onto the new ground plane. To do this, open up the Material Editor, click Diffuse Color in the Maps rollout, and select the vancouver.tga image. See Figure 24.20.

In the map's Coordinates rollout, select Environ to project the image as though it were part of the environment. See Figure 24.21.

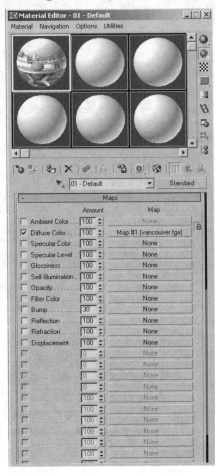

Figure 24.20

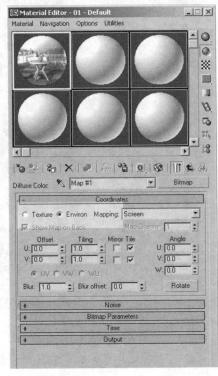

Figure 24.21

Before you render your first frame, be sure the vancouver.tga image is also selected as your environment image, as shown in Figure 24.22.

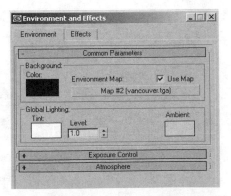

Figure 24.22

Now render an image.

Figure 24.23

If you look at the rendered image closely, you'll see that part of the render with the geometry plane is brighter than the background image. We'll deal with that later. The most important thing is that we now have a ground plane onto which objects will cast shadows. Without shadows, a CG element will never look like it belongs in the shot.

So let's add an object to the scene.

I poked around the web until I found this free fire hydrant at Amazing 3D Graphics (www.Amazing3d.com). This site has a bunch of free 3D meshes that are fun to play around with. I just dropped it into my scene so that it was sitting on the ground plane.

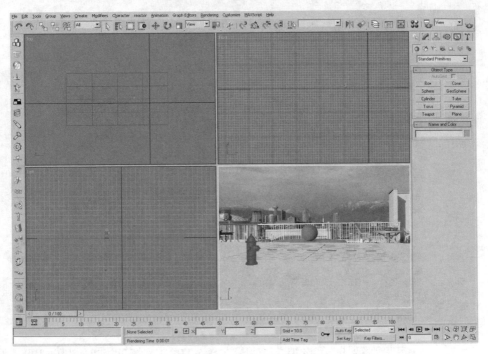

Figure 24.24: Add an object to the scene.

Here's what the first render looks like.

Figure 24.25

The first thing you will probably notice is that the lighting and shading are completely wrong on the fire hydrant. That's okay; we haven't added any lights yet. But you'll notice that the perspective lines look right. The object appears to sit correctly on the ground. That's because we took the time to insert a ground plane and orient our view appropriately.

Adding a single light in the direction of our key light (the sunlight in the background image) will help.

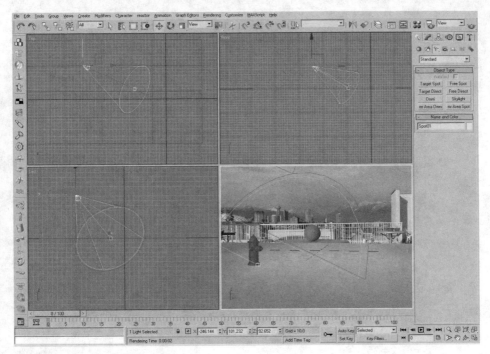

Figure 24.26: Add a light.

If you do a quick render, you'll see that the hydrant is now casting a shadow onto the ground plane.

Figure 24.27

Adding a sky light and turning off any ambient intensity will also really help.

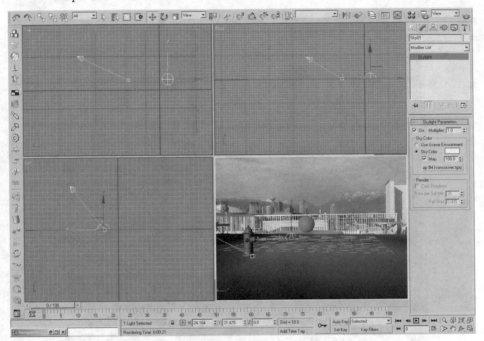

Figure 24.28: Add a skylight and disable ambient intensity.

Now for a quick render. See Figure 24.29.

Figure 24.29

There. That's about the right light intensity and direction. The shadows also look to be about the right density and softness.

And that's pretty much all there is to it.

It's a myth that lighting a CG element in a plate is a difficult job requiring a great deal of skill. If you can identify the light sources in the plate and replicate them with your MAX lighting toolset, it will be just as simple as the example scene we've just completed.

If you'd like to see the completed scene file, check out vancouver.max on the companion CD.

Rendering the Element

We have been learning to match lighting by rendering our elements against the background plate and seeing how well they match up in the render. Under normal production circumstances, however, after you match up the lighting, you will almost certainly turn off the background and render the CG element by itself, usually on a black background. This rendered sequence or still frame will then be handed off to a compositing station where another artist will import both the background plate and the CG element and marry them together. The compositing artist (or *compositor*) who does this marrying will be sure to very carefully match color. He will also add film grain if it is appropriate and soften, blur, sharpen, and adjust contrast, gamma, or color curves, and do whatever else might be necessary to make the CG element look like it really belongs in the image.

Getting the Color Perfect Is Not Your Job

Compositors and their tools are a critical part of the CG process. This is because computer-generated images almost always look CG straight out of the render. They need help such as blurs, grain, natural variations, and color correction. I don't believe the technology is yet mature enough to provide perfectly photo-real CG elements without at least a little compositing help. So when you are spending hours and hours trying to tweak the exact, precise color to match the plate, and the compositor imports it and changes everything anyway, remember this: Your light color will never be perfect simply because you are probably working with an uncalibrated monitor, or at least a monitor that is calibrated differently than that at the compositing station. Get the light shadows, distance, angle, and whatnot perfect, but get the color close. Trying to get the perfect color is a waste of time.

As a matter of fact, chances are the sequence will be color timed after leaving the compositor's station anyway. Color timing occurs when all the shots of the show are edited into proper sequence. Many different scenes — shot on different days, using different lighting, or even all-CG shots — will be played back to back. This is when we discover the wild variation in color from one shot to the next. The color timer goes through all the shots to give them similar color values.

So you see, trying to make lighting color perfect is a big, fat waste of time.

Don't do it!

■ ■ ■

If you look through this chapter you will see a few simple examples of how to identify and replicate the lighting in a photographic plate. I chose simple examples, because the process really is simple. Select a single light source, identify its properties, then place an appropriate lighting tool in your MAX environment to match it. Fiddle with the settings until you're happy. Select the next light source and repeat the previous steps. Once you've done this with all the light sources, your lighting will be complete.

It really is that simple.

If you don't already know how to identify a light source, then you haven't read this entire book. Part I deals intensively with real-world light and lighting properties. Go and read those chapters. When you come back, you will be one with the lighting.

Focus Power.

Lighting Setup Examples

For those of you who prefer concrete examples of lighting setups, this chapter contains a number of such examples. Rather than providing a single setup technique for a sunny day or a room interior, however, I am employing various properties of the lighting tools to demonstrate a number of different techniques for dealing with each lighting scenario. The purpose of this is to demonstrate the flexibility of 3ds max's lighting toolkit and to put into practice the lighting theory and tool descriptions found earlier in the book. By using different tools in different ways to achieve similar results, I hope to demonstrate that almost any lighting can be attained with almost any lighting tools, provided you understand what is needed in the scene and what each light type is capable of. I hope you find these short tutorials useful in describing the many applications of MAX's lighting tools. Feel free to alter each of the following examples by inserting different light types if you like. In fact, I encourage it. If you can get different lighting instruments to work in place of the obvious ones, you're a more powerful and creative lighting artist. You'll be better able to solve the myriad technical problems and create viable workarounds by understanding the capabilities and limitations of each individual light type and property.

Exterior Sunny Day

An exterior sunny day is a very common lighting scenario and a very good place to start since the lighting setup is very simple. If you find yourself in a situation where you must create a lighting setup for an exterior sunny, clear day, the first thing you should do is examine that environment and decide exactly how many light sources exist and what their position, angle, color, and size are.

Typically, exterior sunny days have two or three light sources, depending on the environment. The key light is the sun. It's a bright, slightly amber light source in the color temperature range of 5500 to 5700 degrees Kelvin. That's slightly amber in color and low in saturation; in other words, a very pale yellow-orange. It is relatively small in the sky but is not an omni light, although omni lights can be used for sunlight sources in many cases.

The fill light is the sky. Since we know that the sky itself is luminous, we know that it is diffusing light from the sun and spreading it in all directions, some of which reach our subject or stage. The skylight is very large, hemispherical in shape, and quite blue in hue, in the range of 10,000 to 20,000 K. That equates to a fairly deep mid-blue color.

A third light source, if there is one, is likely to be a reflected light from the ground or perhaps a nearby wall. This is often called a "bounce" light and is usually diffuse, unless it is reflected off a highly specular surface such as water, polished marble, glass, or a mirror. This third source represents real-world "radiosity" in which certain amounts of light energy reflect from one material to the next. This source may or may not be required. For one thing, there may not be enough surface light to justify a bounce source. If you are sitting outside at a table with a white tablecloth, and sunlight is shining directly on the tablecloth, there is most definitely a brightly visible bounce light source in the tablecloth. Any surfaces that are faced toward the tablecloth will pick up a great deal of reflected light. If, on the other hand, you are standing on a freshly paved road, in other words a road that is really black, there probably won't be much bounce light at all. You will have to decide what is needed in your scene through careful analysis. Bear in mind that a subtle bounce will add a great deal of realism to your shot, but it doesn't have to increase your render times.

Let's take a look now at some ways of tackling this problem, beginning with the cheapest render solutions.

Exercise 1: Direct Key, Ambient Fill

For super-fast renders where photo-real quality is not an issue, there are many options, most of which do not include shadows.

Start fresh or reset 3ds max 6, and add a simple ground plane. Then add an object. Any object will do, although we will be able to see the effects of our lighting better with slightly complex objects that have lots of places for shadows and highlights to fall. I picked the following ogre object I made. It's called ogre.max and is on the CD if you want to try it out.

Figure 25.1: The ogre.max object

Add a single directional light from the Create tab and place it so that the shadow will be visible in the render.

Figure 25.2: Add a directional light.

Don't forget to turn advanced raytraced shadows on in the Create panel, the Modify panel, or the Light Lister.

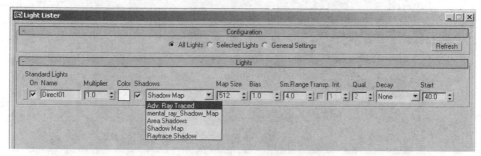

Figure 25.3: Enable advanced raytraced shadows.

The render should look something like the following.

Figure 25.4: Rendered scene

Now, we want to make our sunlight a little more sun-colored. In the Modify tab, under the Intensity/Color/Attenuation rollout, click on the light color square to bring up the MAX Color Selector.

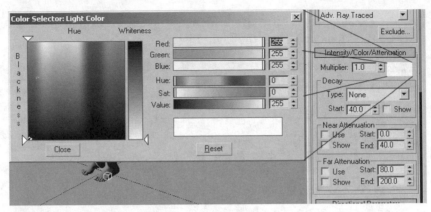

Figure 25.5: Select a color for the sunlight.

I selected an HSV value of 24, 48, 248.

> **Note:** For details on how HSV and RGB color models work, please refer to Chapter 16.

Most people believe sunlight is white. This mainly comes from a lifetime of living in sunlight and believing that all the colors we see are not altered by the natural lighting from the sun. This is not so. Sunlight is amber in color, especially when it comes through our atmosphere and has part of the blue light stripped out by atmospheric particles.

So let's add some blue back into the mix, just as we'd see on a clear, sunny day.

Select the Rendering>Environment menu option.

By clicking on the Ambient color swatch in the Global Lighting section of the Environment tab (see Figure 25.6), you can change the color of ambient light that illuminates the scene. I picked an HSV value of 163, 109, 166 for my ambient skylight. Remember that the value will determine the intensity of the ambient light in your scene. My render looks like Figure 25.7.

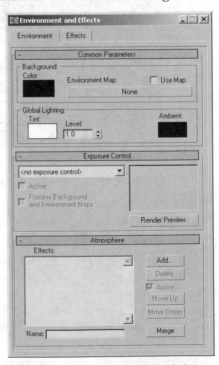

Figure 25.6: Adjust the ambient light.

Figure 25.7: Rendered scene

The completely black areas have been raised in value slightly. I'll increase the direct light multiplier to make it look a little more like a searing sunlight. This looks a little better.

Figure 25.8

That's not bad for a 10-second render. As the goal of this exercise was to create a very fast simulation of exterior daylight, I'd say that's a success, although it's not as beautiful or physically accurate as it could be.

Let's move on to a slightly more accurate method.

Exercise 2: Direct Key, Direct Fill

Instead of using flat ambient intensity as a fill light this time, we're going to use another direct light. The advantage to this is that rather than adding general intensity to all surfaces like the ambient intensity, a direct light will obey geometric shapes and illuminate the surface based on its orientation to the light source, much like a real light source does.

So start fresh with the ogre scene, or load up the Exercise2.max file from the CD with a distant key light and a distant fill light already in the scene. Don't forget to make your ambient light black again if you just carry on from the last exercise.

Figure 25.9

If you take a look at the light settings, you'll see that the second direct light is blue in color and has a lower intensity than the key sunlight. If you remember the earlier chapters of this book, you will identify this as a natural key-fill ratio using a complementary color scheme.

But something is wrong. There is a shadow from the fill light. Skylight does not cause a hard shadow like this. The easiest way to fix this with the least impact on render time is simply to turn off shadows for the fill light. You can do this any way you like. I prefer using the Light Lister.

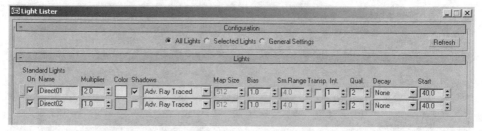

Figure 25.10: Turn off shadows for the fill light.

Figure 25.11: Rendered scene

That looks much better. It doesn't take any longer to render than the light setup in Exercise 1, but looks much, much better.

Exercise 3: Using Shadow Maps

The first thing to remember about using shadow maps is that they have a size parameter that determines how many pixels square the map is. If you spread a small map out over a very large area, you're going to get a very inaccurate shadow. On the other hand, if you use a very large shadow map, rendering times will increase. So it's a good idea to be sure your light cone or cylinder is just large enough to cover the area needed and no larger. For this exercise I've started with a distant light and sized it down to cover the ogre object. I've also enabled Overshoot to be sure there is light outside the light cylinder as well.

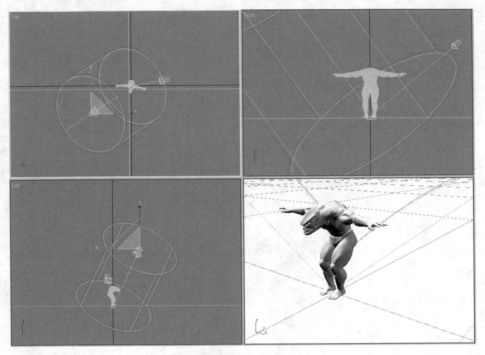

Figure 25.12

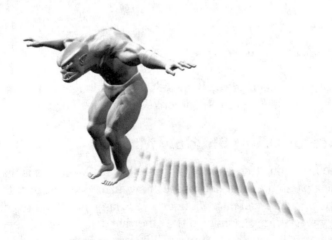

Figure 25.13: A shadow map with too small a resolution renders inaccurately.

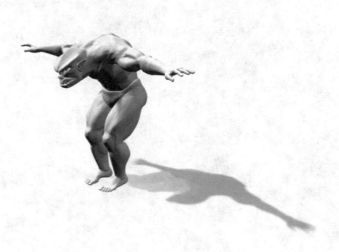

Figure 25.14: A shadow map with too high a sample range will render soft shadows all the way around the shadow edge.

As you can see from Figure 25.14, shadow maps can create nice, soft shadows. While this may be very useful for many situations, and while it has the advantage of render speed, the main problem with shadow maps is that real shadows are harder-edged near the object that is casting them and softer farther away from the object.

In the next exercise, we'll see what makes area shadows so great.

Exercise 4: Area Shadows

Load up the Exercise4.max scene included on the CD or, if you like, you can start fresh and add a couple of lights with area shadows and an object of your choice.

Bear in mind that area shadows take much longer to calculate and render than raytraced, advanced raytraced, or shadow maps. However, the trade-off is physical accuracy and a much nicer-looking render.

Figure 25.15

Area shadow parameters can be tweaked to improve quality at the cost of increased render time. There are also ways to shorten render times at the cost of shadow quality. This is a judgment you will have to make every day depending on your production requirements.

Exercise 5: Using a Skylight for the Fill

Once again we'll improve the quality of our lighting by using a more expensive light type. In this case, we'll get rid of the second direct light that we had been using for the sky fill light source and use a skylight instead.

You can either create your own scene using a direct light as the key and a skylight as the fill, or you can simply load up Exercise5.max from the CD.

Figure 25.16

The main advantage to the skylight is that, unlike a direct light, it emits light from all directions toward the subject, providing that natural "wraparound" lighting that we get from a very large light source such as the sky. Where direct lights, spotlights, and most other light types only illuminate the polygons facing toward the light origin, the skylight exists all around the subject, illuminating it on all sides and causing natural, soft shadows if you have enabled shadows for the skylight. If you don't enable shadows, the skylight will behave much like regular ambient light.

Figure 25.17: Enable Cast Shadows.

Enable Cast Shadows in the Skylight Parameters rollout to get the most out of your skylight.

Figure 25.18: The same render as in Figure 25.16 but with the key light turned off

Figure 25.18 demonstrates just what kind of lighting a skylight can provide for a scene. You can see that there are no hard shadows but plenty of soft, natural illumination.

Keep in mind that the above examples are just a handful of the many, many combinations of light types you can use to simulate outdoor lighting. Spotlights and omni lights do just as good a job in lighting environments like this as do the directional lights that we chose for the exercise scenes.

Exercise 6: mental ray Area Lights

Discreet has been kind enough to gift us with a pair of awesome mental ray lights. Area lights are, by far, my favorite light type because they most closely simulate light from real light sources. The area shadows from standard MAX lights are quite nice, and they simulate the shadows from area lights very well, but they don't provide the light wraparound that you get from real area lights.

One of the great things about mental ray lights is that they render fine with MAX's standard lights. According to the MAX documentation, you can't mix photometric and standard lights (although I have done it successfully numerous times).

Don't forget: If you want to use mental ray lights, you have to assign the mental ray Renderer on the Common tab of the Render Scene panel.

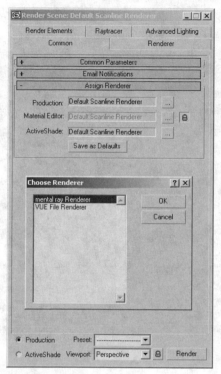

Figure 25.19

Once you have assigned the mental ray Renderer you will notice that your renders come out a little differently than when you use the Default Scanline Renderer. The mental ray engine calculates small squares called "buckets" one at a time, or two or four, depending on how many processors you have and whether or not your render is hyperthreaded.

Figure 25.20

I started this exercise by loading up a wheel and throwing in a mental ray area omni light. This will be my sunlight. I selected a sphere as the area shape. Now you don't really need a sphere, and they calculate slower than a disc, but I threw one in for fun. You can change it in the Exercise6.max scene if you like. The sun is, after all, a sphere, but it is so far away from us that it illuminates the earth just the same as if it were a disc, so the minute differences are irrelevant and invisible to the human eye. Figure 25.21 shows what my first render looked like with just the one key light.

Figure 25.21

The first thing you will probably notice is that the shadows are hard-edged nearest the wheel and get softer farther away. This is the penumbra effect in action and is very natural and physically correct. Perhaps there is a little too much softness for such a small object, which makes the wheel seem larger in scale. I'll make the area omni a bit smaller to tighten up the shadows a little. While I'm at it, I'll ramp up the intensity a little to look more like sunlight.

Figure 25.22

There, that looks better both in terms of intensity and shadow softness. What's really missing now to complete the outdoor look is the skylight filling in the shadows.

Let's throw in a large mental ray area spotlight over the wheel to act as a skylight.

Figure 25.23

That looks much better.

Just for the fun of it, I enabled Final Gather in the mental ray Render Scene panel's Indirect Illumination rollout.

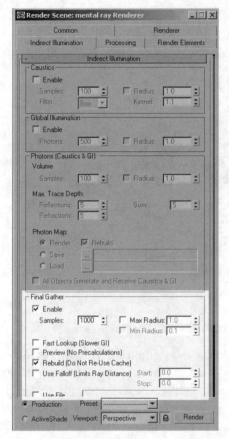

Figure 25.24

This definitely added some time to the render, but just take a look at the beautiful light bounces in the final render.

Figure 25.25 (See color image.)

Exercise 7: Using Photometric Lights

The first thing you should know about photometric lights is that, since they are designed to be real-world accurate, they have certain nitpicky real-world requirements. For example, the scale of your scene should be the same as it would be in the real world. A human, for example, should probably be between 1.5 and 2 meters tall. A teacup on the table should be 10 or 12 centimeters across and so forth. Additionally, you'll need to be careful with your geometry. Geometry must be complete, join well, and not have any holes that will cause "light leaks."

Personally, I find photometric lights to be more work than they're worth, since as a visual effects artist, I'm more interested in the aesthetic look of the final render than I am in the physical accuracy of the light transmission, but here's an exercise using photometric lights nonetheless. You may find you need to use them in your work. Also remember that you'll likely find yourself becoming friendly with the exposure controls if you use photometrics a fair bit. Now, on to the tutorial.

First, I added a two-sided cube to simulate a room interior, added a simple 1 m square plane to act as a tabletop, and placed a 7.5 cm radius teapot on the tabletop.

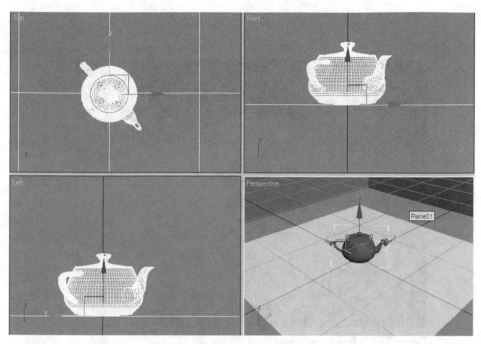

Figure 25.26: Create a room, and add a plane and an object.

Switching to photometric light types, I added a target area light, setting it fairly small, in the 0.1 meter square range.

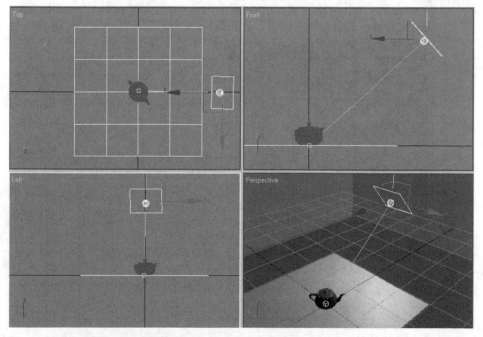

Figure 25.27: Add a target light.

The first render doesn't look that impressive, mainly because we haven't employed any exposure control yet.

Figure 25.28: Rendered scene

In the Environment and Effects Panel, in the Exposure Control rollout, select Logarithmic Exposure Control. Logarithmic is usually the best exposure control since it mimics film exposure more closely than Linear Exposure Control.

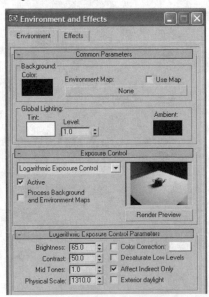

Figure 25.29: Select Logarithmic Exposure Control.

Leave all the default settings as they are and try another render.

Figure 25.30: Rendered scene

Now the table doesn't look blown out. In a moment, we'll look at adding a fill light to the scene. But if you look carefully within the shadows, you'll see "light leaks" from where the geometry is one-sided inside the teapot. It's a pretty ugly artifact but easy to fix. I simply added a double-sided material to the teapot. While I was at it, I made the material reflective, just because it looks nice!

Figure 25.31

That's better. Now let's add some light fill to the scene.

In an interior scene with a single light source such as a lightbulb or lamp, there is no better fill lighting than radiosity. Sure, I could use any one of the photometric lights to fake radiosity fill, but in this case, let's use the Radiosity plug-in.

From the Advanced Lighting tab of the Render Scene panel, add the Radiosity plug-in and leave all the settings at their default levels. Now click the Start button to have MAX calculate a radiosity solution for you.

Figure 25.32: Render using Radiosity plug-in

That provides quite a nice soft fill indeed. Let's try a different trick though. Instead of radiosity, let's place a low-intensity area light over the teapot and tabletop to simulate this radiosity fill. I'll add a few more teapots to better demonstrate the shadow softness as well.

Figure 25.33: Render that simulates radiosity fill

In my opinion, this render looks even nicer than the radiosity render. Of course there are dozens of photometric light parameters you can fiddle with to tweak settings as you desire. As for me, I prefer to use standard or mental ray lights as they offer easier, more predictable results with less hassle.

If you're interested in seeing the scene file for this exercise, it is included on the CD and is labeled Exercise7.max.

Exercise 8: IES Sun and IES Sky

Here are another couple of photometric lighting instruments you can use. IES Sun and IES Sky are physically correct representations of sunlight and skylight. If you are doing an outdoor scene and want your lighting to be as close to physically perfect as possible, these are the tools you'll want to use, although there are tons of other tools you can use that will provide equally pleasing lighting effects and are easier to set up and quicker to render.

So let's get into a quick setup.

First, add a large ground plane into a new scene and put some geometry on it. Any geometry will do.

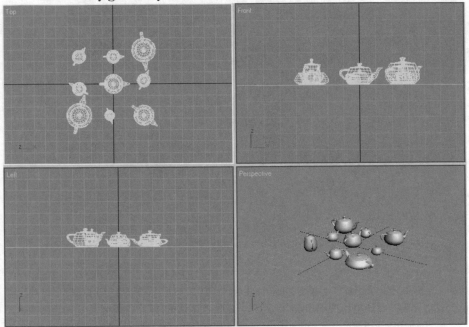

Figure 25.34: Create a ground plane and add geometry.

Before adding IES skylight and IES sunlight, go to the Environment and Effects panel and select Logarithmic Exposure Control.

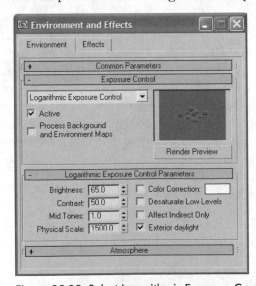

Figure 25.35: Select Logarithmic Exposure Control.

Check the Exterior Daylight check box, and add an IES skylight. In the IES Sky Parameters panel, enable Cast Shadows for the skylight.

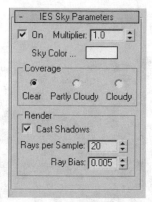

Figure 25.36: Enable Cast Shadows.

Now render a frame to see the results.

Figure 25.37: Rendered scene with IES skylight

That's a pretty nice-looking skylight render, but the render time was painful. This is something you could achieve much more quickly using some of the other techniques.

We'll add IES sunlight to complete the scene. Don't forget to turn on shadows for the light.

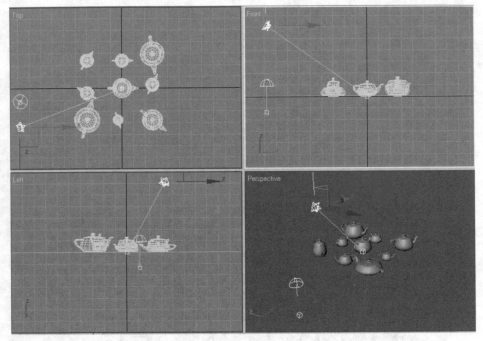

Figure 25.38: Add IES sunlight.

Now render out a frame to see the results. Warning: This is going to take a while!

Figure 25.39: Rendered scene with IES skylight and sunlight

The render is looking nice, but is it worth the massive render time? I don't think so. There are so many other, faster methods for achieving this look that physically correct lighting becomes moot. My advice is to explore cheaper, less physically perfect techniques and let your eye be the judge. The final scene, named Exercise8.max, is available on the CD.

Exterior Scenes with Radiosity

Having now worked through a number of tutorials dealing both with exterior lighting situations and with the use of real and simulated radiosity, it should be easily apparent how to combine the two for effective lighting setups.

Once you have placed your key and fill light sources, you have the option of enabling MAX's built-in radiosity solution. Or you can estimate where the most pronounced radiosity bounces might occur in the scene and place bounce lights at those locations yourself, therefore removing the need to use radiosity. Try this out yourself. If you find it difficult, then work through all the tutorials again. By the time you get back here, I'm sure you will have it figured out.

Why am I not simply providing a detailed tutorial? Well, the purpose of this book is not to provide you with a handful of easy techniques to deal with all lighting scenarios. It is to teach you the tools so that you can develop your own techniques as need be. That is what makes a good lighting artist. I could go on and do dozens of little example scenes like these, but the foundation is laid. You should be able to identify any lighting scenario, identify light positions, types, and properties, choose the most appropriate lighting instruments for your needs (including render times), and proceed to create beautiful and appropriate lighting for your scene.

■ ■ ■

My intention with this chapter was not to help you learn about specific lighting techniques, although many have been used here, but to help you learn about the lights themselves. I hope you have learned more about light and shadow and about the combinations of possibilities that lie at your command with the simple application of a little knowledge and imagination.

My suggestion is to try to use every light type for every type of application. There is usually some way to do it, although the quality and render times may vary greatly and may not be exactly what you had hoped for. Chances are, though, that you will discover some very interesting things along the way. Every time you learn some new way of doing something, even though it may not apply to your current project, it is yet another tool for you to file away in your toolkit. It may be the tool that saves your shot one day. It may be the tool that saves your job or gets you a new one. That may sound melodramatic, but consider how many work hours are spent every day by CG artists all over the world who struggle to attain simple, quality lighting. Many have no idea how to accomplish it and, therefore, waste many hours fruitlessly chasing a lighting setup they don't understand. You must realize that a skilled, knowledgeable lighting artist is going to be a valuable asset. The clever artist will now come up with his own numerous, subtle, and cheap techniques for creating the lighting environments described in this chapter.

Observe the world and learn the tools — that's all there is.

Index

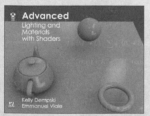

About the CD

The companion CD contains a number of illustrative images, objects, and scenes used in the book. Additionally, all of the figures from the book are located in the Images folder and are organized by chapter.

Warning: By opening the CD package, you accept the terms and conditions of the CD/Source Code Usage License Agreement. Additionally, opening the CD package makes this book nonreturnable.

CD/Source Code Usage License Agreement

Please read the following CD/Source Code usage license agreement before opening the CD and using the contents therein:

1. By opening the accompanying software package, you are indicating that you have read and agree to be bound by all terms and conditions of this CD/Source Code usage license agreement.

2. The compilation of code and utilities contained on the CD and in the book are copyrighted and protected by both U.S. copyright law and international copyright treaties, and is owned by Wordware Publishing, Inc. Individual source code, example programs, help files, freeware, shareware, utilities, and evaluation packages, including their copyrights, are owned by the respective authors.

3. No part of the enclosed CD or this book, including all source code, help files, shareware, freeware, utilities, example programs, or evaluation programs, may be made available on a public forum (such as a World Wide Web page, FTP site, bulletin board, or Internet news group) without the express written permission of Wordware Publishing, Inc. or the author of the respective source code, help files, shareware, freeware, utilities, example programs, or evaluation programs.

4. You may not decompile, reverse engineer, disassemble, create a derivative work, or otherwise use the enclosed programs, help files, freeware, shareware, utilities, or evaluation programs except as stated in this agreement.

5. The software, contained on the CD and/or as source code in this book, is sold without warranty of any kind. Wordware Publishing, Inc. and the authors specifically disclaim all other warranties, express or implied, including but not limited to implied warranties of merchantability and fitness for a particular purpose with respect to defects in the disk, the program, source code, sample files, help files, freeware, shareware, utilities, and evaluation programs contained therein, and/or the techniques described in the book and implemented in the example programs. In no event shall Wordware Publishing, Inc., its dealers, its distributors, or the authors be liable or held responsible for any loss of profit or any other alleged or actual private or commercial damage, including but not limited to special, incidental, consequential, or other damages.

6. One (1) copy of the CD or any source code therein may be created for backup purposes. The CD and all accompanying source code, sample files, help files, freeware, shareware, utilities, and evaluation programs may be copied to your hard drive. With the exception of freeware and shareware programs, at no time can any part of the contents of this CD reside on more than one computer at one time. The contents of the CD can be copied to another computer, as long as the contents of the CD contained on the original computer are deleted.

7. You may not include any part of the CD contents, including all source code, example programs, shareware, freeware, help files, utilities, or evaluation programs in any compilation of source code, utilities, help files, example programs, freeware, shareware, or evaluation programs on any media, including but not limited to CD, disk, or Internet distribution, without the express written permission of Wordware Publishing, Inc. or the owner of the individual source code, utilities, help files, example programs, freeware, shareware, or evaluation programs.

8. You may use the source code, techniques, and example programs in your own commercial or private applications unless otherwise noted by additional usage agreements as found on the CD.

Warning: By opening the CD package, you accept the terms and conditions of the CD/Source Code Usage License Agreement.
Additionally, opening the CD package makes this book nonreturnable.